POISON, PLAY, AND DUEL

Nigel Alexander

POISON, PLAY, AND DUEL

A Study in Hamlet

London
Routledge & Kegan Paul

First published in 1971
by Routledge & Kegan Paul Ltd
Broadway House, Carter Lane, London EC4V 5EL
Printed in Great Britain by
Alden & Mowbray Ltd
at the Alden Press, Oxford
© Nigel Alexander, 1971
No part of this book may be reproduced in
any form without permission from the
publisher, except for the quotation of brief
passages in criticism

SBN 0 7100 6984 7

CONTENTS

		page
PREFACE		ix
1. POISON, PLAY, AND DUEL		1
2. HAMLET AND THE ART OF MEMORY		30
3. THE CENTRE OF CONSCIOUSNESS		58
4. POISON IN JEST: the Play Scene		91
5. THE POWER OF BEAUTY: Hamlet and Ophelia		119
6. THE KING'S JESTER: the Graveyard		153
7. POISON IN PLAY: the Duel Scene		173
BIBLIOGRAPHY		202
INDEX		207

LIST OF ILLUSTRATIONS

facing page

1. The Dream of Scipio (*Raphael*)   68

2. The Three Graces (*Raphael*)   69

3. Allegory of Prudence (*Titian*)   84

4. Amor–Pulchritudo–Voluptas (*Titian*)   85

PREFACE

All quotations from Shakespeare are from the *Complete Works* edited
by Peter Alexander (Collins, 1951). As well as act, scene and line
references to this edition I have given the through line numbers from
the facsimile of *The First Folio of Shakespeare* edited by Charlton
Hinman (Norton, 1968). Where the lines quoted exist in the Quarto
of 1604 but not in the Folio of 1623 the number of the last Folio line
to appear before the Quarto passage is given followed by a Q to
identify Quarto lines and the number of extra lines taken from the
Quarto. Hamlet's seventh soliloquy at 4 iv 32 therefore appears as
2743 Q 26. The last line of the Folio before Hamlet's conversation
with the Captain and the resulting soliloquy is 2743. The soliloquy
itself begins twenty-six Quarto lines later.

Quotations from Jonson are taken from the *Complete Works* edited
by Herford and Simpson (Clarendon Press, 1925–53). Quotations from
The Tragedy of Locrine and *The Tragedy of Hoffman* are taken from the
Malone Society reprints, although the spelling has been modernized.

The footnotes to the text refer to the actual editions used in the
preparation of this book and often include paperback editions of standard and important works which, it is hoped, may be more readily
available to students. The Bibliography lists the first edition except in
cases where a second or revised edition has to be cited on account of
its new material.

I am grateful to the following galleries for permission to reproduce the paintings used as illustrations: The Trustees of the National Gallery, London for Raphael's *The Dream of Scipio* and Titian's *Allegory of Prudence*; the Musée Condé, Chantilly and Photographie Giraudon for Raphael's *The Three Graces*; The Galleria Borghese, Rome and Gabinetto Fotografico Nazionale for Titian's *Amor–Pulchritudo–Voluptas*.

I should like to thank the Trustees of the Henry E. Huntington Library, San Marino, California for a generous summer research fellowship in 1968. I am grateful to the library staff there, and to the staff of the British Museum, the University of Arizona and Glasgow University for their help.

Professor Peter Ure and Professor John Brown read earlier versions of the manuscript and, although I cannot claim their approval, I hope that I have benefited from their constructive criticism. Professor John Lawlor read the final version and made a number of very helpful suggestions.

I owe a particular debt to the scholarship of Erwin Panofsky, Edgar Wind, and Frances Yates. Like all students of the Renaissance I have profited from their work, but any errors in its application to this particular case must remain my own. I am especially grateful to Dr Yates for her personal help and encouragement.

Anyone who writes on *Hamlet* must acquire many intellectual debts. I am conscious of many more than I have been able to record in footnotes. I hope that I have robbed no one in learning from them. I am very grateful to the friends who have listened patiently to the argument of this book over a number of years. These obligations, and the debt of memory and understanding that I owe to Peter Alexander, lie beyond the scope of formal acknowledgment.

Glasgow   Nigel Alexander

Chapter 1

POISON, PLAY, AND DUEL

Hamlet is a play of ideas. The problems of Hamlet exist for an audience as the result of the dramatic presentation of a number of complex intellectual and emotional questions. These moral and political problems are realized within the context of a murder story which involves three families, and an entire state, in a deeply disturbing conflict of love and hate. This discord is enacted in physical and psychological conditions which force an audience towards a definition of the terms of courage, honour, and revenge which the characters use as justification for their actions. The spectator's attention is particularly focused upon these problems through the character of Hamlet, Prince of Denmark.

In a remarkable series of speeches and soliloquies Hamlet, torn by conflicting emotions and divided against himself, asks the tormented and tormenting questions which create the special quality of the play. It is necessary, however, for the critic and the director to observe that the difficulties and doubts experienced by his protagonist are only one of the dramatic methods used by Shakespeare to draw the necessary questions of the play to the attention of his audience. There is a distinction between Hamlet's problems and the problem of *Hamlet*.

The actors who play any of the characters in *Hamlet* may bring a wide range of personal resources and experience to the interpretation of their roles. No such licence, however, can be permitted to the company which intends to present *Hamlet*. They must perform three

I

difficult theatrical tasks supremely well. They must make the way in which the spirit of the dead King walks on to the stage strike the audience as both natural and unnatural. The Ghost must be theatrically acceptable and yet clearly outside normal experience. Their next task is to simulate their own profession and mimic the reception of a court performance as part of the dramatic action. The audience in the theatre must be made to grasp the distinction, and the relationship, between the play and inner-play; between the 'poison in jest' (3 ii 229:2102) played by the actors and the acts of poison performed by the characters. Finally, they must produce a difficult and exciting stage fight. This stage business must be managed in such a fashion that the exchange of rapiers, and the rapid succession of deaths by poison, seem a dramatic and logical conclusion to the Ghost's original revelation of murder by poison.

The dramatist has laboured to establish this connection for his actors. The Ghost gives Hamlet an account of a single death by poison. The inner-play presents the physical act of poisoning twice, once in dumb show and once accompanied by speech. In the final duel four of the main characters die by poison. Shakespeare deploys all the resources of his exceptional sense of theatre, and all the imaginative power of his language, to assist the players in this performance of poison, play, and duel. There are many ways of playing Hamlet, but no performance of *Hamlet* can succeed if it ignores the way in which the repetition of these powerful symbolic actions is designed to dominate and determine the language and the physical behaviour of all the characters on stage. It is this design which will catch the imagination of the audience.

When the play opens Claudius has obtained the crown of Denmark by secretly poisoning the King his brother. One month after the funeral and coronation he has married Gertrude, the wife of his dead brother and the mother of Hamlet. A Ghost, in the shape of the dead King, appears on the battlements of the castle of Elsinore. It discloses the crimes of Claudius, and commands Hamlet to revenge his father's murder. In the play Hamlet's problems develop from the fact that he does not immediately obey this command by killing the King his uncle.

Hamlet is unable to explain this delay and frequently reproaches himself in bitter terms for his failure to kill the King. At a crucial stage of the action, and in the seventh and last of his soliloquies, Hamlet can say (4 iv 43:2743 Q 37):

Hamlet   I do not know
            Why yet I live to say 'This thing's to do',

Sith I have cause, and will, and strength, and means,
To do't.

It is hardly surprising that the question of Hamlet's delay has assumed such critical importance. It is so evidently a problem for Hamlet.

It is here that Hamlet's problems differ in marked fashion from the problem of the play. To accept Hamlet's self-reproaches, and look for some reason, explained or unexplained, which prevented him from killing the King is to accept an important, although generally unstated, assumption. It accepts that the most natural, or the best, solution to the problem of murder and violence in Denmark should be a swift and, if necessary, violent retaliation or revenge. Hamlet never questions the necessity and duty of avenging his father's murder. The duty of revenge, however, is presented in more than one dramatic fashion during the course of the play. The play which Shakespeare wrote does ask its audience to examine and question the assumption made so readily by so many of Hamlet's critics—the assumption that Hamlet's only proper response to the news that his father has been murdered in secret is to become a secret murderer.

The play is not a series of random scenes but an ordered and highly controlled pattern. The metaphorical and symbolic language is used to expand, define, and interpret the physical actions of the characters. Within this poetic pattern of action and language the theme of violent death followed by equally violent revenge and retaliation is repeated in different circumstances by different players. As death answers to death in the play the audience are required to examine the nature of this act of violence. The play is more than a murder story: it is an examination of the kind of response provoked by murder.

Fortinbras, Hamlet, and Laertes all know that their fathers have been killed. All, in their own fashion, revenge their deaths. The desire for vengeance is seen as part of a continuing pattern of human conduct. The way in which that desire is fulfilled or frustrated in the play forces the audience to examine this fashion of human behaviour and the effect that it has upon the lives and fortunes of all of the characters. The varied ways in which individuals meet the challenge of their common humanity are compared and contrasted. The audience are entertained because they are being asked to see, and feel, and understand a little more about the hidden springs of action which are supposed to drive the characters. In being asked to look into the mirror of a stage play and define their own attitudes and sympathies to what they see, they are being given the opportunity to recognize, and per-

3

haps comprehend, something about their own personalities. *Hamlet* is a masterpiece because it is designed to provide intense and unusual possibilities of self-recognition.

The play's pattern of violence is not confined to sons who have lost their fathers. The death of Polonius affects Ophelia as well as Laertes. She is unable to stand the strain imposed by her father's death. Her reaction is violent but it is violence which is turned against herself. Driven insane by the shock, she drowns in circumstances which lead some of the characters to suggest that she has committed the ultimate self-violence of suicide. Her death confirms Laertes in his desire for revenge. That desire, however, makes him a willing instrument of the King. Claudius, too, is engaged in retaliation. He is anxious to counter what he feels to be a threat to his life and throne from Hamlet. He therefore engages Laertes in a plot to murder Hamlet secretly and with the help of poison. Their joint attempt to revenge themselves upon Hamlet succeeds—but it also leads to the death of the Queen and to their own destruction.

As they move passionately but unwittingly to their deaths, Laertes and Ophelia appear to exemplify in conduct the alternative courses of action considered by Hamlet in his soliloquy, 'To be, or not to be' (3 i 56:1710). Ophelia chooses 'not to be' and finds refuge from 'the heart-ache' (3 i 62:1716) of human existence in madness and death. Laertes chooses 'to be' and takes up arms in order to end his troubles by killing his enemy. In this desperate endeavour he meets his own death—knowing that 'I am justly kill'd with mine own treachery' (5 ii 299:3785).

Revenge, madness, and possible self-destruction are all debated passionately in Hamlet's soliloquies. Hamlet's awareness of the possible paths before him, his intense consideration of the issues and their consequences, is only a part of the dramatist's larger awareness of the problem. *Hamlet* dramatizes a number of possible human responses to direct and indirect aggression. It is therefore concerned with the kind of internal psychological pressures which may destroy not only an individual or a society but the human species. The play does not solve this problem. In dramatizing his characters' response and reaction to this situation Shakespeare suggests a number of uncomfortable questions which are usually overlooked by those critics who feel that the problems of Hamlet exist only to provide Shakespeare with an excuse for his dramatic illusion.

The court of Denmark is bound together by the usual ties of kinship and hierarchic social order which can be traced in human society from the 'primitive' tribe to the 'advanced' industrial corporation. The structure of this particular society is influenced by the fact that its present King obtained the crown by murdering his brother. The play dramatizes the way in which Claudius attempts to conceal this fact. Although he is legally and socially accepted as King of Denmark he could hardly count upon the support of his society if the true facts were known. In the course of the play the 'natural' bonds of the society of Denmark are broken in almost every conceivable fashion. As the characters, both men and women, respond to the intolerable pressures created by violence and treachery they become themselves violent and treacherous.

As the play proceeds it becomes clear that Hamlet's problem is not only to combat the violence and treachery with which he is surrounded but to try to control the violence within himself—even when that violence seems 'natural' or even laudable in his situation. The exercise of this control is as necessary, and as difficult, in the twentieth century as it was at the beginning of the seventeenth. It is not surprising that audiences have seen mirrored in Shakespeare's play their own most fundamental problems and ineradicable fears.

It is also not surprising that the play has provoked an enormous moral and critical debate about the nature and fitness of Hamlet's own response to his situation. Critics continue to debate whether Hamlet's conduct is 'normal', 'moral', 'weak', 'selfish', or 'aggressive' because the play forces questions of motive and human responsibility upon the attention of its audience. The play does not solve the riddle of the universe. It does compel its critic to reveal, and sometimes to question, his own concealed assumptions and attitudes to the human predicament. The continuance of this debate is a natural consequence of the play's artistic design and a tribute to Shakespeare's own analysis of the problems. Hamlet's problems are not accidental. They have been created for him by the dramatist.

The moral and psychological questions which grip the attention of the spectator can only exist upon the stage because, in the version of *Hamlet* which was played between 1599 and 1601, Shakespeare had discovered new and brilliant solutions to old intractable dramatic problems. These new solutions made the performance of *Hamlet* as important an event for the Jacobean drama as Marlowe's *Tamburlaine* had been for the Elizabethan. The director, and the critic, of the play must distinguish carefully between the problems presented by the play, which are moral and psychological, and the dramatic and technical problems which Shakespeare solved in order to be able to present his play. The moral problems of *Hamlet* exist because Shakespeare discovered a way in which they could be dramatically expressed.

As a work of dramatic art *Hamlet* is created by five major technical triumphs. These may be listed simply as Shakespeare's use of the Ghost, the device of presenting *The Murder of Gonzago* before the court, the way in which the themes of love and death, involving both Gertrude and Ophelia, are united in the graveyard scene, the way in which the final duel unites the military imagery and the imagery of poison, and, finally, the entire creation of the mind and consciousness of Hamlet. By these methods Shakespeare dramatizes the past, provides dramatic conflict in the present, and prepares a satisfying, but unexpected, future resolution of that conflict.

These are not simple matters but artistic problems of great difficulty and complexity. Hamlet's soliloquies, for example, are one of the most interesting features of the play. Their recurrent themes are conscience, and a consciousness of the human condition which involves an awareness of oblivion and death. Yet Hamlet never steps forward to provide the spectators with a suitable synthesis of safe opinions on these subjects. The soliloquies conspicuously fail to solve the riddle of the universe because they contradict each other. They fail to provide any easily assimilable explanation of Hamlet's own motivation. They express, above all, an appalling awareness of frustration and failure. This uniquely observed dramatization of Hamlet's feelings of personal inadequacy has caused many commentators to assume that anything so strongly expressed must represent the real truth about the character.

The fact that Hamlet feels inadequate does not necessarily mean that he is inadequate. One of the questions raised by the play is precisely what response is adequate in the conditions of Elsinore. Critical attention is usually concentrated upon Hamlet's divided mind and the suggestion is sometimes made that it represents some deep division or sense of personal inadequacy within the dramatist. This fails to observe that the extended presentation of Hamlet's troubled consciousness allows Shakespeare to solve one of the most difficult of his artistic problems.

One of the most helpful critical accounts of this problem is given by Henry James in the preface written for the New York edition of *The Spoils of Poynton*—although the passage quoted actually refers to *A London Life*:

We may strike lights by opposing order to order, one sort to another sort; for in that case we get the correspondences and equivalents that make differences mean something; we get the interest and the tension of disparity where a certain parity may have been in question. Where it may *not* have been in question, where the dramatic encounter is but the poor concussion of positives on one side with negatives on the other, we get little beyond a consideration of the differences between fishes and fowls.[1]

It is evident that one order opposes another in the conflict between Hamlet and Claudius. Hamlet describes it as a duel between 'mighty opposites' (5 ii 62:3565). Under pressure, Claudius naturally resorts to the language of 'divine right' to defend his position as King of Denmark. The cry of 'treason' is still raised at the end of the play when Hamlet stabs the King.

This natural opposition between King and Prince is complicated by two further factors. The audience knows that Claudius obtained the crown by murdering the King of Denmark. In using the language of divine right to sanction his acts as King, Claudius is also implying the possibility of a divine retribution for the act which made him King. It is then possible to regard Hamlet as the agent of this divine retribution. It is equally possible to regard him as a man who has been betrayed by a demon in the shape of his father into an act of damnable impiety. It is clear that this encounter involves more than a poor concussion of positives with negatives.

The contrast between Hamlet and Claudius, however, is only an introduction to the play's major conflict. This takes place in Hamlet's mind. The progress of this mental battle can be traced clearly in the seven soliloquies. Their function in the pattern of the play is to make clear the exact nature of the division in Hamlet's mind. For this reason the soliloquies are not consistent. They vary according to Hamlet's contradictory moods and warring passions. They are not, therefore, a series of wholly positive statements in Hamlet's favour. They present, with an almost mathematical precision, a coherent and logical account of 'the correspondences and equivalents that make differences mean something' in Hamlet's consciousness.

This may be demonstrated briefly by a consideration of Hamlet's fifth and sixth soliloquies. Up to this point the soliloquies have been filled with Hamlet's memory of his father and with his attempt to understand the nature of his own position and role of avenger. He has questioned his own apparent inability to act. Now, on his way to his

[1] Henry James, *The Art of the Novel: Critical Prefaces by Henry James*, ed. R. P. Blackmur, 1934, 132.

mother's closet (3 ii 378:2259), and standing behind the figure of the praying King (3 iii 73:2350), he presents a totally negative image. He no longer mentions conscience. His words provide a complete vocabulary and grammar of intent for an avenger of blood.

It appears to be the duty of exacting a complete and damnable revenge which prevents him from stabbing the King. Yet the seventh soliloquy (4 iv 32:2743 Q 26) returns to a consideration of the earlier problems of conscience and consciousness. Hamlet again debates the questions of honour and action. This soliloquy might be considered to modify the hymn of hate expressed in the fifth and sixth—except that it closes with the words (4 iv 65:2743 Q 59):

Hamlet   O, from this time forth,
          My thoughts be bloody, or be nothing worth!

The feeling of failure and frustration, which Hamlet himself recognizes, is created by this rapid alternation between the language of blood revenge and the language of conscience. These contradictory attitudes can only be reconciled or explained away if the critic chooses to ignore one or more of the soliloquies. Any attempt to resolve the dilemma in this way ignores the problem which has been deliberately created by Shakespeare.

Hamlet is at one moment the Prince who holds in his hand the skull of Yorick, the King's Jester, and uses it to remind himself and the audience of man's mortality. Conscious of his own intelligence, Hamlet naturally questions his place in a universe which may appear at one and the same time to be a 'majestical roof fretted with golden fire' (2 ii 298:1347) and 'a foul and pestilent congregation of vapours' (2 ii 301:1349). At another moment he is a man who hates the King with such determined and implacable loathing that he becomes an avenger who hopes to reach beyond the grave and damn his enemy's soul to eternal hell fire.

These attitudes are difficult to reconcile. They may easily coexist in the same mind. If they do, and it becomes necessary to act on one view or the other, they will create a profound mental disturbance and conflict which cannot be solved by the easy application of moral formulas. It is not possible to be a courtier who is a scholar from Wittenberg and at the same time a courtier who is totally consumed by the passion of blood revenge. Hamlet is a scholar from Wittenberg who is determined to become an avenger of blood. He is consequently judged, by critics of the play, as an over-zealous scholar who proves himself an inadequate avenger, or an inadequate scholar who, neglectful of the doctrines for which the University of Wittenberg was famous throughout Europe, proves himself to be an over-zealous and damnable avenger.

The conflicting accounts of Hamlet's character are themselves evidence that his mind presents a more subtle conflict than 'the poor concussion of positives on one side with negatives on the other'. There is a sense, and I believe it to be a powerful and deeply rooted sense, in which any audience of *Hamlet* longs for the Prince to act in final and decisive fashion against the King. There is also a sense in which an audience must recoil before the entire macabre masque of vengeance— especially when vengeance becomes associated with the techniques of eternal sadism.

Faced with the experience of these contradictory emotions on the part of the protagonist and the audience, it is perhaps natural to conclude that the dilemma is insoluble and that 'the experience of Hamlet, then, culminates in a set of questions to which there are no answers'.[1] It would be a mistake, however, to imply that Shakespeare is content to solve his dramatic problem by representing Hamlet's divided mind and to leave his audience in the same confusion as his characters.

Hamlet's mind is at war with itself because he is aware that more than one single set of answers exists to the problems which face him. These problems, the necessary questions of the play, do not admit of any 'final' or 'ultimate' solution. They must, however, be solved to the extent that in order to act, men have inevitably to judge between particular beliefs and values. The other characters in the play do not hesitate to act because they are sure of their own values and beliefs. Fortinbras and Laertes act because they believe that certain actions are right or honourable. Claudius acts because, although he is aware that his conduct is neither right nor honourable, he intends to survive. Hamlet, as subject as they are to the instinctive pull of human passion, is dramatized as a man who is not only aware of problems which have escaped the notice of the other characters, but is engaged in a search for the right answers.

The dramatist is inevitably involved in moral problems. It is not his task to present his audience with instant recipes for the correct regulation of life or conduct. The kind of art which does present instant recipes is, as Bertolt Brecht and William Burroughs insist, a branch of the international narcotics traffic. The play asks its audience if they are entirely confident that they know that their own answers are right— or whether anyone can know what the right answers are. The play of

[1] Norman Rabkin, *Shakespeare and the Common Understanding*, 1967, 9.

Hamlet culminates in a series of questions to which the audience must find answers. The answers that each individual finds are an expression, a revelation, and a definition of his human personality. This play should also make the spectator wonder if the personality which he has revealed to himself is entirely adequate.

This is precisely Hamlet's own response to the problems of the play. Since Hamlet is unable to bring the inner debate of the soliloquies to a final and satisfactory conclusion, psychology has sought for a final answer to the problem in Hamlet's unconscious. In the Freudian interpretation of the play offered by Dr Ernest Jones[1] Hamlet fails to act, and is unable to explain this failure, because he is suffering from an Oedipus complex. Since he has not resolved his unconscious infantile desires to kill his father and marry his mother he is constitutionally incapable of taking any action against the man who has in fact acted out these fantasy wishes.

This diagnosis is extended to cover the dramatist as well as his creation. This depends upon the critical assumption that Hamlet does not explain his delay because Shakespeare could not explain or understand it. I believe this assumption to be false. Hamlet's delay is a dramatic device which allows the dramatist to question the nature of the act of revenge. This has escaped the notice of many critics and psychologists because they are persuaded that they know the right answer to one of the play's most important and exacting questions. In their view Hamlet ought to kill the King.

It is now traditional for literary critics to decline the whole question by asserting that, however valuable psycho-analysis may be in treating patients, it is not a suitable tool for the analysis of dramatic characters whose existence is purely fictional. This seems to me mistaken. The basis of the dramatist's work is observation of human beings. In this case the observation appears to have been accurate enough to appeal to an audience several hundred years after the play can no longer depend upon local conditions or fashionable appeal. It seems reasonable and probable that this observation could be confirmed by the scientific study of the human mind. There should be no quarrel between literature and science. An unbridgeable difference of opinion exists only between those who think that no scientific explanation of literature is possible and those who imagine that it has already been provided.

Ernest Jones's analysis is inadequate because he has failed to examine one of the major psychological observations of the play. He thinks that Laertes exists in the drama as an example of how Hamlet should

[1] Ernest Jones, *Hamlet and Oedipus*, 1949.

have behaved. The evidence of accumulated criticism indicates that this is a significant response to the events of the play. The audience is, as we have argued, bound to desire Hamlet to execute vengeance upon the King in the same aggressive spirit that Laertes exacts his revenge. The realization that what they desire is a person like Laertes ought to cause the audience more reflection. The reaction of Laertes is a 'normal' and 'human' reaction. It leads to those very normal and human activities of treachery and murder by poison. Jones has made exactly the kind of automatic ethical assumption that the play of *Hamlet* is designed to examine and question. Unthinking aggression is not always necessarily a sign of mental health.

It is possible to argue that Hamlet does display exactly these symptoms of unthinking aggression when he kills Polonius, believing that he has killed the King. This would suggest that he is not as inhibited in his reactions as the Oedipus complex requires, and Jones goes to elaborate lengths to explain away the plain language of the play. It is, however, clear that Hamlet's conduct, the violent reaction natural to his situation, is connected with fundamental instincts of jealousy and sexual affection. The psychology of *Hamlet* is more subtle than the simple observation that infantile relations with one's mother involve sexual feelings which may give rise to adult complications.

The existence of such instincts in the play does not explain Hamlet or help to differentiate *Hamlet* from other similar plays. The protagonist of Henry Chettle's *The Tragedy of Hoffman*, written at approximately the same time as *Hamlet*, spares one of his intended victims, Martha, Duchess of Lunanberg, because he has fallen in love with her. He has murdered her son, Otho, and is now impersonating the dead Prince. Once he has failed to strangle the Duchess in her sleep he has to confess to this impersonation, explain that Prince Otho was drowned in a shipwreck, and persuade her, for a variety of reasons, to permit him to continue his impersonation.

Hoffman's own intentions, as he informs the audience, are unquestionably sexual (H 4 v: 1909):

Hoffman   But, new-made mother, there's another fire
               Burns in this liver; lust and hot desire
               Which you must quench. Must? ay and shall; I know
               Women will like however they say no.
               And since my heart is knit unto her eyes
               If she, being sanctimonious, hate my suit,
               In love this course I'll take, if she deny
               Force her: true, so, *si non blanditus: vi.*

He meets his death in attempting to carry out this plan. He decoys the Duchess to a deserted cave by the sea shore where the skeletons of his dead father and her son hang in chains. She, however, is decoying him and he is surprised by his enemies. He is killed by having an iron crown, heated white-hot, placed upon his head and dies cursing love for betraying his revenge.

It could be argued that Hoffman's failure to complete his revenge is due to the paralysis of his will caused by desire for his 'mother'. Within the analogies of the Freudian system, Hoffman's unresolved desire for his own mother could easily be displaced on to the Duchess. The tragedy of Hoffman is clearly an Oedipus complex. If Hoffman's delay fails to move an audience in the same way as Hamlet's, it is because Hamlet's motives, which he finds inexplicable, have been subjected to a conscious and searching analysis, closely similar to the process of psycho-analysis, on the part of the dramatist. The deliberate creation of Hamlet's 'unconscious' is a technical triumph of Shakespeare's art. It has not yet received the close psychological attention that it deserves.

Hamlet's argument with himself, conducted in soliloquy, is deliberately inconclusive because the dramatist needed to create an unconscious as well as a conscious side of Hamlet's mind. This part of Hamlet's mind, as will be demonstrated, makes a vital contribution to the argument of *Hamlet*. This argument is conducted in the terms of the actions of poison, play, and duel which the actors must perform if they are to present the play. A dramatic argument, however, is a series of more or less accurate observations which have been arranged in a systematic pattern in order to convey the maximum amount of information with the greatest possible clarity to an audience. A dramatic argument is not a divine revelation. It is essential to be as aware of the limitations of the theatre as of its possibilities.

At the end of the play Fortinbras orders Hamlet's body to be borne 'like a soldier to the stage' (5 ii 388:3896) while Horatio prepares, as he had promised, to relate Hamlet's cause 'aright' to the 'unsatisfied' (5 ii 331–2:3823–4). This true and authoritative account of the events of the play ought to resolve all critical doubts about questions of intention and motive. As the actors leave the stage in order to listen to this account they have performed their last exit and the play of *Hamlet* is over. The audience, therefore, must be content to judge the question themselves from what they have seen, and heard, and more or less understood.

Shakespeare declines to be the ultimate judge of his characters.

Horatio's last words to Hamlet (5 ii 351:3849):

Horatio   Good night, sweet prince,
And flights of angels sing thee to thy rest

are, among other things, a reminder that those who seek an ultimate judgment will have to apply to a higher tribunal than the actors on the stage or the audience in the theatre.

The end of the play does not bring its argument to an end. *Hamlet* is a disturbing play because it is about a man who made up his mind. The appalling nature of the decisions in this play, and their equally terrible consequences, leave the spectators on and off the stage—those whom Hamlet calls 'but mutes or audience to this act' (5 ii 327:3819)—still arguing towards a conclusion.

The play, therefore, continually tempts the critic into the confident delivery of the final or ultimate judgments which the author has declined to supply. In this respect it is a notably successful illustration of Hamlet's own critical views on the theatre whose purpose (3 ii 22:1869):

Hamlet   both at the first and now, was and is to hold,
as 'twere, the mirror up to nature; to show
virtue her own feature, scorn her own image,
and the very age and body of the time his form
and pressure.

In *Hamlet* the art of the theatre continually provokes its audience into self-revelation.

Hamlet is so deeply affected by a theatrical performance, the recitation by the First Player of Aeneas' tale to Dido, that he resolves to present *The Murder of Gonzago* before the court. The King is very violently affected by this play. As a result of what he has seen Claudius arranges another court entertainment—the 'play' with foils between Hamlet and Laertes. In each case the 'mirror' of the stage reveals to the spectator his own most fundamental problem in a new and unexpected light. The play asks its audience, as Hamlet asks Gertrude, to 'Look here upon this picture and on this' (3 iv 53:2437) and then turn their eyes upon themselves.

The relevance of the questions asked in the play extends outside the theatre. The answers determine the part that the individual must himself play in the world. The spectators do not share all of Hamlet's problems but their world is also the world of poison, play, and duel.

As Hamlet looks into the empty eyes of death in the graveyard that is Elsinore he speaks to their condition across the gulf of time and circumstance.

Since Shakespeare himself insists on the metaphor of the theatre throughout this play, it is legitimate to say that Hamlet is an actor who has been offered a choice of roles. He is unable to determine which part he ought to play. He has been accused of self-dramatization in the soliloquies. The charge is just. Self-dramatization, however, is an extremely important and valuable human activity.

In his third soliloquy Hamlet compares his own conduct with that of the actor who weeps as he recites the story of Hecuba. In the play scene Hamlet has to become an actor and take part in a play which turns into an unrehearsed happening. The results are spectacular. In the seventh soliloquy Hamlet contrasts his conduct with that of the soldiers of the army of Fortinbras. He is himself called upon to exhibit some of the qualities of a soldier in the duel with Laertes.

In the self-dramatization of the soliloquies Hamlet judges his own conduct to be inadequate because he has so far failed to play the role he feels most essential to him—the role of an avenger of blood. The audience comes to understand the nature of these various roles because Hamlet rehearses them all in the theatre of his own mind. The audience are invited to compare these players' speeches with the actual parts played in action by Hamlet and the other characters of the play. The difference between Hamlet's estimate of himself in soliloquy rehearsal and his actual capabilities in action is one of the methods by which Shakespeare creates the unconscious mind of Hamlet.

In the soliloquies Hamlet blames himself because thought hinders action. Hamlet's thoughts are, however, an examination by the dramatist of the avenger's role that Hamlet desires to play. The competing languages of the soliloquies, the language of thought and conscience and the language of blood and action, define the nature of the incompatible parts that Hamlet feels compelled to play. The soliloquies reveal more than a division and uncertainty in Hamlet's mind. They examine the possibilities of some of the parts open to humanity. Hamlet's divided mind is the best, most economical, dramatic device available for making the power and attraction, and the importance, of these parts clear to an audience in the theatre.

The suggestion that the whole world was a stage for human actors would have been familiar to an Elizabethan audience. When, in *As You Like It*, Shakespeare makes Jaques instruct the Duke and his followers that (2 vii 139:1118):

Jaques   All the world's a stage
And all the men and women merely players:
They have their exits and their entrances;
And one man in his time plays many parts,
His acts being seven ages

he is making use of a figure of thought and speech that had long been familiar in philosophy, art, and literature.

The exceptional importance of this vision of the theatre of the world has been pointed out by Frances Yates:

> Heywood's defence of the theatre is important for the understanding of the real public theatres of the Elizabethan and Jacobean age. The ancient theatre, in the abstract, had gathered a strong emotional and moral appeal, and the theatre of the world as an emblem of the life of man was a *topos* widespread in the Renaissance, whether in the form of memory theatres, or of emblems, or of rhetorical discourses. These associations cannot be entirely separated from the appearance of the real ancient theatres, the public theatres of London.[1]

The morality and mystery plays had shown mankind as a minor but significant actor in the God-created universal drama of heaven and hell, death and judgment. The very name of the Globe theatre was an indication that the actors had not abandoned the claim of their art to have universal applications. *Hamlet* is a play which is peculiarly suited to production in such a theatre of the world. The continual references to plays and playing are direct references to the physical details of the structure of the Globe theatre. They are also a reference to man's continuing performance in the theatre of the greater globe. The idea that life is a performance is naturally associated with the reflection that death provides all of the characters with one undignified universal exit.

The images used by Hamlet in the graveyard to symbolize the triumph of time and fortune are part of this great European tradition. When Hamlet's imagination traces 'the noble dust of Alexander till 'a find it stopping a bung-hole' (5 i 198:3391) it is moving along familiar paths. In a corridor of the Palazzo Trinci at Foligno there are a number of frescoes painted about 1420. One wall shows the great heroes of western tradition, including both Alexander and Julius Caesar, mixing classical and biblical figures. The other wall depicts the seven ages of

[1] Frances A. Yates, *Theatre of the World*, 1969, 165.

man, apparently based upon the descriptions of a French poem of the fourteenth century. In the *Camera delle Stelle* of the same palace the figures of the seven ages of man are repeated. This time they are associated with the hours of the day and the planetary divinities—the Greek and Roman gods whose names had been given to the planets, who ruled the signs of the zodiac and thus determined the fortunes of men.[1]

Shakespeare was familiar with this common association of Time, Fortune, and the Seven Ages of Man. In the same scene in which he delivers his speech upon the theatre of the world Jaques describes his meeting with Touchstone in the forest (*As You Like It*, 2 vii 20:993):

Jaques	And then he drew a dial from his poke,
	And, looking on it with lack-lustre eye,
	Says very wisely, 'It is ten o'clock;
	Thus we may see', quoth he, 'how the world wags;
	'Tis but an hour ago since it was nine;
	And after one hour more 'twill be eleven;
	And so, from hour to hour, we ripe and ripe,
	And then, from hour to hour, we rot and rot;
	And thereby hangs a tale.'

Shakespeare allows his audience to laugh at Touchstone's heavily moralized view of Fortune and the hours of the day before he makes Jaques remind them that such folly is another expression of an inescapable reality. Even the road through the Forest of Arden leads to old age and death.

Shakespeare uses this familiar comparison for new and unexpected dramatic purposes in *Hamlet*. The theatre is not now an image of an orderly progression through the seven ages of man. The players have to choose their parts without time to reflect or enough information to allow them to order the anarchy of their own imaginations. In choosing their parts they are also choosing the manner of their own deaths. All the available parts end in the grim dumb show of the graveyard where the politician, the courtier, the lawyer, and Yorick, the King's Jester, all wear the anonymous mask of a death's-head.

The parts of the theatre of the world seem interchangeable. The pride of possession and the lust for power, even the heroic triumphs

[1] J. Seznec, *The Survival of the Pagan Gods*, Harper Torchbooks, 1961, 130–2; Mario Salmi, 'Gli affreschi del Palazzo Trinci a Foligno', *Bollettino d'Arte*, xiii (1919), 139–80; E. Mâle, *L'Art Religieux de la fin du Moyen Age en France*, 1908, 324 ff.

of Alexander and Julius Caesar, make little sense when compared to the overwhelming fact of man's mortality. Yet in another moment Hamlet will be grappling with Laertes over Ophelia's grave asserting his love for that most useless of all inanimate objects, a human corpse. The play is a dance of death in which it can still matter how the individual parts are played.

The metaphor of the theatre of the world in *Hamlet* is more than a literary commonplace. It is a symbol which provides a convenient and essentially theatrical method of referring to more than one series of fairly complex ideas. The metaphor of 'playing a part' can have more than one connotation. Claudius, for example, plays the part of King of Denmark in two ways. He appears as the legitimate elected ruler but he has also, in murdering his brother, managed to assume a role to which he is not entitled. During the play the crazed face of the murderer slowly becomes clearer behind the mask of the King.

The first time that Hamlet appears on stage he defends himself against the charge that he is playing a part in continuing to mourn for his father's death (i ii 76:257):

Hamlet   Seems, madam! Nay, it is; I know not ' seems '.
'Tis not alone my inky cloak, good mother,
Nor customary suits of solemn black,
Nor windy suspiration of forc'd breath,
No, nor the fruitful river in the eye,
Nor the dejected haviour of the visage,
Together with all forms, moods, shapes of grief,
That can denote me truly. These, indeed, seem;
For they are actions that a man might play;
But I have that within which passes show—
These but the trappings and the suits of woe.

'Playing' and 'seeming' are both key terms in the argument of *Hamlet*.

In the sense used by Hamlet 'seem' has the implication of deceit or 'false-seeming'. Duke Vincentio uses it in this sense in *Measure for Measure* when he comments upon Angelo's assumption of power (i iii 53:345):

Duke   Hence shall we see,
If power change purpose, what our seemers be.

'Play' can mean more than the art of acting. It is associated with children's play and it can also mean sexual play. All three meanings are vividly present in Leontes's speech in *The Winter's Tale* (i ii 187: 269):

Leontes   Go, play, boy, play; thy mother plays, and I
                  Play too; but so disgrac'd a part, whose issue
                  Will hiss me to my grave. Contempt and clamour
                  Will be my knell. Go, play, boy, play.

These meanings of false-seeming and playing are an essential part of the theatrical metaphor in *Hamlet*.

The King agrees to the presentation of the play entitled *The Murder of Gonzago* before the court as the kind of 'child's play' which may divert Hamlet from his melancholy. The actual performance, however, is a play about false-seeming in which sexual play is preceded by the act of murder. Hamlet is 'playing' with the King—as a cat plays with a mouse or an angler plays a fish. He also 'plays' upon words in his conversation with Ophelia. The double meanings have clear overtones of sexual 'play'.

The inner-play is the most extended and important use of the theatrical metaphor in *Hamlet*. As Maynard Mack has described it:

On the stage before us is a play of false appearances in which an actor called the player-king is playing. But there is also on the stage, Claudius, another player-king who is a spectator of this player. And there is on the stage, besides, a prince who is a spectator of both these player-kings and who plays with great intensity a player's role himself. And around these kings and that prince is a group of courtly spectators—Gertrude, Rosencrantz, Guildenstern, Polonius, and the rest—and they, as we have come to know, are players too. And lastly there are ourselves, an audience watching all these audiences who are also players. Where, it may suddenly occur to us to ask, does the playing end? Which *are* the guilty creatures sitting at a play? When is an act not an 'act'?[1]

This use of *The Murder of Gonzago* is a brilliant solution to a technical problem. It presents, in concrete terms, the dramatic and logical argument of *Hamlet* to the audience.

The inner-play is, in the first instance, an instrument of Hamlet's will. It satisfies him that the Ghost is an 'honest' Ghost. It convinces him that Claudius is indeed a murderer and that his own task of vengeance is justified. These are in themselves sufficient reasons for its dramatic existence. Its real function is, however, to solve some of Shakespeare's dramatic problems. This inner-play allows the dramatist to exercise complete control over the past, the present, and the future in the time scheme of his play.

[1] Maynard Mack, 'The World of *Hamlet*', *The Yale Review*, xli (1952), 502–23.

The inner-play is a representation of the past whose present performance has an instant psychological effect so powerful that it determines
future action. After the play, the killing begins. The deaths which
occur after *The Murder of Gonzago* are, however, a direct consequence
of the deaths that are dramatized within it. Up to this point the
audience have only heard of the murder of Hamlet's father. Now they
have seen it. The inner-play dramatizes events which occurred before
the beginning of the action of *Hamlet*. This presentation of the past is
one of the most difficult problems facing any dramatist.

The past represented in the inner-play is an act of poisoning. This
act is performed twice before the watching King and court. The
audience are bound to remember, since this scene is designed to
remind them of that specific fact, that King Hamlet was murdered by
having poison poured into his ear. They may also remember the
earlier words of the Ghost (1 v 35:722):

Ghost   'Tis given out that, sleeping in my orchard,
               A serpent stung me; so the whole ear of Denmark
               Is by a forged process of my death
               Rankly abus'd; but know, thou noble youth,
               The serpent that did sting thy father's life
               Now wears his crown.

Claudius has poisoned the ear of Denmark with false reports, just as he
poisoned the ear of Denmark's King with 'juice of cursed hebona in a
vial' (1 v 62:747).

It has often been pointed out, perhaps most notably by Caroline
Spurgeon, that 'in *Hamlet* there hovers all through the play in both
words and word pictures the conception of disease, especially of a hidden corruption infecting and destroying a wholesome body'.[1] There is,
however, some disagreement among the characters about the source
of the infection which they recognize is spreading through the body-
politic of Denmark.

The Ghost and Hamlet believe that Claudius is the source of this
poison. Polonius and Laertes, on the other hand, see Hamlet as a
possible origin of the 'canker' (1 iii 39:502) or 'contagious blastments'
(1 iii 42:505) which they fear threaten Ophelia. Claudius describes
Hamlet as a disease raging in his blood which can only be cured by
the King of England. The cure is the execution of Hamlet (4 iii 65:
2730):

[1] Caroline Spurgeon, *Shakespeare's Imagery*, 1935, 213.

King   Do it, England:
     For like the hectic in my blood he rages,
     And thou must cure me. Till I know 'tis done,
     Howe'er my haps, my joys were ne'er begun.

On the other hand, if Claudius is the source of the infection, then the inner-play may be regarded as the beginning of a cure.

This is, perhaps, lightly suggested in the 'medical' imagery which follows upon the success of Hamlet's stratagem (3 ii 290:2168):

Guildenstern Good my lord, vouchsafe me a word with you.

Hamlet   Sir, a whole history.

Guildenstern The King, sir—

Hamlet   Ay, sir, what of him?

Guildenstern Is, in his retirement, marvellous distemp'red.

Hamlet   With drink, sir?

Guildenstern No, my lord, rather with choler.

Hamlet   Your wisdom should show itself more richer to signify this to his doctor; for, for me to put him to his purgation would perhaps plunge him into far more choler.

The presentation of *The Murder of Gonzago* convinces Claudius that he is diseased. He diagnoses this disease as Hamlet and attempts to cure himself by sending the Prince to execution in England. When that scheme fails he arranges the fencing match in which a poisoned cup and a poisoned rapier are used. This attempt is both successful and fatal. Hamlet is killed but the King dies of his own poison. Curing oneself of disease by the use of poison is a risky occupation. The image of the past in the inner-play is an image of poison. Its performance causes further poisoning.

The 'mirror up to nature' (3 ii 23:1870) which reflects this image of poison brings Claudius literally face to face with his own past. The use of the term 'mirror' for a stage play or other work of literature has a long history in art and philosophy. One of the implications of the term is that the mirror does not simply reflect: it reflects the truth even when that truth may be unwelcome. Mirrors may be magical. As Otto Rank writes:

It is a man's reflection in a mirror (originally water) which provides a more life-like image of the self than the dark featureless shadow.

In Greek mythology, we find traditions bearing out this creative significance of the mirrored image for artistic inspiration. One of the most primitive deities in prehistoric Greece, Dionysos, known through his mysterious cults, was said to have been conceived by his mother Persephone as she admired herself in a mirror. He himself, according to Procules' account, created the world of things after his miraculous re-birth in the following manner: one day Dionysos gazed at himself in a mirror, the work of the mythical artisan Hephaistos, and, seduced by the reflection, created the external world in his own image.[1]

In the mirror which Hamlet has placed before him Claudius can see the way in which he created the present world of the court. Claudius as he is now, the King, is faced by Claudius as he was then, a murderer. He realizes that both are images of the same person. The play does not reveal this truth about the past to the other spectators—apart from Hamlet and Horatio who already know it. Art provides an opportunity for recognition rather than revelation. The most important effect of the inner-play is to force Claudius to recognize a crime whose full horror he had succeeded in concealing from his own consciousness. The inner-play performs the exact function predicted for it by Hamlet: it catches the conscience of the King.

In the privacy of his chamber Claudius falls upon his knees in prayer. He is attempting to wipe away from his mind the hideous reflection of the murderer. He believes that the murder of his brother is recorded in heaven. There he will be called upon to give a true account of his actions before the bar of a court which cannot be deceived by false-seeming but will compel him to give evidence for the prosecution. He also believes that it is possible to obtain pardon; that the grace of God can offer mercy even to those who have committed the crime of Cain and murdered their brothers.

In order to obtain forgiveness, however, he knows that he must repent. He must admit, not only to himself but to the world, that the image presented by the play was true. He must give up (3 iii 54:2330):

King   those effects for which I did the murder—
          My crown, mine own ambition, and my queen.

This, as he recognizes, he is unable to do. As he is in the very act of acknowledging that, for him, repentance is impossible the image of retribution—an avenger of blood with drawn sword—comes and stands behind him.

[1] Otto Rank, *Beyond Psychology*, Dover Books, 1958, 97.

The King cannot alter the past but he could obtain forgiveness if he were prepared to abandon playing his present part as King. Unwilling to change roles, he now finds that his future actions are conditioned by his former role as a murderer. If he is to remain King he must continue to be a false-seemer and play a part. It is evident, however, that Hamlet intends to interfere with the King's acting. He appears, somehow, to have obtained information which has allowed him to catch a glimpse of the murderer beneath the King. There is some danger that he may spoil the performance by unmasking the King.

Having gained the crown by poisoning the King, his brother Hamlet, Claudius must now attempt to keep it by murdering the Prince, his nephew Hamlet. The representation of his crime before him on the stage thus compels him to attempt to repeat his previous success in the role of murderer. The mirror image of the play has shown Claudius a true and exact reflection of his own nature. He now proceeds to prove that he is, as Hamlet says, 'a murderer and a villain' (3 iv 96: 2475).

The inner-play forces the audience on stage to reveal the parts that they have chosen for themselves in the theatre of the world, both in the past and for the future. It acts as a mirror for Hamlet as well as the King. *The Murder of Gonzago* is first performed by the actors in a dumb show and followed by a spoken play. Both dumb show and play present the same argument—the poisoning of a king.

On his first appearance the poisoner is necessarily an unknown and anonymous figure, a 'fellow'. In the spoken play he is carefully identified. He is named by Hamlet, rather than by the actors, as (3 ii 238: 2112) 'one Lucianus, nephew to the King'. Hamlet even speaks some of the actor's lines for him—or invents the kind of speech he ought to use, since the lines quoted by Hamlet are not spoken by the player. Hamlet may intend his line 'the croaking raven doth bellow for revenge' (3 ii 247:2122) as a parody of the high revenge style. The language he uses in his own fifth and sixth soliloquies bears a more than striking resemblance to the melodramatic language spoken by the actor who plays the part of Lucianus.

The act of poisoning is repeated during *The Murder of Gonzago* because Shakespeare is using the inner-play to represent two separate occasions on which poison is used. The inner-play mirrors the murder that is past, the murder of a king by his brother, and the murder that is yet to come, the killing of a king by his nephew. This is the event which the audience have been anticipating ever since they heard the command of the Ghost. The image which they now see enacted in the mirror of the play is rather unexpected. The different roles of murderer and avenger appear to be played by the same actor. The two functions seem to coexist in one part.

The inner-play thus gives the questions of the soliloquies a new direction. Instead of the question that Hamlet asked himself, why does he hesitate to kill the King, the play substitutes a different question, 'Is Hamlet going to play the part of Lucianus?' It is evident, from the evidence of critical commentary, that many spectators of the play feel that Hamlet ought to play his chosen role of avenger. Others feel that he ought not to play it but that he does, in fact, come to accept it. It is because he thinks that he has accepted it that Hamlet postpones the execution of vengeance on the praying Claudius. He intends to wait until the King is engaged in an act 'That has no relish of salvation in't' (3 iii 92:2367). The fifth and sixth soliloquies, and the action of the prayer scene, at least make clear to the audience that the role of avenger is also the role of the secret murderer Lucianus.

After the prayer scene Hamlet is no longer free to choose his own role. The exact nature of the parts that remain available to the characters is determined by the King's casting of parts in his own court entertainment. This is the 'play' with foils which Claudius has devised as an answer to the threat contained in the inner-play.

The duel scene which ends the play is thus the logical consequence and counterpart of the play scene. The immediate consequence of the inner-play had been, not the murder of the King, but the death of Polonius. This death abruptly reverses the apparent roles of Hamlet and Claudius. Hamlet may still be an avenger, but he is also the object of a son's vengeance. The King, knowing that Hamlet represents a threat to his life, is quick to turn this situation to his own advantage.

After the death of Polonius, Hamlet is sent to England in the custody of Rosencrantz and Guildenstern. This first attempt on Hamlet's life is a disastrous failure. Hamlet substitutes his own forged commission for the royal death warrant. After the engagement with the pirate ship Hamlet is landed again in Denmark while Rosencrantz and Guildenstern sail on to their execution in England.

Claudius now uses Laertes and his natural desire for vengeance as the instrument of his own deadly intent. The actual act of fencing is correctly described as 'play'. It is also a 'play' in the theatrical sense since Claudius and Laertes are acting elaborate parts in a masque of their own devising. Only they can know how the action of this masque is supposed to develop since only they (apart from the theatre audience) know that certain of the properties employed, like the poisoned sword and poisoned drink, are genuinely deadly.

In using an unbated rapier which he has also anointed with poison during what purports to be a friendly wager on a contest of skill, Laertes breaks the honourable code of conduct which was supposed to govern the art of fencing. He becomes a false-seemer in search of a complete, bloody, and satisfying revenge. This point about the ethics of revenge is made clearly and deliberately by Shakespeare. It is Claudius who believes that 'Revenge should have no bounds' (4 vii 128:3118) and Laertes who is prepared to violate sanctuary or break his own code of honour to achieve it.

This counterstroke of the King follows upon Hamlet's success in the play, prayer, and closet scenes. Claudius bases the plan for his court entertainment upon his estimate of the characters of Laertes and Hamlet. He imagines that he can safely predict their reactions. He is right in his assessment of the considerations which would affect Laertes. The total success of the plan depends upon two other factors. Hamlet must fail to notice that one of the rapiers is sharp, and Laertes must be able to hit him with its point. The King has decided to allow for a certain margin of error and has prepared a poisoned cup as well.

The plan fails because Claudius has made a serious mistake in his casting of parts. Hamlet ought to behave in an honourable but in-efficient fashion. It turns out that he is a more accomplished actor and a far more dangerous opponent than Claudius imagined. Hamlet's unexpected performance cannot save him from death but it does expose 'the foul practice' (5 ii 309:3798) of his opponents.

The double part of Lucianus, as poisoner and avenger, predicted in *The Murder of Gonzago* has now been filled and the role has been played out to the end. Claudius and Laertes, the original murderer and the new avenger, are seen as partners and allies in guilt and death. The role of Lucianus is now seen to be self-defeating and self-destructive—like the foul disease which constantly appears in the imagery of the play. The poisoned pearl or 'union' used by Claudius to rid himself of Hamlet also concludes the poisoned union of his own incestuous marriage by killing the Queen. The story of *Hamlet* ends, as it had begun, in death by poison.

The violent action of the fencing match between Hamlet and Laertes provides an obviously exciting and theatrical end to the play. It expresses in physical action the violence which has long been present in the language and which has been constantly predicted by the dramatist and expected by the audience. The idea of the duel is one of the great images which dominate the action of the play.

The first information that the audience receives from Horatio after the appearance of the Ghost is an account of the famous duel fought between King Hamlet and King Fortinbras of Norway. This was a combat of champions 'well ratified by law and heraldry' (1 i 87:104) and its result should have been legally binding upon both states. Instead, Denmark is now being forced to make hasty preparations to defend itself against an army of irregular mercenaries led by young Fortinbras.

This attack is diverted by prompt diplomatic manœuvre and Fortinbras leads his army against Poland instead of Denmark. Every time that the attention of the audience is directed to Norway—as when the Danish ambassadors leave the stage or return bringing peace with honour, or when Hamlet encounters the army of Fortinbras—they are reminded of the original heroic combat fought by Hamlet's father.

Images of war and rumours of war are continually present in the language of the play. Like the images of poison and disease the images of war have a structural as well as a decorative function. Hamlet once refers to the struggle between himself and his uncle as a duel of 'mighty opposites' (5 ii 62:3565). The military imagery exists, as Kenneth Muir has suggested, 'to emphasise that Claudius and Hamlet are engaged in a duel to the death, a duel which does lead ultimately to both their deaths'.[1]

The nature of the duel between Hamlet and Claudius is complicated by the way in which it has to be conducted. From the beginning of the play Claudius, suspicious of Hamlet's manner and language, has interposed other people between the Prince and himself. He has summoned Rosencrantz and Guildenstern home to act as his agents. He allows Polonius to use Ophelia as a bait for information. When that fails he agrees to use Gertrude in a similar role.

At this point *The Murder of Gonzago* is performed, the mouse-trap snaps shut, and Polonius is killed behind the arras. Claudius now uses Rosencrantz and Guildenstern, who may be unaware of their true function, as the instruments of murder. When they perish in the execution of what they conceive to be their duty, the King, knowing only that they have failed, turns to Laertes as a man who does not

[1] Kenneth Muir, 'Imagery and Symbolism in *Hamlet*', *Études Anglaises*, xvii (1964), 352–63. R. B. Heilman, in 'To Know Himself: An Aspect of Tragic Structure', *Review of English Literature*, v (1964), 36–57, makes the same point: 'It is a world of war: the duel writ large.'

scruple to contemplate secret murder. Only when Laertes falls mortally wounded is the King completely exposed and even then his last words are a call for further help. The action of the play can be seen in terms of a long duel of wits which eventually becomes a physical duel with weapons.

The inner-play is obviously a crucial moment in the conduct of this duel. The play has a special moral reference for both Hamlet and Claudius. It provokes them both into violent and self-revelatory action. It is perhaps the most double-edged and deadly weapon in *Hamlet*. At the moment of its performance the past is an act of murder by poison, the present a play about poison, and the future a duel in which the combatants, and some of the spectators, will die by poison.

Poison, play, and duel are not only the dominant symbols of the action of *Hamlet*. They recur at every stage of the plot and are used to structure the entire language of the play. It is not possible to discuss the acts of poisoning, the performance of the inner-play, and the duel between Hamlet and Laertes as entirely distinct actions. Each act of poisoning is part of the 'play' of the court and the duel between Hamlet and Claudius. Each act of playing is part of the search for an advantage in the duel of wits and is a search for information about poison or a disguise for the actual administration of it. Each stroke in the duel of wits between Claudius and Hamlet is a 'play' upon words concerned with poison until the words themselves become barbed, poisonous, and turn into the poisoned weapons of the duel scene.

The audience first sees the Ghost of the King who had fought a famous duel and been murdered by poison. The revelation of the Ghost leads to the performance of the inner-play with its double presentation of poison. His defeat in this duel of wits leaves Claudius with the alternatives of repenting or continuing his course of poison. He chooses to repeat his crime in the shape of the duel. Against this basic action Shakespeare counterpoints the intricate pattern of his verse which repeats the pattern in every scene, sometimes in almost every line, to achieve the final ironic and deadly harmony of *Hamlet*. The complex structure of the language, and the evident interaction of these dominant images, express the essential distinctions of character and motive which form the intellectual and emotional basis of the drama. Upon these distinctions rests its psychological power as a play.

The duel dramatized by Shakespeare is not simply an actors' fencing match. It is a duel in the mind of Hamlet, and in the mind of the audience, between fundamental human instincts, impulses, and affections. These instincts and affections cannot all be satisfied since they often demand different and contradictory courses of action. The choice between them may have tragic consequences. Shakespeare's play investigates the exact nature of that choice, and the human limitations which circumscribe the characters' freedom of action.

The problem of *Hamlet* exists because Hamlet does not step forward to speak a divinely-inspired soliloquy destined to put an end to war and human misery and to man's tyranny over his fellow-men. The problem of *Hamlet* will be solved when that soliloquy has been written. A large part of the commentary on this extraordinary play has been an attempt by its critics, ironically encouraged by the dramatist, to write such a soliloquy. What alienates Hamlet from us is his humanity.

This humanity is expressed in Hamlet's unusual awareness of the possible paths before him, in his intense consideration of the issues, and his acceptance of the necessity of following his chosen course to what can only be a bitter end. Like Oedipus, Hamlet relies upon the weapons of the human intellect and the power of human thought. Like Oedipus, he finds that they are not strong enough to protect him from the operation of time and fortune, or the dark pull of instinctive human passions over which the intellect has only a tenuous control. Yet in *Hamlet*, as in the *Oedipus Tyrannus* of Sophocles, the power of the human mind, the union of understanding and love which the Elizabethans called conscience, is not entirely defeated.

The Murder of Gonzago caught the conscience of the King. It also makes clear that the role which Hamlet desires to play, the role which he reproaches himself for not playing, is both barbarous and disgusting. The success of the inner-play appears, in the fifth and sixth soliloquies, to have reduced Hamlet to the level of Claudius. Yet the fact that it makes Hamlet determined to play the part of a secret murderer also removes from him for ever the opportunity of playing that role. When the King rises from prayer it will be to deliver a deadly series of counter-strokes which will cost Hamlet his life. The scenes in which Hamlet instructs the players in their art are the last scenes in which Hamlet is in command of his destiny.

Yet this moment is sufficient. The fact that the play does catch the King's conscience makes it Hamlet's successful act of revenge against the King. Once the limed soul of the King has failed to struggle free, once he has no hope of freeing himself from his guilt, once he is determined never to give up his throne, or his ambition, or his Queen, Claudius can do nothing else except attempt to repeat his original crime. This time he fails. It is not possible for him to repeat his success in the role of Lucianus.

The prayer scene marks the end of the opportunity for secret revenge in *Hamlet*. If the King had repented then Hamlet would never have been given the opportunity to damn his soul as well as his body. The grace of God would have frustrated the code of vengeance. Since, however, the King has had the opportunity to repent he can never again be an unsuspecting victim. It is one of the great ironies of the play that he destroys himself in his effort to achieve security.

In wrestling with his own conscience Hamlet blames himself for substituting words for action (2 ii 578:1623):

Hamlet   Why, what an ass am I! This is most brave,
That I, the son of a dear father murder'd,
Prompted to my revenge by heaven and hell,
Must, like a whore, unpack my heart with words,
And fall a-cursing like a very drab,
A scullion.

Criticism and psychology have often agreed with this condemnation. In *Art and Artist* Otto Rank comments on Hamlet's preoccupation with words:

> Taking Hamlet as the type of the passive, inactive hero, whose indecisiveness has led to so many discussions and commentaries, what he really expresses is just this characteristic word-magic of the hero. Though he does occasionally despise himself for venting himself only in words, the whole play is substantially built up on a faith in words which are imagined capable of improving men and altering circumstances.[1]

In presenting *The Murder of Gonzago*, however, Hamlet is neither passive nor inactive. The words are not a substitute for an attack upon the King. They are an attack. Hamlet's choice of weapons is correct. Words are a weapon against which the policy and poison of Claudius is ineffective. Sitting at a play the King is poisoned by a mortal self-knowledge. He plunges through the mirror to self-destruction.

Hamlet despises his own words and thoughts because he recognizes that it is the power of consciousness or conscience which makes him too 'cowardly' to act instantly as a secret and bloody avenger. The action of the play, and the conduct of the other characters, suggest that to hesitate before committing the act of murder, or to avoid the kind of blind passion which exacts instant retribution for every real or imagined wrong, may not be as cowardly or as despicable as Hamlet

[1] Otto Rank, *Art and Artist*, tr. Charles Francis Atkinson, 1943, 284.

imagines. Claudius may not be hindered by the cowardice of conscience but it is still his conscience, or his lack of it, which kills Claudius. In *Hamlet*, as in the theatre of the world, words are capable of altering circumstances. Ideas are also weapons of war.

Chapter 2

HAMLET
AND THE ART OF MEMORY

The appearance of the Ghost upon the battlements of Elsinore is a striking theatrical effect which introduces an audience abruptly to the problems of Hamlet. Its first appearance is designed to communicate a sense of fear and wonder from the stage to the audience—and this fear is independent of their belief in ghosts. The veterans of the guard are alarmed by the armed figure of the King of Denmark. Despite its military appearance, this figure is clearly outside the scope of their duty and warlike preparation. It even causes Horatio, the scholar they have summoned to help them, to 'tremble and look pale' (1 i 53:68). The 'fearful summons' (1 i 149:148) of the crowing cock ensures that the Ghost's response to the formulas of religion and scholarship is as uncertain as its imperviousness to partisans is clear.

Doubt and uncertainty surround every appearance of the Ghost. This means that the first half of the play is shadowed by a malign sense of threatening ill-fortune which is the more menacing because it is never clearly defined. The presence of such a supernatural figure raises acute moral and theological questions for the actors and the audience. It is also Shakespeare's solution to one of the most pressing artistic problems of the play.

It is essential to make and preserve the distinction between the moral questions raised by the Ghost and the dramatic problems solved by the Ghost. This character, above all others in the play, exercises an unusually powerful temptation which continually tantalizes commen-

tators. It offers the illusion of certainty. The instant that Hamlet himself sees the Ghost he expresses the dilemma which haunts criticism
(1 iv 40:625):

Hamlet   Be thou a spirit of health or goblin damn'd,
                Bring with thee airs from heaven or blasts from hell,
                Be thy intents wicked or charitable,
                Thou com'st in such a questionable shape
                That I will speak to thee.

Horatio is more certain. On the two occasions on which he sees the
Ghost he treats it as if it might be an evil spirit. He is afraid that it may
represent a threat to Hamlet's reason and life.

The Ghost fulfils Horatio's fear. It does affect Hamlet's reason and
his life. The question, however, of whether it is a 'spirit of health' or
'goblin damn'd' is never satisfactorily resolved in the course of the
play. After talking with his father's spirit Hamlet can assure his friends,
and the audience, that 'It is an honest ghost' (1 v 138:831) but in his
third soliloquy he is still troubled by the thought that (2 ii 594:1638):

Hamlet   The spirit that I have seen
              May be a devil; and the devil hath power
              T'assume a pleasing shape.

This is one of Hamlet's main reasons for presenting *The Murder of
Gonzago* before the King.

After the inner-play, it is true, he tells Horatio that he will 'take the
ghost's word for a thousand pound' (3 ii 280:2158). It is evident that
Claudius is a murderer. The fact that the Ghost has told the truth
about the murder of King Hamlet does not necessarily resolve all
doubts about its origin. It is possible for the devil to tell the truth for
his own purposes. If those purposes were to turn Hamlet into the
damnable figure of Lucianus then the Ghost could still be a demon.[1]

The moral problems of the play would appear much simpler if the
audience and the commentators could make up their minds unequi-
vocally about the nature of the Ghost. If it is a 'spirit of health' carrying
the command of heaven then Hamlet's duty of revenge is binding in
both honour and conscience. His delay in killing the King is then both
unnecessary and inexplicable. If the Ghost is a 'goblin damn'd' then

---

[1] Eleanor Prosser, in *Hamlet and Revenge* (1967, 112), demonstrates this point
beyond reasonable doubt.

Hamlet has been ensnared by an agent of hell in his father's shape and the whole act of revenge may be dismissed as a device of the Devil.

Hamlet's own doubts about this question appear to make the Ghost what Dover Wilson calls the 'linchpin' of *Hamlet*.[1] A great deal that has been written about this difficult critical problem is succinctly summed up by Morris Weitz:

> The basic problem for Hamlet as well as for his audience, consequently, was: Is the Ghost that Hamlet has seen and conversed with his father's spirit, a devil—as he seems to be in the cellarage scene—or an angel? Until we understand that this was a crucial problem for Hamlet and his audience, much of the drama, especially Hamlet's expressed motive for the play (2 ii 585–601:1629–45), remains unintelligible.[2]

Critics of the play remain sharply divided about this question. Before committing himself to confident pronouncement, it is important for any commentator to notice that he is left to reach after certainty alone. No one in the play offers to make up the mind of the audience about this question. The doubts which exist in the minds of the characters are always expressed in conditional form. In order to convince himself the critic must rely upon contemporary evidence and treatises on the nature of ghosts and demonic possession. In order to achieve moral certainty it is necessary to abandon the text of the play.

It can be argued that Shakespeare was appealing to beliefs that were so firmly fixed in the minds of his audience that it was unnecessary to make more definite statements. The kind of certainty, however, offered by such evidence is entirely different in kind from the certainty which Shakespeare usually offers his audience in such matters. In *Othello*, *King Lear*, or *Macbeth*, however ambiguous the motives of the main characters may be, the instruments of darkness are always clearly identified. Before these plays end evil is not only recognized: it is openly and frequently named as evil upon the stage.

It is impossible for an audience to question the malevolence of Iago, to misunderstand the cold calculation of Edmund, or to doubt the fiendish nature of the Weird Sisters. It is possible to argue that Shakespeare uses this emphasis in his later tragedies because he had been dismayed at the tendency to misinterpret the Ghost. This clarity, however, is also found in the early comedies. In the light of Shakespeare's usual dramatic practice it seems reasonable to argue that the nature of the Ghost is intended to be an open question.

[1] John Dover Wilson, *What Happens in Hamlet*, 1935, 52.
[2] Morris Weitz, *Hamlet and the Philosophy of Literary Criticism*, 1964, 118.

The Ghost raises more questions than can be solved by Horatio's 'philosophy' (i v 167:864) or by our own. It is a spirit which seems to have risen from the grave. In particular, it is a father's spirit calling upon his son for revenge. Such an apparition is bound to make a powerful psychological appeal to any human audience. It is also bound to leave them in a state of doubt and uncertainty. The questions of heaven and hell, death and judgment, were answered, but scarcely solved, by the Elizabethan theologians. The Ghost, however, is more powerful and more primitive than the careful catalogues of the theologians. Fundamentally its appeal is pre-Christian and prehistoric. It is not an appeal that the most sophisticated audience can ignore.

The problem of the Ghost is not solved within the play because its essence eludes the intellectual grasp of the characters in the same way that its form escapes their partisans. It does not escape the dramatist's definition. The logic of the drama does not require a solution to the theological problems raised by the Ghost. Its dramatic function is more important than its moral reference. If Shakespeare had chosen to be more specific about the Ghost he would actually have limited his own dramatic freedom.

The Ghost exists to create Hamlet's problems, not to solve them. The most necessary question of the play is not what Hamlet, or the Elizabethan audience, thinks about the Ghost. It is what Hamlet intends to do about the Ghost's revelation of murder, adultery, and incest. Only Hamlet can translate the Ghost's command into action. The responsibility for that action is Hamlet's alone. The question of Hamlet's responsibility for his actions is raised in its most acute form once he is sure that the Ghost has spoken the truth. To define the Ghost more fully would be to limit Hamlet's own responsibility for dealing with the murderer who is also his uncle and the King of Denmark. The chief dramatic function of the Ghost is not to start a theological debate, although theological questions are inseparable from its appearance, but to concentrate the attention of the audience upon the really vital conflict of the play—the division within Hamlet's mind and will.

This dramatic function is not confined to establishing an atmosphere and giving the audience essential information. The actual command to Hamlet to revenge his father's 'foul and most unnatural murder' (i v 25:710) is delayed until more than five hundred and fifty lines have been spoken. When that moment comes, the growing intensity of the reactions of Bernardo, Marcellus, Horatio, and Hamlet compel the audience to give the maximum attention to words which determine the future course of the action. Shakespeare, however, is seldom content to compel attention without offering his audience the opportunity of understanding.

The importance of the comparatively slow opening of *Hamlet* may be illustrated by a comparison with the opening of Henry Chettle's *The Tragedy of Hoffman*. It is possible that Chettle was imitating the obviously successful features of *Hamlet* in his play. In his opening, Hoffman's first soliloquy appears to give the audience as much information in twenty-eight lines as the entire first act of *Hamlet* (*The Tragedy of Hoffman*, B 1 r:3):

Hoffman   Hence clouds of melancholy
I'll be no longer subject to your schisms.
But thou, dear soul, whose nerves and arteries
In dead resoundings summon up revenge,
And thou shalt hate—but be appeas'd sweet hearse
The dead resemblance of my living father
   (*strikes ope a curtain where appears a body*)
And with a heart as air, swift as thought
I'll execute justly in such a cause.
Where truth leadeth, what coward would not fight?
Ill acts move some, but mine's a cause is right.
   (*thunder and lightning*)

The thunder and lightning are explained as heaven's anger at Hoffman's tardiness in executing his revenge. The audience can have no reason for such a complaint. By the end of this speech, Hoffman visits a 'promont's top' where he observes his first victim cast by shipwreck into his power. Almost before the audience have had time to identify the characters the first act of revenge has been committed. This act is made memorable by heating an iron crown white-hot and placing it on the victim's head.

A scene which reveals a skeleton behind a curtain and moves on to murder with an iron crown is bound to compel attention. This, however, is the limit of Chettle's competence as a dramatist. He can offer his audience no understanding of the events they witness. His only dramatic resource is to repeat, with variations, the original revenge murder until Hoffman falls in love. This provides the excuse for his enemies to dispatch him with the same burning crown.

Shakespeare's opening scene is as dramatic and arresting as Chettle's. The difference is that Shakespeare introduces all the themes that are later developed in the pattern of the play. This pattern presents the audience with a number of possible ways in which the action can develop. It forces them to compare alternative courses of action and discriminate between them. The more an audience is forced to exercise its own choice and judgment, the more it will understand of the action. Shakespeare's opening prepares his audience for the desperate decisions which face Hamlet. It does not reveal more of this choice of action at the beginning of the play than an audience can easily comprehend.

In the interval between the Ghost's first appearance and Hamlet's acceptance of the duty, or the burden, of revenge, Shakespeare establishes a number of important dramatic relationships. Claudius and Gertrude are shown performing their roles as husband and wife who are also King and Queen in circumstances which only Hamlet seems to regard as in any way abnormal. The name of Fortinbras is introduced and repeated often enough for the audience to remember it. The military situation is explained. In a brief scene the vital, and fatal, triangle of love and affection that binds Ophelia and Laertes to Polonius is sketched.

Hamlet's own relationship to the other characters is established before the Ghost's command creates the intolerable pressures which shatter the court of Denmark. These pressures exist as the result of past actions. Hamlet is already upset by the past actions of his uncle and mother. In order to understand, as well as observe, Hamlet's condition it is necessary for the audience to hear the history of actions that belong to the story of the play but which have occurred at a point in time before the dramatic plot of the play begins. The Ghost is a triumphant solution to this extremely difficult problem of how to dramatize the past—the problem that Henry James called 'the eternal time question'.

James discusses the problem in the preface to the New York edition of *Roderick Hudson*:

> This eternal time question is accordingly, for the novelist, always there and always formidable; always insisting on the *effect* of the great lapse and passage, of the 'dark backward and abysm', by the terms of truth, and on the effect of compression, of composition and form, by the terms of literary arrangement.[1]

James uses Prospero's words to Miranda in *The Tempest* (i ii 49:139):

Prospero   What seest thou else
            In the dark backward and abysm of time?

in order to help him define the problem.

[1] Henry James, *The Art of the Novel: Critical Prefaces by Henry James*, ed. R. P. Blackmur, 1934, 14.

Miranda's faint and incomplete memory of her childhood is used as a rapid method of informing the audience of the events which took place in Milan. It thus forms the 'historic' background of the play. This is an important distinction. The plot of The Tempest begins with the shipwreck observed by Prospero and Miranda. The story of The Tempest began when Antonio seized the dukedom and set his brother Prospero adrift in an open boat with his baby daughter.

The plot of Hamlet begins with the appearance of the Ghost. The story of Hamlet began with the murder of King Hamlet by Claudius. In both plays 'historic' past actions which belong to the story have present 'dramatic' consequences which affect the plot. Both plays are therefore committed to explaining this past to the audience. There is clearly a distinction between 'dramatic' action which can simply be presented and 'historic' action which must somehow be narrated.

The difficulty which faces the dramatist is that there is almost no end to the 'historic' explanation which he could give. There is always something which could be further explained. It is evident that more explanation could be given of the motives which lay behind Antonio's act of usurpation in The Tempest. The love affair of Gertrude and Claudius in Hamlet could be developed into a different play. The dramatist must select his 'historic' explanation in such a way that he does not find himself committed to an infinite regress of perpetual explanation which destroys his dramatic plot.

This problem was clearly in Aristotle's mind when he produced his celebrated definition that a play ought to have a beginning, a middle, and an end:

> A beginning is that which is not itself necessarily after anything else, and which has naturally something else after it; an end is that which is naturally after something itself, either as its necessary or usual consequent, and with nothing else after it; and a middle, that which is by nature after one thing and has also another after it.[1]

It is clear that a murder, a crime, or some other act which requires retribution, expiation, or revenge, makes an excellent beginning. It can be accepted without too much explanation and it has obvious consequences. It was, for this and other important reasons, as favourite a device with the Elizabethan dramatists as it had been with the Greeks.

It is possible, from this point of view, to describe both Hamlet and The Tempest as revenge plays. It is important, however, to notice that

[1] Aristotle, Poetics 1450b, in Aristotle on the Art of Poetry, tr. Ingram Bywater, 1909, 40.

Aristotle's definition applies to the beginning of the story rather than the beginning of the plot. It is important for the dramatist that the event which begins his story, and does not require explanation, should take place at an earlier point in time than the beginning of the plot. He can thus provide the illusion of explanation without finding himself committed to the infinite regression of the historian.

In both *Hamlet* and *The Tempest* Shakespeare uses the beginning of his story as the 'historic' explanation of his 'dramatic' plot. He does not develop this explanation in quite the same way. A comparison of the plays provides an instructive example of the way in which a dramatist's treatment of the past has a profound effect upon the nature of his play. I believe that the celebrated exchange at the Cannes Film Festival in 1966:

Clouzot	But surely you agree, M. Godard, that films should have a beginning, a middle part and an end?
Godard	Yes, but not necessarily in that order.[1]

is, like many similar critical arguments, a dispute about the correct way to dramatize the past. *Hamlet* is an interesting example of how the beginning, middle, and end of the story can be 'not necessarily in that order' in the plot of the play.

In *The Tempest* Prospero uses the apparent destruction of the ship to relate the history of his brother's conduct to Miranda. It is, therefore, no surprise to the audience that the usurping Duke of Milan, Antonio, should suggest to Sebastian, brother of the King of Naples, that they should seize the throne of Naples by killing the King and his councillors while they are asleep. It is, he suggests, their destiny (*The Tempest*, 2 i 243:946):

Antonio   to perform an act
              Whereof what's past is prologue, what to come
              In yours and my discharge.

The theatrical metaphor draws the attention of the audience to the fact that Antonio is trying to repeat, in more deadly fashion, the crime he committed against his own brother in the past.

Prospero's art, however, exists to ensure that the crimes of the past cannot be repeated on the enchanted island. The spiritual experience to which the characters are subjected influences their minds and allows them to escape the consequences of their actions. This art is itself not

[1] Kenneth Tynan, 'Verdict on Cannes', *The Observer*, 22 May 1966, 24.

without its dangers. The history of the enchanted island is darkly illumined by the name of the witch Sycorax. Her influence is exemplified by her monstrous son, Caliban. Once Prospero has brought the past under control and arranged the new future of Ferdinand and Miranda he abjures even the art which permitted him this magic licence. In the world of men, Prospero will rely upon the neglected arts of self-knowledge and self-control.

This treatment of the past marks an important difference between tragedy and comedy. *The Tempest* is designed to allay anxieties about the past and give the audience a glimpse of a hopeful future. *Hamlet* raises anxieties about the past and buries all hope for the future. The past continually overtakes the characters and ensures that no one escapes all the possible consequences of their actions.

On the enchanted island Prospero can say (*The Tempest*, 5 i 25:1975):

Prospero   Though with their high wrongs I am struck to th'quick,
               Yet with my nobler reason 'gainst my fury
               Do I take part; the rarer action is
               In virtue than in vengeance.

Forgiveness is exchanged in *Hamlet* as well, but those who offer and accept it are already dying by poison. There is no equivalent to Prospero's art in *Hamlet*. Chance and circumstance make even the operation of the reason dangerous. Reason encourages some of the characters to attempt to repeat the crimes of the past. The difference in the tone of the plays depends, to some extent, upon the different solutions adopted by the dramatist to 'this eternal time question'.

Shakespeare appears to have given exceptional care and thought to the problem of dramatizing the past in *Hamlet*. He may have done so because it had proved a particularly difficult problem in *Julius Caesar*. This play, which was probably written immediately before *Hamlet*, seems still to have been in the dramatist's mind. Horatio recalls the strange sights seen in Rome before Caesar's death. Polonius had actually acted the part of Caesar at his university.

One of the most remarkable features of *Julius Caesar* is that Caesar himself very seldom refers to his own past. He relies upon his authority —but he bases his claim to that authority upon the fact that, unlike other men, he is incapable of change[1] (*Julius Caesar*, 3 i 58:1266):

[1] J. L. Simmons's 'Shakespeare's *Julius Caesar*: The Roman Actor and The Man', (*Tulane Studies in English*, xvi (1968), 1–28) is an important study of the way in which the theatrical metaphor contributes to the irony of *Julius Caesar*.

Caesar   I could be well mov'd, if I were as you;
                      If I could pray to move, prayers would move me;
                      But I am constant as the northern star,
                      Of whose true-fix'd and resting quality
                      There is no fellow in the firmament.

The conspirators choose this moment to prove that Caesar bleeds, at least, like other men. Their grounds for making Caesar bleed are the ironic ones that Caesar, once he has become king, may change into a tyrant.

This irony is one method of dealing with the extremely complex dramatic problems of the play. Caesar's myth of constancy means that there is no need, and no possibility, of dramatizing his past actions in order to show how he became the public figure which he presents to Rome. There is consequently no danger that Caesar's past achievements may dwarf the act of assassination. It also makes the grievances of the conspirators have a personal rather than a political bias.

In his speech to Brutus at 1 ii 90:188 Cassius maintains that Caesar, who is an even weaker mortal than Cassius, is now treated as a god. He recalls two episodes from Caesar's past—the challenge to swim the Tiber and the fit of fever in Spain, to justify this assertion. This is the only account of Caesar's past which the audience receives from the conspirators.

Brutus knows of no personal reason for him to act against Caesar. His political reasons depend upon Caesar's possible future actions. Yet it is Caesar's past, dramatized upon the stage in the Ghost which appears to Brutus in his tent, which eventually overwhelms all the conspirators.

Over Caesar's dead body Antony had predicted the appearance of this spirit (*Julius Caesar*, 3 i 271:1498):

Antony   And Caesar's spirit, ranging for revenge,
                      With Ate by his side come hot from hell,
                      Shall in these confines with a monarch's voice
                      Cry 'Havoc!' and let slip the dogs of war,
                      That this foul deed shall smell above the earth
                      With carrion men, groaning for burial.

In his funeral speech in the market place Antony begins to make his own prophecy come true by reminding his hearers of Caesar's past actions. He mentions the ransom money paid to the state. He reminds them that Caesar wept for the poor. He recalls Caesar's refusal of a crown at the Lupercalia. One solitary, powerful, personal reminiscence terminates Antony's argument. He has been reminding his hearers of matters that were common knowledge. His sudden appeal to his private memory of Caesar putting on the mantle in which he was murdered, on a summer's evening after the defeat of the Nervii has an extraordinary rhetorical force. It seems to guarantee the truth of his other statements about Caesar. It is this spirit, in part created by Antony, which then controls the future of the play.

The logic of the play has required Shakespeare to present Caesar first as an unchanging figure without a past; then to use all the dramatic and historical resources at his disposal to create the immensely powerful 'spirit of Caesar'. This is a solution, but not an entirely satisfactory one, to the immense dramatic problems posed by the subject of the play. It is a tragedy in which the characters are all overtaken by the consequences of their past actions. These consequences depend upon the nature of Caesar's history. Yet Caesar's history is, to a very large extent, a blank in the play which bears his name. The overtaking past is never really dramatized.

In *Julius Caesar* it is fair to say that Caesar is presented as a historical figure but not as a 'historical' character. We may now define a 'historical' character as one whose past has not only been accounted for but dramatized within the play. This definition is of some importance for criticism. In Maurice Morgann's *Essay on the Dramatic Character of Sir John Falstaff* (1777) there is a celebrated, or notorious, footnote which ends with this observation:

> If the characters of Shakespeare are thus *whole*, and as it were original, while those of almost all other writers are mere imitation, it may be fit to consider them rather as Historic than Dramatic beings; and, when occasion requires, to account for their conduct from the *whole* of character, from general principles, from latent motives, and from policies not avowed.[1]

This footnote has caused some critics to dismiss the whole of Morgann's essay with scorn. He is accused of committing what A. J. A. Waldock has called 'the documentary fallacy'.

Waldock uses this phrase to describe 'one of the commonest, and perhaps also one of the most serious, of all critical errors'. He illustrates this error by examining an article of Harold Goddard's on Ophelia.[2]

---

[1] Maurice Morgann, *An Essay on the Dramatic Character of Sir John Falstaff*, ed. W. A. Gill, 1912, 62.
[2] Harold Goddard, 'In Ophelia's Closet', *The Yale Review*, xxxv (1946), 462–74.

Goddard's argument is that Hamlet never made the visit to Ophelia which she describes at 2 i 75:971. Her whole description of his conduct to her father is the first clear symptom of the madness which later overwhelmed her. Waldock comments:

> The premise is that *Hamlet* is a document: that it is a literal transcript of fact: that it somehow records what, at that given time and place, an interlinked set of people said and did. This is the concealed assumption; and once this assumption is made it is clear that Mr Goddard's line of inquiry is perfectly right. Indeed, his investigation could have been much more searching and thorough; all the instruments of historical research, all the power of modern psychology, might justifiably be brought to bear, not merely on this one scene, but on every issue raised by the play. For it is obvious that—such an assumption once made—the whole ground of the inquiry is shifted. A document, preserving by some miraculous means the record of what really took place, would open up endless possibilities of conjecture; not a trifle, not the obscurest detail, but might be a key to the ultimate truth.[1]

Waldock permits himself to make something of a rhetorical Roman holiday of Goddard's article but the attack is not unfair.

It might be argued that Maurice Morgann is committing the 'documentary fallacy' on a grand scale. Morgann's actual critical purpose is different. His method should be distinguished from attempts to treat the text as a historical document. In the rest of his essay Morgann makes it quite clear that he is aware that he is talking about a work of art. His famous footnote is the result of a technical confusion. The point that he is trying to make is an extremely important one.

When Morgann attempts to distinguish the 'historic' characters of Shakespeare from the 'dramatic' characters of other dramatists he is actually referring to two kinds of dramatic character. Morgann is wrong in supposing that only Shakespeare can create the kind of character whose past has been dramatized. He is right in assuming that there is a difference between a 'historic' dramatic character and an ordinary, purely functional, dramatic character.

This distinction is important because there is still current a critical controversy waged between those who claim to study the play as a poem, and those who believe in 'character criticism', which is said to have been practised by Morgann, A. C. Bradley, and others. This

[1] A. J. A. Waldock, *Sophocles the Dramatist*, 1951, 15.

controversy is one of the great pseudo-problems of criticism. It is not possible to separate the actors from the action of the play. Everything that a dramatist cares to tell us about the actors may be relevant to our understanding of the action. The 'documentary fallacy' involves a separation of actors and action. It concentrates attention upon details of the 'lives' of the characters which have not been dramatized by the author and which consequently have no relevance to the action of the play. A similar separation, however, is involved if the critic fails to take account of the dramatist's involvement in the 'eternal time question'. This is the presentation, within the plot of the play, of details about the past lives of the characters which are essential to the story but which cannot be accommodated in the plot in their normal chronological order. It is evident that *Henry IV* is filled with such 'historic' details of the life of Falstaff.

The Ghost in *Hamlet* is, in this sense, a 'historical' character. It is one of the means used by the dramatist to make Hamlet a 'historical' character by dramatizing his past. The Ghost is not simply the traditional Ghost whose function is to explain past events to the audience. The concern of this imposing figure in full armour is not with the audience but with the other characters on stage. It is stressed that the reason that it 'harrows' Horatio is that it looks like the dead King. This terrifying resemblance leads Marcellus to question the reasons for their own 'strict and most observant watch' (I i 71:87). Horatio's explanation of Denmark's military preparation is the first dramatic step in establishing the 'historic' character of the Ghost. The account of the duel between King Hamlet of Denmark and King Fortinbras of Norway has immense consequences for the whole course of the play.

Fortinbras had challenged Hamlet to single combat out of 'most emulate pride' (I i 83:100). Such a combat was a recognized part of the chivalric code, ratified by the laws of heraldry. Horatio's careful use of legal terminology emphasizes that it was also an international agreement which was intended to be binding on both parties to the dispute. The duel between the Kings, with the territorial wager attached, is presented as a recognized part of the *ius gentium*—the concept of a law governing the conduct of states.

Young Fortinbras proposes to upset this legal agreement by force. He has 'shark'd up a list of lawless resolutes' in the 'skirts of Norway' (I i 97–8:114–15) and intends to substitute his own 'terms compulsatory' (I i 103:120) for those 'well ratified by law and heraldry' (I i 87:104). Denmark is arming against this threat. Bernardo, at least, is convinced that the appearance of the King 'that was and is the question of these wars' (1 i 111:124 Q 4) must be connected with this foreign danger.

It is extremely significant that the Ghost is associated in this way with the ideals of military honour and chivalry. Within the recognized framework of society, King Hamlet had acted in a perfectly correct and legal fashion in his duel with King Fortinbras. The actions of Young Fortinbras are illegal, but they are perfectly 'natural' and understandable. It is extremely difficult to enforce an agreement of this nature. Fortinbras wishes to avenge his father's memory. He also assumes that an agreement arrived at by force can be changed by force. Justice, as so often in international affairs, has become the interest of the stronger. Denmark appears to have no choice but to defend itself against this threat. Horatio's comparison between the appearance of the Ghost and the 'sheeted dead' (1 i 115:124 Q 8) who appeared in the Roman streets is the first ironic indication that the situation is now beyond military control.

Horatio suggests that the Ghost's continued silence means that they must (1 i 169:168)

Horatio   impart what we have seen tonight
    Unto young Hamlet; for, upon my life,
    This spirit, dumb to us, will speak to him.

The scene of the Ghost's double appearance to the guard has lasted from midnight, when Francisco was relieved, until daylight. Immediately before Horatio mentions Hamlet's name the language is filled with spectacular images of dawn. Horatio even describes it as if it were an approaching figure visible from the stage (1 i 166:165):

Horatio   But look, the morn, in russet mantle clad,
    Walks o'er the dew of yon high eastward hill.

Horatio, the student of the classics, links the crowing of the cock—the 'trumpet to the morn' (1 i 150:149) and the 'bird of dawning' (1 i 160: 159)—to the god of day. Marcellus connects it with the birth of Christ. The dark night of the watch, troubled by the ominous presence of the Ghost, is lightened by dawn and Horatio's assurance that the Ghost will speak to Hamlet.

When the Ghost does speak to Hamlet it lays upon him the command which directs the future course of the action. This command depends upon the King's murder by his brother Claudius. It is clear that this past event is so essential to the story that the audience must be informed of it at an early stage of the action. It is also clear that such an event cannot form part of the chronological order of the plot without seriously disturbing the balance of the play.

Yet the event is so crucial to the plot that it is not enough to have it described. It must, somehow, be dramatized. Consequently the audience receives its early information in the tense and intimidating midnight meeting of father and son. Hamlet's determination to test the truth of the Ghost's story gives the dramatist a good fictional reason for dramatizing the actual act. The audience do not merely hear of the murder of King Hamlet. During *The Murder of Gonzago* they watch it happen upon the stage.

The history of the Ghost therefore forms an important part of the design of the play. In this design the middle of the play also represents the beginning of the story. The dramatization of the past is a continuous process which lasts throughout the play. Past events constantly appear to repeat themselves in the present actions of the characters. If the history of King Hamlet begins with the account of the duel fought with Fortinbras, the story of Hamlet ends with his duel against Laertes. The Ghost is an agent of the past which haunts the lives of all the inhabitants of Elsinore and from which there is no escape.

The fact that the characters cannot escape the past does not necessarily mean that they are completely determined by it. The Ghost's command awakens more than one memory of the past and appeals to emotions which may be contradictory as well as complementary. The past may limit their freedom of action, but the future still depends upon the decisions, passions, and conduct chosen by the characters.

The meeting between Hamlet and his father is more than a convenient way of delivering otherwise unobtainable information. It develops the consciousness of Hamlet upon which the rest of the action depends. The Ghost makes three requests. At this moment of the action all three requests seem so interrelated that they are part of a single command. It is, however, a relationship which may be understood in more than one way. The way in which it should be understood is one of the great questions of the play.

The Ghost describes itself as an inhabitant of some unidentified eternal prison. This could be purgatory or hell. It is certainly a place of expiation, where the spirits are still troubled by the affairs of this world (i v 9:694):

Ghost   I am thy father's spirit,
         Doom'd for a certain term to walk the night,
         And for the day confin'd to fast in fires,

> Till the foul crimes done in my days of nature
> Are burnt and purg'd away.

It then directs Hamlet to his first, and most obvious, duty. He must revenge his father's murder.

Hamlet's response appears simple and unequivocal (1 v 23:708):

Ghost   If thou didst ever thy dear father love—

Hamlet   O God!

Ghost   Revenge his foul and most unnatural murder.

Hamlet   Murder!

Ghost   Murder most foul, as in the best it is;
But this most foul, strange, and unnatural.

Hamlet   Haste me to know't, that I, with wings as swift
As meditation or the thoughts of love
May sweep to my revenge.

The choice of images, however, is curious and significant. An avenger usually has to rid himself of all thoughts of love and meditate only upon his revenge. These words are likely to remain in the memory of the audience. They are the first indication that the play will be concerned with more than a single-minded concentration upon vengeance.

The audience now hear for the first time the history of the murder. The Ghost disposes of the false report that King Hamlet was stung by a serpent while sleeping in his orchard. Claudius first won the love of Gertrude, and then poisoned her husband by pouring 'juice of cursed hebona' into his ear. Vengeance is demanded for incest and adultery as well as murder—and yet the Queen herself is to be spared (1 v 81: 766):

Ghost   If thou hast nature in thee, bear it not;
Let not the royal bed of Denmark be
A couch for luxury and damned incest.
But, howsomever thou pursuest this act,
Taint not thy mind, nor let thy soul contrive
Against thy mother aught; leave her to heaven,
And to those thorns that in her bosom lodge
To prick and sting her.

It may well be asked—and the action of the play ensures that the question is asked—how a Ghost which condemns all murder as 'foul'

45

can demand vengeance, since vengeance will almost certainly involve the act of murder.

Is it possible, in these circumstances, for Hamlet to avoid tainting his mind? The Queen is to be left to heaven and her conscience. Why should God's judgment be anticipated in the case of the King? These doubts are not immediately apparent. The need for revenge seems evident and necessary. As the Ghost leaves the stage its last words to Hamlet form a third and final command—a command in the form of a farewell (i v 91:776):

Ghost   Adieu, adieu, adieu! Remember me!

These words are seized upon by Hamlet and repeated so that they become the theme of his next soliloquy. The command to 'remember' is therefore the one that is most vividly pressed upon the mind of the audience. Memory and remembrance have become one of the great themes of the play.

Hamlet's immediate reaction to the revelation of murder by poison had been to offer to sweep to his revenge. As he now dedicates himself to his task he swears to remember rather than to revenge—although vengeance is no doubt implied in the act of remembrance. The words of Hamlet's soliloquy, however, form a description of his own mind and memory (i v 92:777):

Hamlet   O all you host of heaven! O earth! What else?
And shall I couple hell? O, fie! Hold, hold, my heart;
And you my sinews, grow not instant old,
But bear me stiffly up. Remember thee!
Ay, thou poor ghost, whiles memory holds a seat
In this distracted globe. Remember thee!
Yea, from the table of my memory
I'll wipe away all trivial fond records,
All saws of books, all forms, all pressures past,
That youth and observation copied there,
And thy commandment all alone shall live
Within the book and volume of my brain,
Unmix'd with baser matter. Yes, by heaven!
O most pernicious woman!
O villain, villain, smiling damned villain!
My tables—meet it is I set it down
That one may smile, and smile, and be a villain;
At least I am sure it may be so in Denmark.
So, uncle, there you are. Now to my word:

It is 'Adieu, adieu! Remember me'.
I have sworn't.

In the memory created by this soliloquy, the audience will see reflected the great problems of the play.

I have argued elsewhere that the 'word' chosen by Hamlet at the end of this soliloquy should be understood as a technical 'word' used as an aid to memory in the Classical and Renaissance systems of the art of memory.[1] Quintilian advised his students to remember rhetorical passages by remembering one word on the page which would act as a trigger, calling the entire passage to mind. Hamlet's choice of 'Remember me' and its frequent repetition in the soliloquy is a deliberate mnemonic device which allows Hamlet to call all the details of the Ghost and his command to instant and complete remembrance. Hamlet is not only impressing his task upon his own mind. He is stamping one of the play's most important features upon the memory and imagination of the audience. In *Hamlet* the past is dramatized through the art of memory. As Dr Frances Yates has shown,[2] this art has many unexpected philosophical and religious implications in the Renaissance.

For this reason the way in which this scene is played is of great importance for the actors and the audience. It is usual to make Hamlet produce a property notebook at the end of the speech and write down that 'one may smile, and smile, and be a villain'. It is, as J. L. Styan has argued,[3] possible to play the scene in this way. The actor, however, must be careful to treat his book, if he uses one, as part of the art of memory and not a convenient property which allows him to give an obvious meaning to words which he does not understand. The sudden act of writing (an act which is not mentioned in the Quarto or Folio stage directions) is often used to associate this soliloquy with the 'antic disposition' (I v 172:868) or the 'wild and whirling words' (I v 133: 825) that he speaks to Horatio. Hamlet's memory, however, is the necessary starting point for most of the vital distinctions and discriminations of the play. The actor is given a soliloquy whose controlled design is a model of dramatic clarity—provided the actor understands what he has to do. This opportunity is too often thrown away.

Real or imagined, the 'tables' at the end of the speech are clearly associated with the 'table of my memory' at the beginning. Through-

[1] Nigel Alexander, '*Hamlet* and the Art of Memory', *Notes and Queries*, New Series, xv (1968), 137–9.
[2] Frances A. Yates, *The Art of Memory*, 1966.
[3] J. L. Styan, *Shakespeare's Stagecraft*, 1967, 59–60.

out the soliloquy Hamlet compares his mind and imagination to a book, or tablet of wax or slate, upon which ideas and impressions may be written—or erased. He now intends to 'wipe away' all thoughts 'that youth and observation copied there'. The Ghost and its command remain as the sole content of the 'book and volume of my brain'.

This same connection between 'tables' and 'memory' is central to Sonnet 122. Shakespeare is there making the precise point that he does not need written records to remind him of his love:

> Thy gift, thy tables, are within my brain
> Full character'd with lasting memory,
> Which shall above that idle rank remain
> Beyond all date, even to eternity;
> Or at the least so long as brain and heart
> Have faculty by nature to subsist;
> Till each to raz'd oblivion yield his part
> Of thee, thy record never can be miss'd.
> That poor retention could not so much hold,
> Nor need I tallies thy dear love to score.
> Therefore to give them from me was I bold,
> To trust those tables that receive thee more.
>   To keep an adjunct to remember thee
>   Were to import forgetfulness in me.

The author abandons the 'tables' or books since he has already 'character'd' them within his brain with words which will remain until eternity. These words will last at least until his own brain and heart have yielded to oblivion. He has therefore given away the 'tables' or notebooks since the 'tables' of his memory are a more reliable instrument for the recording of love. The argument implies that while the sonnets themselves may last till eternity Shakespeare has within that 'which passes show' (I ii 85:266) and so requires no written records to recall the memory and reality of his love.

Hamlet's soliloquy expresses the same kind of emotion as the sonnet. The 'seat' of memory within the castle of Elsinore is now within Hamlet's mind. The metaphor can be associated with riding, in the sense of holding one's seat on a horse, and it can also be used as if Hamlet were conducting a military defence of the castle of his memory. It is evident that he is aware that he must guard his memory against the corrupt 'show' of the King and his court as well as from the threat offered to his reason by the terrifying power of the supernatural.

Memory is now seen as the only fixed point in a 'distracted' world. If madness is involved it is a madness or 'distraction' which belongs to the world, not to Hamlet. What Hamlet remembers is the image of his living father, and the court as it existed before the act of murder turned Denmark into a mad-house where all values have been corrupted. Hamlet therefore characters the fact 'that one may smile, and smile, and be a villain' upon the tables of his memory and assumes the 'antic disposition' as a defence which conceals his own fatal knowledge from the world of lunatics who surround him.

Polonius uses exactly the same image when he is exhorting Laertes to store his mind with precepts useful for life in the city of Paris (I iii 58:523):

Polonius   And these few precepts in thy memory
              Look thou character.

Hamlet, forced by the King to remain at Elsinore, has now received advice from his father which contains rather different precepts from those of Polonius. It will be difficult to remain true to them and true to himself. This difficulty can be measured by the fact that Laertes will find his own return to Elsinore a far greater threat to his integrity than anything he encountered in France.

The entire design of the play's opening has led to this moment of the special creation of Hamlet's memory or consciousness. Hamlet is the only character, apart from the Ghost and Claudius himself, who knows of his uncle's guilt. The isolation of this knowledge is now emphasized by the dramatist. Horatio and Marcellus arrive, concerned for Hamlet's safety. Hamlet withdraws himself and his affairs from their concern by taking refuge in a joke. The Ghost's revelation was (I v 123:814):

Hamlet   There's never a villain dwelling in all Denmark
            But he's an arrant knave.

Horatio is further alarmed by Hamlet's levity and the Prince has to make it clear that the matter is no joke. He refuses, however, to take his friends into his confidence.

Hamlet insists upon swearing his friends to secrecy in a formal oath. This ceremony is three times interrupted by the Ghost calling from the 'cellarage' below the stage. On these occasions Hamlet shifts his ground and begins the ceremony again. Such conduct upon the part of modern actors is liable to cause laughter and, for that reason, it is seldom seen upon the stage. It is however so important that the director should make his actors brave even laughter in order to make the dramatist's point.

It is frequently argued that the point of this scene is to suggest that the Ghost may be a devil. It is true that the Devil is capable of being 'hic et ubique' (I v 156:853) and that Hamlet may be indicating the devilish character of the Ghost by using such phrases as 'truepenny' or 'old mole'. Yet if this is a well-known way of dealing with devils it is surprising that Horatio only describes it as 'strange' (I v 164:861). The oath-taking ceremony maintains the ambiguity of the Ghost because it ends with words which are not likely to be acceptable to the Devil (I v 179:875):

Hamlet	this do swear
	So grace and mercy at your most need help you.
Ghost	Swear.
(beneath)	
Hamlet	Rest, rest, perturbed spirit.

The 'judicious' were likely to have doubts about the nature of the Ghost whatever statement Shakespeare had made about it. Instead of resolving these doubts the cellarage scene effectively cuts off all discussion of them.

The only witnesses to the appearance of the Ghost are silenced—and they are silenced in a way which the audience are not likely to forget. The nature of the Ghost, therefore, never becomes a subject for discussion as Macbeth and Banquo, for example, discuss the nature of the Weird Sisters. Whatever the problem may be it is one that has to be approached through the imagination of Hamlet alone. The difficulty and the pressure of that problem is demonstrated in the way in which future scenes follow the pattern of the Ghost's commands.

The play scene, the prayer scene, and the scene in Gertrude's closet are all closely connected with Hamlet's desire to make his father's memory live again in the minds of those who have consigned him to oblivion. This desire to make the King and Queen understand their own past actually causes Hamlet to reverse the original command of the Ghost. The play catches the conscience of the King. In the closet scene Hamlet revenges himself upon his mother by speaking 'daggers' to her. This reversal is itself an indication that Hamlet finds the pressure of the past upon him a burden that it requires all of his courage to bear. This awareness is made plain as Hamlet leaves the stage at the end of the cellarage scene (I v 189:885):

> The time is out of joint. O cursed spite,
> That ever I was born to set it right.

The problems encountered by Hamlet in his endeavour to set the time right are, logically and dramatically, independent of the theological or moral 'problem' of the Ghost.

The contrast between past and present runs throughout the play. The first court scene is concerned with different, indeed contradictory, attitudes to the past, and begins an argument which is still in progress at the end of the play. This clash of opinion is emphasized by the clash of colours in the clothes of the actors. The court glitters with the ceremony of a new reign and a recent wedding. Hamlet wears black— the colour of remembrance for the dead.

The argument falls naturally into two parts. Before the court Claudius uses all the persuasive and concealed coercive power of the state to make his own position clear. He appears to remember his dead brother. His actual intention is to make everyone, including Hamlet, forget him as soon as possible. For this purpose Shakespeare has given the King a powerful and convincing 'rhetoric of oblivion'—so convincing that it has persuaded one critic that:

> Claudius's advice to the mourning Hamlet on acceptance of death
> as a law of nature, conceived in direct contrast to the strained and
> over-elaborated speech of Hamlet which it answers, is not merely
> sensible: his long speech is *the* one indispensable passage in our
> whole literature for help on such central occasions.[1]

The critic has forgotten what Claudius wants him to forget—that death is not always 'natural'. The argument about death as a law of nature is resumed in different circumstances in the graveyard.

Hamlet does not make any reply to the King's argument before the court. His reply is contained in the soliloquy spoken immediately after the court has left the stage. His own vital rhetorical question (I ii 142: 326):

Hamlet   Heaven and earth!
          Must I remember?

establishes the 'doctrine of remembrance' which will eventually shatter and destroy the 'rhetoric of oblivion'.

Yet in his opening speech Claudius displays a firm and impressive grasp of that rhetoric. In a series of striking phrases, he combines ideas

[1] G. Wilson Knight, *Shakespeare and Religion*, 1967, 14.

of opposite meaning in an attempt to persuade his audience that, having weighed the arguments, he is pursuing a reasonable course of action. The rhetoric thus conceals the fact that his forceful and aggressive behaviour is based only upon one of the opposed views which he mentions (1 ii 1:179):

King   Though yet of Hamlet our dear brother's death
The memory be green; and that it us befitted
To bear our hearts in grief, and our whole kingdom
To be contracted in one brow of woe;
Yet so far hath discretion fought with nature
That we with wisest sorrow think on him,
Together with remembrance of ourselves.
Therefore our sometime sister, now our queen,
Th'imperial jointress to this warlike state,
Have we, as 'twere with a defeated joy,
With an auspicious and a dropping eye,
With mirth in funeral, and with dirge in marriage,
In equal scale weighing delight and dole,
Taken to wife.

The speech appears to start as a formal tribute to the memory of his dead brother. It soon appears that 'discretion' has been so successful in its battle with 'nature' that 'memory' for Claudius now means 'remembrance of ourselves'. This is the King's great fixed point of principle, from which he never departs during the play. In these circumstances 'dole' may be weighed against 'delight' but the scale is hardly equal.

Claudius intends to make his own actions appear natural. In fact he describes how he has contracted the 'brow' of Denmark into something approaching the leer of a satyr. Amid the fine phrases about 'defeated joy' the most vital information contained by the speech, 'our sometime sister, now our queen', appears as simply another rhetorical figure. More is involved than a manner of speaking. Claudius has designed this masterpiece of Machiavellian policy because his marriage requires him to consign the 'green' memory of his 'dear brother' to swift obliteration.

There are two immediate obstacles in his way. Young Fortinbras remains as a threat to the kingdom and a reminder to court and audience of the heroic combat fought by King Hamlet. Having dealt with this matter in expeditious and efficient fashion, Claudius is free to turn the full force of his rhetoric on Hamlet. The Prince compels this attention from the King since his obvious and conspicuous remembrance of his father draws attention to what the King is striving to forget and prevents the discreet triumph of 'remembrance of ourselves'.

In his first speech Claudius conceded that 'discretion' had to fight with 'nature' in order to allow him to marry Gertrude. Now he uses both 'nature' and 'reason' in order to condemn Hamlet's conduct. Forgetfulness, according to Claudius, is natural and remembrance a fault (I ii 92:274):

> *King*   But to persever
> In obstinate condolement is a course
> Of impious stubbornness; 'tis unmanly grief;
> It shows a will most incorrect to heaven,
> A heart unfortified, a mind impatient,
> An understanding simple and unschool'd;
> For what we know must be, and is as common
> As any the most vulgar thing to sense,
> Why should we in our peevish opposition
> Take it to heart? Fie! 'tis a fault to heaven,
> A fault against the dead, a fault to nature,
> To reason most absurd; whose common theme
> Is death of fathers, and who still hath cried
> From the first corse till he that died today,
> 'This must be so'.

The appearance of the Ghost at the beginning of the play has already, ironically, made impossible that wiping away of the past that Claudius desires. Before Claudius has begun his second speech, Shakespeare has introduced the theme of 'playing' in Hamlet's response to his mother's appeal. This metaphor provides a further ironic context for the speech of Claudius—a context which the audience will come to appreciate in the course of the play as it becomes clear how expert an actor the King is.

Like Hamlet, the King has 'that within which passes show'. Unlike Hamlet, he would gladly forget this deadly knowledge. Since the death of King Hamlet was not natural the major premise of his speech is false. It is not Hamlet but Claudius who has committed 'a fault against the dead, a fault to nature'. The rhetorical climax of the speech with its survey of human history 'from the first corse till he that died today' is a particularly unfortunate example. The first corpse was that of Abel, murdered by his brother Cain. In making his appeal to the natural law Claudius is inevitably condemning himself.

The King argues that Hamlet's continued mourning is obstinate, excessive, and neurotic. Hamlet himself feels the force of these arguments. He later accepts that he may be suffering from 'melancholy'. He is also firm in his conviction that the sudden marriage of Gertrude and Claudius was not a natural or a normal reaction. If a union of this kind is 'natural' then the world is an 'unweeded garden' (1 ii 135:319) possessed by things 'rank and gross in nature' (1 ii 136:320). The fact that the wedding took place within a month of the funeral is stressed three times in the course of the speech.

The vital information that Claudius is a murderer has been withheld for good dramatic reasons. It is essential that the audience should see, hear, and understand Hamlet's reaction to the court before he even knows of the Ghost's existence. Hamlet's first soliloquy is concerned with remembrance untinged by any idea of revenge. In the course of the play it will be suggested not only that remembrance comes before revenge but that it may be more important than revenge.

The kind of remembrance displayed by Hamlet is, therefore, of great importance. He sees Claudius as a satyr compared to Hyperion the sun-king, now eclipsed by the long night of death and mourning. His mother is a fit mate for such a satyr since she has proved herself lower than 'a beast that wants discourse of reason' (1 ii 150:334). A careful distinction is made between her attitude to her husband (1 ii 143:327):

Hamlet   She would hang on him
As if increase of appetite had grown
By what it fed on

and her conduct after his death (1 ii 156:340):

Hamlet   O, most wicked speed, to post
With such dexterity to incestuous sheets!

Appetite, in this context, means the appetite of the senses. It is not the sexual act itself, but his mother's lack of all other feelings, which appals Hamlet. This lack of feeling implies a total lack of understanding which makes her worse than a beast.

Memory, according to St Augustine, is one of the three powers of the soul. The other powers are Understanding and Will. If the Queen's memory has failed her then there is no check exercised by the consciousness of sin upon the operation of her will. Without understanding, or 'discourse of reason', she can prefer the satyr Claudius to Hyperion.

Memory, as Frances Yates has pointed out,[1] is also considered by Thomas Aquinas as a part of Prudence—and is an important element in the soul's progress to salvation. Prudence is closely connected with Time since its three parts are Memory, Intelligence, and Foresight. These are the qualities that Hamlet refers to in his seventh soliloquy when he again links reason with prudence—and its absence is the mark of a beast (4 iv 33:2743 Q 27):

> Hamlet   What is a man,
> If his chief good and market of his time
> Be but to sleep and feed? A beast, no more.
> Sure he that made us with such large discourse,
> Looking before and after, gave us not
> That capability and godlike reason
> To fust in us unus'd.

Gertrude's total forgetfulness indicates that she is not in command of her soul. Her present and her future actions are therefore neither reasonable nor prudent and it is a reasonable conclusion on Hamlet's part that 'it is not, nor it cannot come to good' (1 ii 158:342).

If the Queen lacks memory and understanding then all of her former actions—her love for her husband and her ostentatious grief at his funeral—come into the category of 'actions that a man might play' (1 ii 84:265). Gertrude has found no difficulty in casting off her inky clothes and posting with naked dexterity to 'incestuous sheets'. According to Hamlet it is this acceptance of oblivion on the part of Claudius and Gertrude which is contrary to 'reason' and 'nature'. Remembrance may, even in terms of worldly wisdom, turn out to be a more reasonable response to death than the forgetfulness advocated by the King. His attitude implies a total cessation of human contact since, in the end, he considers himself alone.

Hamlet's attitude now receives strong dramatic support with the entry of Horatio, Marcellus, and Bernardo. Hamlet may be isolated in the court but his remembrance does not seem 'most absurd' to those who have just seen the armed ghost of his father. The half-joke (1 ii 184:372):

> Hamlet   My father—methinks I see my father.
>
> Horatio   Where, my lord?
>
> Hamlet   In my mind's eye, Horatio

[1] Frances A. Yates, *The Art of Memory*, 1966.

is deliberately placed in order to draw attention to the fact that Hamlet's own memory is about to be stirred not only by the mind's eye of memory but by all his 'faculties of eyes and ears' (2 ii 559:1606).

In praising his father Hamlet says (1 ii 187:376):

Hamlet   'A was a man, take him for all in all,
          I shall not look upon his like again.

The guard now summon him to the dark of the battlements to look upon his likeness. The dark/light imagery of the play now takes a new development. Horatio, at the beginning of the first scene, had associated Hamlet with the colours of the dawn. This symbolism is sharply reversed during the first court scene. Claudius appears to be the sun-king while Hamlet appears in the colours of night. He tells Claudius that he is 'too much in the sun' (1 ii 67:247) while the Queen appeals to him to 'cast thy nighted colour off' (1 ii 68:248).

Hamlet is now led to the dark in order to hear the true story of how his father the sun-king was eclipsed in love and life by the satyr Claudius. The glitter of the court is now seen to be the dark light of murder while the one hope of dawn and the restoration of the rule of Hyperion in Denmark is contained in the dark clothes which symbolize Hamlet's remembrance of his father. The imagery is not developed in this fashion until the graveyard scene when the total reversal of 'natural' values in Denmark has become apparent. The dramatist slowly educates his audience into an appreciation of the symbolism and imagery of the play.

The revelation of murder, adultery, and incest does not, as is often claimed, poison Hamlet's mind. It confirms his suspicions of the 'un-natural' basis of the court of Denmark. What has disturbed Hamlet is his mother's lack of affection. He believes that all human love must be an illusion. If this were true, however, it would mean that his own doctrine of memory had no validity. In proving that it does have validity Hamlet cures himself and the state of Denmark. It is the art of memory which destroys the King and Queen. Claudius and Gertrude are not simply overtaken by vengeance. They are overtaken by their own memory and recognition of the past.

Once memory, the first power in the soul, has been awakened, Gertrude is horrified by her own conduct. Claudius is equally horrified and is reduced to praying for forgiveness. Forgiveness and repentance, however, require all three powers of the soul to operate. Claudius remembers his crime and now, perhaps for the first time, understands it. He still lacks the will to repent. In order to avoid the consequences of this failure to repent he determines to repeat the act of murder and kill Hamlet. This act is not prudent. On this second occasion Claudius shows an astonishing lack of intelligence and foresight. It costs him his life.

The 'historical' character of the Ghost is essential to the dramatic structure of the play. It fulfils one usual dramatic function in giving the characters and the audience information which they could not otherwise obtain. It exceeds that function in that it provides the ideal excuse for the dramatization in action of events that occurred in the 'dark backward and abysm of time'. In delivering a triple command to remember, to avenge his father's death, and yet to respect his mother, it creates Hamlet's memory and the division between the powers of his mind. His will leads him on to murder and even matricide. His understanding holds him back in the way which he despises when he says that 'conscience does make cowards of us all' (3 i 83:1737).

In drawing attention to the power of memory the Ghost allows Shakespeare to define one of the great issues which divide Hamlet from Claudius. It also provides a suitable resolution to Hamlet's dilemma by making Claudius's memory the instrument of his destruction. In solving the 'eternal time question' it gives the dramatist an assured control over the past, present, and future of his play. It allows him to create the pattern of poison, play, and duel through which he confronts the audience with Hamlet's problems and with their own. The past has to be continually dramatized throughout the play in order that the audience may understand the significance of the present action. The remembrance of things past represented by the Ghost is the introduction to the vital moral distinctions of the play.

Chapter 3

THE CENTRE OF CONSCIOUSNESS

Hamlet's actions and decisions are the main focus of interest in the play. In order to dramatize the conflict within Hamlet's mind Shakespeare has taken every opportunity of presenting his intellect in operation. The result is an unparalleled series of soliloquies, meditations, and arguments in which Hamlet questions his own actions and attempts to analyse his own motives.

It is possible to say that the first act of the play is designed to admit the spectator into Hamlet's mind and that the rest of the play exhibits the full range and quality of his consciousness. The action brings Hamlet into frequent contact with the other characters. As he engages in verbal duels with the King, or attempts to explain himself to Horatio, the dialogue defines some of the problems and pressures which face him. In the soliloquies the audience see Hamlet brought face to face with himself.

Perhaps the most remarkable feature of the entire play is that this self-encounter is indefinite and inconclusive. The end and purpose of the soliloquies appear to be to reveal that Hamlet does not understand his own motives. The soliloquies do appear to sound Hamlet 'from my lowest note to the top of my compass' (3 ii 358:2237) but they fail, as Hamlet says Rosencrantz and Guildenstern fail, to 'pluck out the heart of my mystery' (3 ii 357:2236). Hamlet's failure to solve his own problems in the soliloquies has caused a great deal of critical confusion. In dealing with the soliloquies it is even more important than usual to maintain the basic critical distinction between the problems presented in the soliloquies and the dramatic difficulties solved by the soliloquies.

It is frequently assumed that Shakespeare would have made Hamlet explain his own motives if he had been able to do so. The obvious absence of a satisfactory explanation must mean that Shakespeare had no explanation to offer his audience.[1] From that point it is a simple step for the commentator to attempt to supply the motives that are so strangely missing from the text. The psycho-analysts only carry this process a stage further when they ascribe Hamlet's difficulties to the fact that Shakespeare shared with his creation an unresolved Oedipus complex.

This critical position rests upon the assumption that Hamlet's divided mind is the sole content of the play. It fails to take into account that this division of purpose—and the apparent delay and indecision on the part of Hamlet—is deliberate. The dramatist is not in the least confused or indecisive about the effects that he is trying to obtain. He presents an extremely common and traditional idea—the battle waged within the mind or soul of the individual—in traditional terms which yet achieve an extremely complex and unexpected psychological effect.

Shakespeare does not make Hamlet explain his own motives for the good dramatic and psychological reason that no explanation could ever be complete. It has already been suggested that any attempt at a complete 'historical' account of the action would involve the dramatist in an infinite regress of explanation. So any attempt to define all of the instincts, affections, and sensibilities which influence the operation of Hamlet's mind would involve an infinite progress of psychological speculation.

Shakespeare does not provide an explanation. What he has done is to dramatize the process of psychological speculation as Hamlet hunts for the hidden springs of his own actions and motives. These motives are difficult to define because Hamlet is driven by a number of violent, instinctive, and largely irreconcilable human passions. In order to present the competing claims of human passion the dramatist has to know when the rest of his psychological explanation has to be silence.

The mind of Hamlet has been designed by Shakespeare as a precision instrument through which the audience may view the events of the play. That carefully-directed vision makes the entire play a mirror in

[1] John Lawlor (*The Tragic Sense in Shakespeare*, 1960, 45–73) is one of the rare critics who argue that 'Shakespeare's triumph is to make the hero fail to understand himself'.

which the audience has the opportunity of recognizing, perhaps for the first time, their own fundamental agony of inescapable choice. Hamlet's long struggle to understand and control the powers of his intellect and emotions helps the audience to interpret the terror which they feel at their own tragic existence. The dramatic function of the battle in Hamlet's soul is to convince the audience that they have been conscripted, by the fact of their human birth, to fight in the same war.

The significance of any dramatic act may be measured by the quality of an actor's response. When Christopher Marlowe brings Helen of Troy upon his stage he does not attempt to describe the girl—he dramatizes her effect upon Faustus. His passionate reaction (*Doctor Faustus*, 5 i 99):

Faustus   Was this the face that launch'd a thousand ships,
             And burnt the topless towers of Ilium?

helps to create the beauty to whom the words are addressed. They make their significance felt even when, as in the Royal Shakespeare Company's 1968 production, the actress uses the extreme beauty of her nude body to give the maximum physical impact. The words give to Helen's entrance a psychic as well as a physical effect.

Words, however, are not essential. In Samuel Beckett's *Acte sans paroles* the human importance of the situation does not depend upon the stage machinery of palm trees, scissors, carafe, and cubes. It depends upon the way these objects, in their irrational arrivals and disappearances, affect the consciousness of the solitary actor. Once the mime is over that consciousness has been fully expressed and dramatized although no word has been spoken.

The author uses the consciousness of the character or the actor to make clear the significance of his dramatic action to the audience. There is a sense, therefore, in which the entire process of dramatization is made to occur in the actor's mind. This use of consciousness exists in most kinds of literature but it has received remarkably little critical attention. The best account of it is probably still the preface which Henry James wrote for the New York edition of *The Princess Casamassima*.

It can, of course, be argued that it is absurd to attempt to apply the critical criteria of an idiosyncratic late nineteenth-century author to the plays of Shakespeare. James himself, however, uses Hamlet as the supreme example of what he means by his phrase 'the centre of consciousness'. In his analysis of his own practice as a novelist he has taken the essential first step in the examination of Hamlet's role in the play.

James begins by emphasizing the important effect that this consciousness has upon the audience:

This in fact I have ever found rather terribly the point—that the
figures in any picture, the agents in any drama, are interesting only
in proportion as they feel their respective situations; since the
consciousness, on their part, of the complication exhibited forms for
us their link of connection with it. But there are degrees of feeling—
the muffled, the faint, the just sufficient, the barely intelligent, as
we may say; and the acute, the intense, the complete, in a word—
the power to be finely aware and richly responsible. It is those
moved in this latter fashion who 'get most' out of all that happens
to them and who in doing so enable us, as readers of their record,
as participators by a fond attention, also to get most. Their being
finely aware—as Hamlet and Lear, say, are finely aware—*makes*
absolutely the intensity of their adventure, gives the maximum of
sense to what befalls them.[1]

It is, however, a very broad critical category that includes Hamlet
and Lear as examples of characters who are 'finely aware'. They could
be selected as examples of entirely opposed kinds of 'dramatic awareness'. James now elaborates, and narrows, this argument.

I confess I never see the *leading* interest of any human hazard but in
a consciousness (on the part of the moved and moving creature)
subject to fine intensification and wide enlargement. It is as mirrored
in that consciousness that the gross fools, the headlong fools, the
fatal fools play their part for us—they have much less to show us
in themselves. The troubled life mostly at the centre of our subject—
whatever our subject, for the artistic hour, happens to be—
embraces them and deals with them for its amusement and its
anguish; they are apt largely indeed, on a near view, to be all the cause
of its trouble. This means, exactly, that the person capable of feeling
in the given case more than another of what is to be felt for it,
and so serving in the highest degree to *record* it dramatically and
objectively, is the only sort of person on whom we can count not
to betray, to cheapen or, as we say, give away, the value and beauty
of the thing. By so much as the affair matters *for* some such
individual, by so much do we get the best there is of it, and by so
much as it falls within the scope of a denser and duller, a more vulgar
and more shallow capacity, do we get a picture dim and meagre.[2]

---

[1] Henry James, *The Art of the Novel: Critical Prefaces by Henry James*, ed. R. P.
Blackmur, 1934, 62.   [2] Ibid., 67.

James frequently maintained that no story was complete without its fools. The difference between the fools and the recording consciousness is not only that one is more intelligent than the other. It is that one has a greater capacity for emotion and can therefore feel and understand more than the other. The recorder is distinguished by his capacity for response as much as by his powers of analysis. Like some of the Renaissance philosophers, James believes that the emotions and the intelligence are interdependent. This distinction has to be remembered when James proceeds with his argument:

> Edgar of Ravenswood for instance, visited by the tragic tempest of *The Bride of Lammermoor*, has a black cloak and hat and feathers more than he has a mind; just as Hamlet, while equally sabled and draped and plumed, while at least equally romantic, has a mind still more than he has a costume.[1]

The soliloquies are, therefore, of crucial dramatic importance. They create Hamlet's recording, responding, and searching mind. The quality of that consciousness, as James argues, makes the intensity of *Hamlet*. The emotions expressed by the soliloquies may seem contradictory, their arguments inconclusive. The dramatization of Hamlet's consciousness provided by the soliloquies, however, is both logical and coherent.

There are seven soliloquies and it has already been argued that the first two are concerned with the art of memory. The next two are concerned with 'act' and 'action' and introduce the idea of conscience. In the third soliloquy (2 ii 543–601:1590–1645) Hamlet examines the passion which made the actor weep while reciting the speech on the grief of Hecuba. The power of the play makes him determined to 'catch the conscience of the King' (2 ii 601:1645). The fourth soliloquy (3 i 56–88:1710–42) argues that 'conscience does make cowards of us all' (3 i 83:1737) and, as a result, 'enterprises of great pitch and moment' (3 i 86:1740) may be said to 'lose the name of action' (3 i 88:1742).

The Latin word *conscientia* means knowledge or consciousness. Its moral sense of 'conscience' is derived from the knowledge of right and wrong, good and evil. It is evident that both senses of knowledge are present in the account in the Book of Genesis of how Adam and Eve acquired 'conscience' through eating the forbidden fruit of the tree of knowledge in the Garden of Eden. Both usages of conscience, as knowledge or consciousness and more specifically as the faculty which allows

[1] Ibid., 68.

us to distinguish between good and evil, are well established for this period. The word is used in both senses within the play.

If, therefore, the first two soliloquies are concerned with memory and the next two are powerful instruments of inquiry that examine human knowledge and understanding, it becomes less surprising that the fifth (3 ii 378–89:2259–70) and sixth (3 iii 73–96:2350–71) soliloquies should be a passionate expression of Hamlet's will to kill the King. The battle within Hamlet's mind and conscience is expressed in the traditional terms of the three powers of the soul—Memory, Understanding, and Will.

The seventh soliloquy (4 iv 32–66:2743 Q 26–60) sums up, but deliberately fails to solve, the argument about memory, understanding, and will. It begins with a consideration of man's 'capability and godlike reason' (4 iv 38:2743 Q 32) and then moves on to the fact that Hamlet can find no reason 'why yet I live to say "This thing's to do" '. He believes that he has 'cause, and will, and strength, and means' (4 iv 45: 2743 Q 39) to do it. The example of Fortinbras's army reminds him that at least one other prince has no difficulty in exercising his will in the service of his honour. Hamlet also remembers that his 'cause' is 'a father kill'd, a mother stain'd' (4 iv 57:2743 Q 51)—very much more powerful reasons than the 'fantasy and trick of fame' (4 iv 61:2743 Q 55) which appears to drive the soldiers on to their graves in Poland.

The compelling dramatic reasons which prevent Hamlet from explaining why he still lives 'to say "This thing's to do" ' now become more apparent. What Hamlet cannot understand is why his will to kill the King does not find expression in action. In the circumstances of Elsinore, however, the killing of the King must be an act of secret murder. The fifth and sixth soliloquies express fully the hatred which drives Hamlet on to think such an act desirable. Hamlet is conscious of this overmastering hatred. He is less conscious of the considerations of memory and understanding, dramatized in the earlier soliloquies, which have hindered or prevented him from performing this act.

It is often pointed out that Hamlet does not question at any stage the propriety of taking revenge upon the King. There is no soliloquy which shows him actually wrestling with his conscience over this matter. It does not therefore follow that his conscience has not been dramatized. It means that Shakespeare was aware of one of the most difficult dramatic problems which may also cause perplexity in the theatre of the world.

If a character walks to the front of the stage and says, 'I am determined to prove a villain' (*Richard III*, 1 i 30:32), he is assured of the interest and to some extent the sympathy of his audience. A man who stands upon a stage, warmly congratulates himself upon his own virtue and conscience, and assures the audience of his integrity, is clearly playing the part of a hypocrite.

One of the reasons that the virtuous are notoriously difficult to portray in works of literature is that there must be someone else to sing their praises. Villains can describe, display, and even defend their own villainy. This dramatic, philosophic, and psychological principle has been summed up in a phrase attributed to Groucho Marx: 'There is only one way to find out if a man is honest. Ask him. If he says "yes" you know he's a crook.'

In the soliloquies, therefore, Shakespeare dramatizes a mind endeavouring to find its way through the labyrinth of poison, play, and duel in order to play the part of an avenger of blood. This is Hamlet's expressed and constant intention. He finds his failure to act disgusting and calls himself a coward, a villain, and a whore. Yet these soliloquies do not only reveal the doubts and questions of which Hamlet is conscious. They also disclose feelings and emotions of which he is not conscious. They provide evidence for a rather different estimate of his character. The fact that Hamlet despises himself does not compel the audience to adopt the same opinion. Shakespeare's dramatic and psychological triumph is to have dramatized the contrast between the conscious and the unconscious processes of the imagination.

In order to do so he makes use of the familiar idea of a division or war between the powers of the soul. This idea was old when Plato created the great image of the horses and charioteer of the soul in the *Phaedrus*. It occurs so frequently in medieval and Renaissance thought that it would be absurd to attempt to find a 'source' for Shakespeare's deployment of memory, understanding, and will. It is true, however, that Giordano Bruno's remarkable sonnet sequence, *De gli eroici furori*, published in England in 1585 and dedicated to Sir Philip Sidney, makes use of the traditional imagery of the sonneteers for his own philosophic purposes. Shakespeare's aims in *Hamlet* are not identical with Bruno's. In the *Sonnets*, and in *Hamlet*, Shakespeare uses the traditional imagery of the Renaissance for his own specific dramatic design. While no argument can be based upon the possibility that Shakespeare had read Bruno, a comparison of the way in which they use similar imagery to describe similar emotional situations is instructive.

In the first dialogue of *De gli eroici furori* Tansillo offers, as a commentary upon a sonnet using the military imagery of love, the following explanation:

The captain is the human will which sits at the stern of the
soul and with the little rudder of reason governs the affections of
the inferior potencies against the surge of their natural violence.
With the sound of the trumpet, that is to say, by determined
election, he summons all his warriors; that is, he calls forth all the
potencies of the soul (warriors we call them because they are in
continual conflict and opposition), or the effect of those potencies
which are the conflicting thoughts, some of which incline toward
one, and others toward the other contrary; and he seeks to assemble
them beneath a single banner for a determined end.[1]

The captain is described as putting to death those 'traitor' thoughts
who will not assemble under the banner, and banishing the 'madmen'
who are incapable of rational action from his camp, 'proceeding against
the former with the sword of anger, and against the latter with the
whip of disdain'.

Hamlet attempts to assemble his thoughts under a single banner for
the determined end of revenge. It is hardly surprising, therefore, that
the battle or voyage which he describes in the imagery of the soliloquies is a desperate situation. Hamlet's passions are not controlled with
the calm appropriate to a Stoic philosopher. His very intelligence and
power of feeling made him react strongly to his father's death. The
passions which call for him to revenge that murder are fundamental
to the parental bond. It would be inhuman not to respond to them.
At the same time, in order to respond to them, it appears necessary to
become a secret murderer and therefore, like Claudius, capable of
inhumane cruelty.

Bruno also expresses this dilemma when he writes:

The human heart contains two summits, which rise progressively
from one root; and in the spiritual sense, from a single passion of
the heart proceed the two contraries of hate and love. For Mount
Parnassus has two summits rising from the one foundation.[2]

It is, in one sense, the passion of love and remembrance which
threatens to overwhelm Hamlet and turn him into a murderer. It is
this same kind of passion which destroys Ophelia, Gertrude, Laertes,
and Claudius. Hamlet searches for the summit of hatred. It is not
necessarily disgraceful that he fails to reach it. In order to understand
the precarious control won in the soliloquies over Hamlet's revealed

[1] P. E. Memmo Jr, *Giordano Bruno's The Heroic Frenzies: A Translation with
Introduction and Notes*, 1964, 87.
[2] Ibid., 86.

passions the audience must consider (and a performance will compel consideration by making them watch) the actions which occur as a result of the soliloquies. The contradictory emotions of the damnation soliloquy, and the self-reproach of the soliloquies on conscience, are the clearest, and perhaps the only, way of making Hamlet's situation comprehensible to an audience in the theatre.

Giordano Bruno believed that the battle in the soul could only be solved by a god. Henry James is of the same opinion. He therefore warns an author that any attempt to provide a godlike explanation of his human characters is likely to lead to artistic failure:

> If persons either tragically or comically embroiled with life allow us the comic or tragic value of their embroilment in proportion as their struggle is a measured and directed one, it is strangely true, none the less, that beyond a certain point they are spoiled for us by this carrying of a due light. They may carry too much of it for our credence, for our compassion, for our derision. They may be shown as knowing too much and feeling too much—not certainly for their remaining remarkable, but for their remaining 'natural' and typical, for their having the needful communities with our own precious liability to fall into traps and be bewildered. It seems probable that if we were never bewildered there would never be a story to tell about us; we should partake of the superior nature of the all-knowing immortals whose annals are dreadfully dull so long as flurried humans are not, for the positive relief of bored Olympians, mixed up with them.[1]

Shakespeare is wiser than the critics who feel that he should have solved the problem of Hamlet. He has solved the problem of *Hamlet* by making his protagonist a man faced by philosophical, psycho-logical, and practical problems which could be completely solved only by a god. It is a fair statement of the human condition. The creation of Hamlet's consciousness, his astonishing range of awareness and appreciation of the issues which face him, remind the audience of the psychic cost of any particular practical solution of these problems.

The soliloquies, therefore, are not passages of poetical thought in which Hamlet avoids the practical problems of the play. They are the practical problems of the play. In order to make this clear Shakespeare does not treat the argument of the soliloquies in isolation. Their themes recur in passages where Hamlet is talking to other characters but his

[1] Henry James, *The Art of the Novel: Critical Prefaces by Henry James*, ed. R. P. Blackmur, 1934, 63–4.

words have a clear reference to his own thoughts as expressed to the audience in soliloquy.

It is convenient to refer to these passages as 'meditations'. At the risk of straining critical credulity it is now maintained that there are seven meditations which correspond to the seven soliloquies and complete the dramatization of Hamlet's conscious and unconscious thoughts for the audience. The relationship between the soliloquies and the meditations in the argument of the play is perhaps best expressed in diagrammatic form as shown in Figure 1.

A description of the order of the soliloquies and meditations provides a brief account of the plot of the play. This combined commentary on the operation of memory, the action of the inner-play, the meeting in the graveyard, and the final duel reveals both inward and outward aspects of Hamlet's mind. The soliloquies concentrate upon his own vital inner concerns. The meditations apply this emotional experience to the wider problems of the general human condition. The meditations show that the war being conducted in the mind is the expression of a total personality. The soliloquies illumine the desperate single engagements. Both are essential to an audience's understanding of *Hamlet*.

The chief dramatic task of both soliloquies and meditations is the comparison and analysis of the emotions. They exist to organize states into sentences. The comparisons of the first soliloquy do more than reveal Hamlet's troubled consciousness: they establish a ratio which allows the audience to measure, according to Hamlet's scale, the whole condition of Denmark. In the first instance King Hamlet is compared to Claudius through the medium of Gertrude. He appears as 'Hyperion to a satyr' (I ii 140:324). When this comparison is repeated at the end of the speech, a new dimension is introduced (I ii 149:333):

Hamlet   why she, even she—
      O God! a beast that wants discourse of reason
      Would have mourn'd longer—married with my uncle,
      My father's brother; but no more like my father
      Than I to Hercules.

The comparison is no longer simply between two brothers: Hamlet is comparing himself to his father.

If Claudius is a satyr who has turned the court into an 'unweeded garden' where passion runs riot, it will require a man who is at least comparable to King Hamlet to check this unnatural growth. Such a task is indeed 'Herculean' and Hamlet clearly feels that the labour of

FIGURE 1

Soliloquies

S 1 (1 ii 129–59:313–43)
'O, that this too too solid flesh would melt'

S 2 (1 v 92–112:777–96)
'O, all you host of heaven'

S 3 (2 ii 543–601:1590–1645)
'O, what a rogue and peasant slave am I!'

S 4 (3 i 56–90:1710–42)
'To be or not to be'

S 5 (3 ii 378–89:2259–70)
''Tis now the very witching time of night'

S 6 (3 iii 73–96:2350–71)
'Now might I do it pat'

S 7 (4 iv 32–66:2743 Q 26–60)
'How all occasions do inform against me'

Meditations

M 1 (1 iv 8–38:612–21 Q 22)—To Horatio and Marcellus:
'The King doth wake tonight and takes his rouse'

M 2 (2 ii 292–311:1340–57)—To Rosencrantz and Guildenstern:
'What a piece of work is a man!'

M 3 (3 ii 1–43:1849–93)—The advice to the actors
M 4 (3 ii 54–85:1907–38)—To Horatio:
'Give me that man/That is not passion's slave'
M 5 (3 ii 338–64:2216–43)—To Rosencrantz and Guildenstern:
'O, the recorders!'

M 6 (5 i 179–210:3372–403)—The graveyard:
'Alas, poor Yorick!'
M 7 (5 ii 81–210:3587–673)—To Osric and to Horatio:
'Not a whit, we defy augury'

1. The Dream of Scipio (*Raphael*)

2. The Three Graces (*Raphael*)

cleansing the Augean stables of Denmark is beyond him. It is this difficult and unwelcome task which is laid on him one scene later.

The first meditation, spoken to Horatio and Marcellus on the battlements while the King drinks in ceremonious style below, is equally concerned with the growth of unsuspected evil. Just as the drinking habits of the Danes damage the reputation of Denmark, so an individual, whose reputation is one of his most precious possessions, may find it totally destroyed by 'some vicious mole of nature' (1 iv 24: 621 Q 8) or 'the o'ergrowth of some complexion' (1 iv 27:621 Q 11) for which he can scarcely be held responsible. The battle in any individual's soul must be influenced by the customs of his country and the facts of his heredity. Both weigh heavily in Hamlet's internal struggle.

This struggle, however, appears to be given new strength and direction by the revelation of the Ghost. Indeed in Hamlet's dedication to revenge his father's memory the conflict seems resolved. The inherent difficulties begin to reappear in the second meditation whose argument is closely linked to that of the third and fourth soliloquies. Since it is also an account of the causes of Hamlet's melancholy it evolves naturally out of the first soliloquy and meditation.

In this speech Hamlet both welcomes and unmasks Rosencrantz and Guildenstern, commanded to court by the King in order to play the parts of old and close friends (2 ii 294:1342):

Hamlet   I have of late—but wherefore I know not—lost all my mirth, foregone all custom of exercises; and indeed it goes so heavily with my disposition that this goodly frame, the earth, seems to me a sterile promontory; this most excellent canopy the air, look you, this brave o'er-hanging firmament, this majestical roof fretted with golden fire—why, it appeareth no other thing to me than a foul and pestilent congregation of vapours. What a piece of work is a man! how noble in reason! how infinite in faculties! in form and moving, how express and admirable! in action, how like an angel! in apprehension, how like a god! the beauty of the world! the paragon of animals! And yet, to me, what is this quintessence of dust? Man delights not me—no, nor woman neither, though by your smiling you seem to say so.

Like the first soliloquy this is an exercise in scale and proportion. Hamlet admits the possibility of beauty, truth, and rarity in the human condition but confesses that, for him, the world is a 'sterile promontory' and man a 'quintessence of dust'.

Hamlet, too, is wearing a mask. The disclaimer 'but wherefore I know not' is intended to emphasize the gap between the facts as they are known to the audience and Hamlet, and the facts as they must appear to Rosencrantz and Guildenstern. The audience is no longer in any doubt about the cause of Hamlet's melancholy. Hamlet has himself accepted the task of purging it and the troubles which afflict Denmark. The disillusion which is expressed in this meditation is still clearly caused by the comparison between the lost golden world of the sun-king Hyperion and the satyr-like present. As the only member of the court who has noticed the contrast, it is hardly surprising that Hamlet is depressed.

Put on his guard by the transparent evasions of his former friends Hamlet makes clear, by his last cryptic words, that he is aware of their function in the world of Claudius (2 ii 371:1422):

Hamlet   But my uncle-father and aunt-mother are deceived.

Guildenstern   In what, my dear lord?

Hamlet   I am but mad north-north-west; when the wind is southerly I know a hawk from a handsaw.

The terms are unusual, but are of considerable importance for the play.

The south wind is particularly helpful for those of a melancholic temperament, according to Timothy Bright's *Treatise of Melancholie*. Bridget Gellert has demonstrated that:

> The same treatise by Bright contains an elaborate series of analogies comparing the soul and the instruments it commands to various natural phenomena and human artifacts. The hawk is used as an example of an instrument that though obedient to command, has life and character of its own; the hand is an example of an instrument that has no freedom, though it is alive; while the saw, the lowest grade, has neither freedom nor life.[1]

Hamlet claims to be able to distinguish between those who have lives and character of their own, and those, like Rosencrantz and Guildenstern, who are merely instruments of the King. Yet Hamlet's own melancholy is now in part a disguise, assumed in order to conceal from his friends that he has himself become the instrument of the

[1] Bridget Gellert, 'A Note on *Hamlet*, 2 ii 356–357', *Notes and Queries*, New Series xv (1968), 139–40.

Ghost's command. It remains to be seen whether Hamlet is a 'handsaw' who will commit murder merely on command, or whether he is a 'hawk' with a life and character of his own and the power to form and act upon his own judgments. In introducing the Players to Elsinore, Rosencrantz and Guildenstern have provided Hamlet with an excellent way of discovering the difference between hawks and handsaws in the court of Denmark. The consideration of the First Player's speech and the nature of a stage play is a natural development of this argument.

In his third soliloquy Hamlet establishes a new emotional ratio between the actor's responses and his own. He imagines that the part of Prince and avenger would be played in more dramatic and bloody fashion by a man who is capable 'but in a fiction, in a dream of passion' (2 ii 545:1592) of weeping for Hecuba (2 ii 553:1600):

Hamlet What would he do,
Had he the motive and the cue for passion
That I have? He would drown the stage with tears,
And cleave the general ear with horrid speech;
Make mad the guilty, and appal the free,
Confound the ignorant, and amaze indeed
The very faculties of eyes and ears.

In contrast, Hamlet protests that he can 'say nothing' (2 ii 563:1609).

The fact that he cannot take his 'cue for passion' and perform his chosen part makes Hamlet ask himself whether he is a coward. His answer is interesting. He concludes that, just as he can 'say nothing' for his father, so he would be unable to make an honourable answer to an opponent who (2 ii 568:1614):

Hamlet gives me the lie i'th'throat
As deep as to the lungs.

The tests for cowardice suggested by Hamlet are all provocations which demand a duel to satisfy the injured honour of the person insulted. Hamlet concludes that he would accept the insult in cowardly fashion and not fight.

If he did possess the courage required to fight a duel in these circumstances he believes that he would already have performed his act of revenge and (2 ii 574:1619):

Hamlet fatted all the region kites
With this slave's offal.

The only possible reason for not doing so is that he is 'pigeon-liver'd'

(2 ii 572:1617) and lacks 'gall to make oppression bitter' (2 ii 573: 1618).

This consideration of his own cowardice leads Hamlet to utter an outburst of passion against the King which threatens to drown the stage in words rather than tears. Hamlet has no difficulty in finding something to 'say'. Words alone, however, are no longer enough to satisfy him (2 ii 578:1623):

> Hamlet   This is most brave,
> That I, the son of a dear father murder'd,
> Prompted to my revenge by heaven and hell,
> Must, like a whore, unpack my heart with words,
> And fall a-cursing like a very drab.

In calling himself a whore for cursing, Hamlet appears to reject the weapon of words.

Yet it is to words that he now turns when he proposes to put on a play before the King. The intention of this performance is certainly to 'make mad the guilty and appal the free'. It is designed to make murder 'speak', and Hamlet himself performs the part of an actor, not by expressing his passion in weeping for Hecuba, but in using the 'dream of passion' of the play to compel the King to weep, or at least to start up in astonishment, at his own past crimes.

The question now is, what kind of an actor is Hamlet? The Prince himself apparently believes that the play is a surgical probe designed to 'tent' Claudius 'to the quick' (2 ii 593:1637). Once this probe has exposed Claudius as the infected sore which is poisoning Denmark it will be a simple matter to cure it by the speedy surgery of revenge. He still believes, that is to say, that the proper way to perform his part will be to slaughter the King the instant he is sure that he is a murderer. The debate which now develops in the meditations round the inner-play is designed to question this assumption of Hamlet's.

In instructing the Players how to deliver the speech that he has inserted into *The Murder of Gonzago* Hamlet recommends that the actor should (3 ii 17:1865) 'suit the action to the word, the word to the action; with this special observance, that you o'erstep not the modesty of nature'. It is evident that Hamlet's own peculiar difficulty is to find the exact words and actions that will 'suit' the passions within him. It also seems possible that if he succeeds in playing the part of the avenger of blood, Hamlet will become one of a kind of actor he despises—one who should be whipped 'for o'erdoing Termagant; it out-herods Herod' (3 ii 13–14:1861).

72

The proper performance of the play will expose, for almost the first time, the figure of the murderer behind the smiling King. It will therefore make it almost impossible for Claudius to 'suit the action to the word, the word to the action' without overstepping the modesty of nature and playing the absurd part of a tyrant. In adopting the role of the actor Hamlet is engaged in an act of remembrance directed at the memory, the moral conscience and the understanding of the King. Even as he calls himself a coward, therefore, Hamlet has taken the first major step which will, in the end, sweep him to his revenge.

The inner-play, therefore, is not mere confirmation of Hamlet's role as an avenger. It is part of his search for a new role in which he may deal with Claudius without becoming like Claudius. It makes it seem possible that Hamlet has not entirely missed his own 'cue for passion'. The fact that, despite his apparent certainty that he must perform the avenger's part, Hamlet is still looking for a role is found in the fourth soliloquy.

There the question has suddenly become 'To be or not to be' (3 i 56: 1710). The militaristic imagery in which the choice of existence is expressed gives an immediate impression of how violent, and how desperate, is the struggle within Hamlet's own mind. The lines present a military situation in which final defeat is inevitable (3 i 57:1711):

Hamlet   Whether 'tis nobler in the mind to suffer
              The slings and arrows of outrageous fortune
              Or to take arms against a sea of troubles,
              And by opposing end them?

The abrupt reversal of the imagery has a notable effect upon the logic of the speech.

It might be possible to suffer or endure a sea of troubles. Waves and tempest can be survived. It is highly impractical to take up arms against it. It might be possible to reply effectively to, or even defeat, an assault with slings and arrows. If they are simply endured they will inevitably overwhelm the object of their attack. Where both active and passive resistance must meet with failure, death, the choice 'not to be', is seen not only as inevitable but as a welcome relief. It suddenly appears to be the one certain cure for the 'heartache and the thousand natural shocks' (3 i 62:1716) that trouble humanity.

If this is true it becomes difficult to understand why a man should accept the burden of his existence, bearing 'fardels' (3 i 76:1730) or 'grunt and sweat under a weary life' (3 i 77:1731). It would only take so small an instrument as 'a bare bodkin' (3 i 76:1730) to bring relief.

Death itself, however, is divided into sleep, which is desirable, and dreams, which may be even harder to endure after death than during the present hopeless battle conducted under burdened conditions.

It is the fear of something after death which paralyses the will and prevents it seeking relief in self-destruction (3 i 78:1732):

Hamlet   But that the dread of something after death—
              The undiscover'd country, from whose bourn
              No traveller returns—puzzles the will.

The image of the traveller who does not return has caused some difficulty. It is argued that the Ghost is an example of a traveller who has returned. The Ghost, however, is forbidden to reveal the secrets of the country or prison that he inhabits. By no effort of the will can he return from death to life. The decision to cross the boundaries of that country is irreversible. If bad dreams exist across that border they will have to be endured. It is hardly surprising that the decision is one which puzzles the will.

The conclusion of this argument is perhaps the most remarkable part of this soliloquy (3 i 83:1737):

Hamlet   Thus conscience does make cowards of us all;
              And thus the native hue of resolution
              Is sicklied o'er with the pale cast of thought,
              And enterprises of great pitch and moment,
              With this regard, their currents turn awry
              And lose the name of action.

There is a clear relationship between 'conscience' and 'consciousness' or the power of thought in this passage. It is the 'pale cast of thought' which turns the 'native hue of resolution' pale and sick. Yet the kind of thought which prevents men from committing suicide is not far from a moral conscience. It has been too readily assumed that since the meaning of 'coward' seems unambiguous the meaning of 'conscience' must be made to fit it.

The effect of the whole passage, however, is to make the audience consider what they mean by 'cowardice'. If it is brave to kill oneself, and cowardly to remain alive, then conscience makes cowards of us all. Hamlet has already made it clear that to stay alive commits a man to the unequal battle of the fight against the sea of troubles or the endurance of the missiles of fortune. Hamlet calls the ability to cross the border between life and death courage, the ability to stay alive and bear the fardels of the human condition cowardice. Hamlet's intellect makes him prefer the courage of death at the same time that his actions proclaim him the coward of conscience. The continual quest of the human soul for thought, conscience, or understanding is, however, a more powerful force than is allowed for in Hamlet's present philosophy. In this battle only the coward of conscience can be a brave soldier.

The 'enterprise' that Hamlet refers to in the last lines of the soliloquy returns to the imagery of a sea voyage. 'Pitch' and 'moment' may refer to the movement of a ship, to the flight of a weapon towards its mark, or the descent of a hawk on its prey. The 'currents' may be the path of the voyage or the flight path of a weapon through the air. It is clear, at any rate, that the tide of this enterprise operates in the same fashion as the tide referred to by Brutus in *Julius Caesar* (4 iii 216:2217):

Brutus   There is a tide in the affairs of men
               Which, taken at the flood, leads on to fortune;
               Omitted, all the voyage of their life
               Is bound in shallows and in miseries.
               On such a full sea are we now afloat,
               And we must take the current when it serves,
               Or lose our ventures.

Hamlet's 'enterprise' is afloat upon an equally full sea. He blames the power of thought and understanding for not allowing him to make the most of his opportunity.

Fortune, Chance or Occasion, and Opportunity are all concepts which appealed to the Renaissance and appeared in the allegory of emblem and the symbolism of painting and poetry. Chance is regularly depicted as a female figure with a flying forelock of hair who must be pursued and seized before she turns away for ever. The concept is closely linked with Aristotle's good counsel to deliberate slowly, but then act very fast.[1] Conscience, or thought, which Hamlet feels inhibits action, may be a very necessary part of that slow haste which ensures that the action performed is the right one.

The soliloquy is justly famous as expressing the play's central meaning. If, like the play, it appears rather enigmatic it is because this centre turns out to be a process of choice. Formally, the speech is a generalized expression of doubt about the possibility of escaping from the troubles of humanity through death or suicide. It is also an earnest particular self-examination of the reasons that prevent Hamlet from acting.

[1] Edgar Wind, *Pagan Mysteries in the Renaissance*, Penguin, 1967, 100–4.

Action, in this sense, appears to imply killing the King or killing himself. The play scene which follows looks back to the third soliloquy and gives the term 'act' a new dimension.

The 'enterprise' from which Hamlet is held back by questions of 'conscience' may be 'of great pitch and moment' but it also requires close scrutiny. Colour is an extremely important part of the soliloquy. The colour of thought is pale—even, Hamlet asserts, sickly. Hamlet, however, is already engaged upon the enterprise of presenting the inner-play. This enterprise was first suggested to him when the actor turned pale with emotion at the description of Hecuba: 'all his visage wann'd' (2 ii 547:1594). The play will have succeeded if it makes Claudius 'blench' (2 ii 593:1637)—or turn white with fear. The Ghost itself, it is established, looked pale rather than red. The colour of thought appears to be white.

This colour is contrasted with 'the native hue of resolution'. It is not an unreasonable assumption that this colour is the colour of red cheeks or the colour of blood. Red is more than the colour of health: it is the colour of revenge. Black and red are the colours which appear in the First Player's speech connected with Pyrrhus whose black arms and complexion slowly turn red as he bathes in the blood of the slaughtered Trojans.

Pyrrhus had been black while he lay 'couched in the ominous horse' (2 ii 448:1496). Hamlet describes himself as being like 'John-a-dreams, unpregnant of my cause' (2 ii 562:1608). If he were pregnant with his cause he might emerge from the womb, like Pyrrhus, to spread blood and death. Hamlet clearly desires to exchange his present black of remembrance for the red of the avenger. He is about to present a play in which the ominous figure of Lucianus joins the list of figures—Pyrrhus, Termagant, Herod—who act out violence. The pale cast of thought appears to be holding Hamlet back from self-destruction or from murder.

The 'act' that Hamlet intends to perform after the inner-play has convinced him of the guilt of Claudius is the act of revenge. The fifth and sixth soliloquies will express a depth of hatred for the King and a passionate desire for vengeance which comes close, as we have argued, to the language of Lucianus. The actual performance of the play, however, places this act in a rather different light. Before the soliloquies of will come the meditations on the nature of passion and the harmony of the human mind. The first is addressed to Horatio immediately before the play, the second immediately after it to Rosencrantz and Guildenstern. They suggest that Hamlet may not be as completely 'passion's slave' as he appears to be in the soliloquies of will and blood.

The phrase occurs in the speech by which, immediately after his advice to the Players, Hamlet summons Horatio back into the action of the play (3 ii 61:1914):

Hamlet　　Since my dear soul was mistress of her choice
　　　　　　And could of men distinguish her election,
　　　　　　Sh'hath seal'd thee for herself; for thou hast been
　　　　　　As one, in suff'ring all, that suffers nothing;
　　　　　　A man that Fortune's buffets and rewards
　　　　　　Hast ta'en with equal thanks; and blest are those
　　　　　　Whose blood and judgement are so well comeddled
　　　　　　That they are not a pipe for Fortune's finger
　　　　　　To sound what stop she please. Give me that man
　　　　　　That is not passion's slave, and I will wear him
　　　　　　In my heart's core, ay, in my heart of heart,
　　　　　　As I do thee.

The lines are justly famous since they are themselves a concentrated effect of reason and passion and provide a brief poetic summary of the argument of the battle in the soul.

Horatio is required to act as an independent witness of Claudius's reaction to the inner-play. The information concerning his function as spectator is given to the audience in the second half of Hamlet's speech. The dramatic function of the speech is to provide a necessary contrast to the passionate action of the inner-play and Hamlet's passionate reaction to it.

Horatio is a man who is in command of his soul. His 'blood and judgement'—the intellect and emotions—are so well balanced that he has been able to withstand the 'slings and arrows', or 'buffets and rewards', of Fortune. His nature cannot be changed either by good fortune or by bad. This means, and it is a very important point in the context of the inner-play, that his love or friendship cannot be changed or bought by a change in fortune. He does not respond to the music of time since he is not 'a pipe for Fortune's finger'. Instead he produces his own harmony, the harmony of a well-governed soul, which can never be 'passion's slave'.

The image of the mind as a musical instrument which may be played upon is repeated by Hamlet immediately after the inner-play. The appearance of Rosencrantz and Guildenstern is used by Shakespeare to continue the argument. Hamlet begins, in his usual ambiguous fashion, by insisting that he cannot be expected to answer their questions since they know that the balance of his mind is disturbed (3 ii 307:2185):

Guildenstern   Nay, good my lord, this courtesy is not of the right breed. If it shall please you to make me a wholesome answer, I will do your mother's commandment; if not, your pardon and my return shall be the end of my business.

Hamlet   Sir, I cannot.

Rosencrantz   What, my lord?

Hamlet   Make you a wholesome answer; my wit's diseased. But, sir, such answer as I can make, you shall command: or rather, as you say, my mother.

Hamlet's wit is diseased only by the standards of the court of Denmark. Since Rosencrantz and Guildenstern are the mere 'handsaws' or instruments of that court, without any judgment or understanding of their own, they cannot comprehend a wholesome answer. They are only capable of the kind of diseased reasoning appropriate to a kingdom that has been infected by Claudius.

Hamlet now demonstrates their ignorance and lack of understanding by calling for the recorders which the players have just brought in (3 ii 335:2216):

Hamlet   O, the recorders! Let me see one. To withdraw with you—why do you go about to recover the wind of me, as if you would drive me into a toil?

Guildenstern   O my lord, if my duty be too bold, my love is too unmannerly.

Hamlet   I do not well understand that. Will you play upon this pipe?

Guildenstern   My lord, I cannot.

Hamlet   I pray you.

Guildenstern   Believe me, I cannot.

Hamlet   I do beseech you.

Guildenstern   I know no touch of it, my lord.

Hamlet   It is as easy as lying: govern these ventages with your finger and thumb, give it breath with your mouth, and it will discourse most eloquent music. Look you, these are the stops.

Guildenstern But these cannot I command to any utterance of harmony; I have not the skill.

Hamlet   Why, look you now, how unworthy a thing you make of me! You would play upon me; you would seem to know my stops; you would pluck out the heart of my mystery; you would sound me from my lowest note to the top of my compass; and there is much music, excellent voice, in this little organ, yet cannot you make it speak. 'Sblood do you think I am easier to be play'd on than a pipe? Call me what instrument you will, though you can fret me, yet you cannot play upon me.

The fact that Guildenstern cannot play the recorder is an indication that he is like the man referred to in *The Merchant of Venice*, 5 i 83: 2496 who 'hath no music in himself' and is therefore fit for 'treasons, stratagems and spoils'.

Since music depends for its performance upon concord and harmony it is an obvious symbol for the divine harmony which governs the universe. The Pythagorean concepts of number, harmony, and proportion, and the music of the spheres had been adapted by the philosophers of the Renaissance into a complete account of the world. The *Harmonia mundi* of Francesco Giorgi (Venice, 1525) had set out the 'world music' of the macrocosm and its echoes or parallels in the harmonious composition of the microcosm.[1]

These meditations suddenly reveal Hamlet as aware of the harmony of the universe, and the harmony which can be created in the individual soul, just at the moment that he is himself in danger of destroying his own concord through the passion of revenge. Hamlet scorns Guildenstern who is unable to play the recorder and yet imagines that, like a crafty politician, he can play upon Hamlet. There is a clear contrast established in the play scene between Rosencrantz and Guildenstern, and Horatio. They are false friends who, having no understanding of music and harmony, are themselves merely the instruments played upon by the King. Horatio is a true friend exactly because he is at harmony with himself and neither passion's slave nor a pipe for Fortune's finger.

[1] Frances A. Yates, *Theatre of the World*, 1969, 36.

In Horatio the audience sees and hears the kind of man that Hamlet claims to admire. In Rosencrantz and Guildenstern are revealed those 'fatal fools' whom he despises and comes to hate for the deadly work which they enjoy without understanding. In the next two soliloquies Hamlet will attempt to transform his own personality into the kind of person that he despises and hates. After the soliloquies on conscience, and the meditations on harmony, it is hardly surprising that the audience do not believe that the soliloquies of passion are the entire content of Hamlet's consciousness.

What is expressed, therefore, in Hamlet's 'conscious' mind in the soliloquies is the mounting pressure of his hatred for the King and his intense desire to play the role of aggressive and triumphant avenger. Hamlet only once considers that questions of love, conscience or social responsibility might hold him back. He asks Horatio, in rhetorical fashion, whether it is not now 'perfect conscience' (5 ii 67:3571) to kill the King. In the soliloquies and meditations the dramatist has ensured that these questions are inescapable for the audience.

Shakespeare reveals a delicate balance or harmony of memory, understanding, and will in Hamlet's mind which Hamlet is himself determined to destroy by dedicating all of his passions to his murderous will. The operation of love, conscience, and understanding is expressed as a part of Hamlet's mind of which he is not fully conscious. The play does, as the psychologists have claimed, reveal Hamlet's unconscious wishes and desires. In the 'unconscious' dramatized by Shakespeare, however, there is more than an exclusive sexual attachment to his mother. Shakespeare is concerned with the growth of conscience or love that finds its expression in regard for the interests of others.

That these powers of the psyche have their origin in close physical contact with a mother and with other bodies is now beyond all reasonable doubt.[1] The bond of affection between mother and son is emphasized repeatedly in the play. The most damaging thing about Gertrude's marriage to Claudius is that it has made Hamlet see love itself as a violent and destructive force. The way in which Hamlet restores the harmony of his own soul is dramatized in the meditations and in his relationship with Ophelia.

Hamlet tries to destroy the power of love and conscience in order to dedicate himself to the primitive passion of revenge. The powers which hold him back, however, are as primitive and as strong as the

[1] Harry F. Harlow, 'Love in Infant Monkeys', *Scientific American*, 200 (June 1959, No. 6), 68–74; Harry F. and Margaret Kuenne Harlow, 'Social Deprivation in Monkeys', *Scientific American*, 207 (November 1962, No. 5), 136–46.

aggressive drive to kill. They are the twin peaks of Parnassus referred to by Bruno in *De gli eroici furori*. It is this conflict of interest between the aggressive drives and the power of affection and human love and understanding which Shakespeare has dramatized in the creation of Hamlet's consciousness. What is unnatural in Elsinore is not Hamlet's abrupt swings of emotion. It is the dedication of the King to complete, total, and therefore criminal, self-absorption.

It would, of course, be a simple matter to solve this conflict by making conscience the instrument of reason and having Hamlet renounce revenge in sentiments of suitable piety. Such a method does not solve the problem of the human instincts and does disservice by its feeble and inexact psychology. The power of Shakespeare's play depends upon his awareness of the enormous and deep pull of both of these systems of feeling and his dramatization of the way in which both currents meet with nearly equal force in the mind of Hamlet. To make Hamlet's conscience a conscious force would be to weaken its dramatic effect.

This may be demonstrated by a consideration of the way in which the aggressive nature of Polonius comes through his barrage of multi-moralled platitudes. The other characters express sentiments of honour, love, or affection at the same time as their unconscious aggressions are clearly working in their own interests. Hamlet expresses hatred, but the very expression of that hatred reveals the strength of his memory and understanding working to create a new consciousness. In the soliloquies of 'conscience' Hamlet had blamed himself for inaction and lack of passion. The soliloquies of blood now guarantee the force of Hamlet's passion. Between them they create the opposition of instinct to instinct and reason to reason which is vital to the dramatic tension of the play.

The fifth and sixth soliloquies, therefore, appear to negate everything that Hamlet has said. For that very reason they are an important part of the debate on conscience and responsibility which runs through the play. In the damnation soliloquy Hamlet appears as the paradigm of the Italianate revenger. He is concerned to damn his victim's soul to eternal torment by killing him while he is engaged in mortal sin.

It can, of course, be argued that these sentiments would be easily comprehensible and even acceptable to a seventeenth-century audience aware that it was watching a 'revenge' play. The difficulty of this argument is that it invokes the reactions of a hypothetical seventeenth-century audience precisely at the point where the reactions of a twentieth-century one cannot be relied on. A twentieth-century audience may not be surprised at this exercise in what has come to be called the theatre of cruelty. In order to accept this as heroic conduct, however, it would have to abandon many of its currently held ethical and social beliefs. The historical imagination would have to be exercised in favour of the 'revenge' code. If this mental juggling act has to be performed at such a crucial stage of the action then it is probable that *Hamlet* has ceased to act as a theatrical experience for our time.

Dr Johnson believed that the speech was 'horrible'. He offered it as evidence for the barbarousness of Shakespeare's sensibility. Modern commentators have tended to argue that it is offered by Shakespeare as evidence of the barbarousness of Hamlet's sensibility. Attempting to damn Claudius, Hamlet overreaches himself. He succeeds only in tainting his own mind while fatally delaying his revenge, and becomes himself a 'smiling, damned villain' (I v 106:791). This appears, then, to be the crucial point in the play where Shakespeare is forced, by the logic of his own argument, to turn Hamlet from the 'hero' to the 'villain' of the play. The Ghost is thus revealed as a damned spirit, if not the Devil himself. Hamlet is either the deadly, dedicated instrument of the powers of darkness or, at best, an incompetent who dies unconscionably pleased with this botched piece of viciousness.

It is clear that the soliloquy raises in acute form some of the serious moral problems associated with revenge. Many Elizabethan dramatists turn their avengers into villains in just this fashion. They follow this course because it is inherent in the convention and the social situation which made that convention a possible form of human behaviour. In seventeenth-century Europe it is clear that blood revenge was both practised and condemned; expected, yet execrated.

This kind of moral contradiction is familiar to our own age. It is likely to be familiar to those who come after us. The vital questions for humanity occur in that borderland between men's actions and their professions of faith. Many, if not most, great works of dramatic art are concerned with that difficult territory.

The important question for the critic of *Hamlet* is, does Shakespeare examine this moral contradiction in the play? Is there any evidence that he was even aware of it? It is plain that Hamlet is not aware of any contradiction as he abandons the language of conscience for the rhetoric of the avenger of blood. This lack of awareness on the part of the protagonist may cause the critic to hold opinion with William Empson that:

Many critics of the last century, including Bernard Shaw, thought that Shakespeare couldn't say plainly what he thought about revenge because he was morally so much in advance of his coarse audience; and I should fancy they were right, except that he was about ten years behind it.[1]

It has been argued, and that argument will be reinforced later, that Shakespeare does say very plainly what he thinks about revenge in *Hamlet*. The obvious difficulty of the play, from the critical point of view, is that Hamlet plainly says that he approves of it. It is evident that the scene of the King at prayer offers an unrivalled opportunity for a speech of conscientious scruple which would have established the character of the 'noble heart' and 'sweet prince' beyond the reach of commentary.

Instead Shakespeare writes this extraordinary speech which throws all into confusion. It is confusing because it is a Machiavellian speech which is not followed by any demonstration of the exercise of Machiavellian policy. It promises an elaborate scheme of revenge—but this scheme is never performed. On the other hand, it is an accurate prediction of the way in which Claudius does meet his death. At the play with foils Claudius is gaming, since he has wagered on the outcome; drinking, from a cup which he poisons; and is about an act 'that has no relish of salvation in't' (3 iii 92:2367) since it is the act of murder.

Arguments about whether Hamlet does or does not mean what he says in this soliloquy rather miss the point. The soliloquy is essential to dramatize the extremes of human passion within Hamlet's mind. It is possible to assert that no performance of Hamlet is successful unless it makes its audience hope that Hamlet will settle his accounts with the King and finish the matter by a single sword-thrust. It is also true that no performance can be successful which does not use all the surrounding indications that such an act would 'finish' nothing and that the emotions it involves are obscene and self-defeating. The history of *Hamlet* criticism is good evidence that the play does involve its audience in just such a debate about vengeance and conscience, understanding and passion. It is successful because it is a more exact representation of the truth about the nature and force of human passion than the conventional moral and psychological systems by which it is judged.

The gap between the conventional systems and the psychological facts they are meant to explain is dramatized by Shakespeare throughout this scene. Claudius, immediately after his disastrous exit at the

[1] William Empson, '*The Spanish Tragedy*', in *Elizabethan Drama*, ed. Ralph J. Kaufmann, 1961, 80.

play, is seen acting with speed and resolution to retrieve his situation. He declares that Hamlet is 'mad' and must be sent to England. No one pauses to ask what Hamlet's madness had to do with the King's reaction at the sight of murder by poison. Rosencrantz and Guildenstern accept the King's commission to convey Hamlet to England in language which is a superb and careful expression of the conventional wisdom concerning kingship in Tudor England (3 iii 7:2279):

Guildenstern   We will ourselves provide.
Most holy and religious fear it is
To keep those many many bodies safe
That live and feed upon your Majesty.

Rosencrantz The single and peculiar life is bound
With all the strength and armour of the mind
To keep itself from noyance; but much more
That spirit upon whose weal depends and rests
The lives of many. The cease of majesty
Dies not alone, but like a gulf doth draw
What's near it with it. It is a massy wheel,
Fix'd on the summit of the highest mount,
To whose huge spokes ten thousand lesser things
Are mortis'd and adjoin'd; which when it falls,
Each small annexment, petty consequence,
Attends the boist'rous ruin. Never alone
Did the king sigh, but with a general groan.

This speech is an example of the way in which Shakespeare uses the political and moral opinion of his own time to ask questions which have continuing relevance. The political philosophy expounded by Rosencrantz and Guildenstern could be made to appear reasonable and respectable in many human situations. They use the old symbolic image of the turn of Fortune's wheel as it rolls downhill to describe the relationship between a king and his subjects.

At the time that *Hamlet* was written there was a fairly strong consensus of established opinion, particularly in government circles, that a subject had no right to act against his sovereign. A king could be judged only by God and his own conscience. Even a usurper might be the chosen instrument of God, sent to punish a faithless and perverse generation.

This consensus was overtaken and destroyed by the revolutions of 1640 and 1688. Long before that time the conventional wisdom had

3. Allegory of Prudence (*Titian*)

4. Amor–Pulchitudo–Voluptas (*Titian*)

difficulty in accommodating rulers with criminal tendencies. It was a problem which the political philosophers of the sixteenth and seventeenth centuries found particularly intractable. The terms of the problem have now changed, but its solution is not necessarily closer.

Shakespeare has designed this argument to cut both ways so that the speech which appears to support Claudius recoils upon the King and his courtiers. Rosencrantz argues that an individual has the right to defend himself against personal attack. The King, therefore, has a much greater duty to protect himself since the welfare of his subjects depends upon his personal safety. If, however, it could be proved that the King was a murderer whose rule represented a threat to the welfare of his subjects, might they not have a right and duty to act, in self-defence, against him?

Since the King does use Rosencrantz and Guildenstern as his instruments in the plot to send Hamlet to England, is Hamlet not justified in striking back at them and at the King? Is it more in accordance with reason and 'natural law' to support Claudius or to defy him? Rosencrantz and Guildenstern utter the conventional pieties about the nature of a king's government in a context which completely contradicts all their words.

The attitude of Rosencrantz and Guildenstern is not simply disproved by the implications of their own philosophy. If the King can only be judged by God and his own conscience, it could be argued that Claudius has already brought himself to trial before that bar. The King's prayer is a careful pattern of legal metaphors in which he finds himself compelled to give evidence for the prosecution. He knows that the only possible verdict is guilty.

At this moment Hamlet appears behind him and reveals both the force of his own hatred for the King, and the appalling trap that such hatred can be for the human spirit. Hamlet's speech is the conventional wisdom for avengers just as the King's speech contains the traditional attitudes to repentance and forgiveness. All three major speeches, therefore, in the prayer scene present traditional views of moral and political action which are negated by the action on stage and the position of the characters who speak the lines.

The courtiers' words are appropriate to true friends and loyal servants. Loyalty to Claudius, however, means the performance of treachery and murder. Claudius, who kneels in prayer to ask pardon for his first murder, will soon be on his feet to arrange the details of his second. Hamlet intends to damn the King's soul but is prevented by the fact that he has just succeeded in catching the King's conscience.

Conscience ironically now restrains him from killing the King, as it had earlier prevented him from killing himself.

Hamlet's hatred of the King is, therefore, carefully set within a context which emphasizes the importance of memory and conscience at the same time as it allows Hamlet to express emotions which are, according to the usual dramatic conventions, only uttered by villains. In this play, however, the opposition between vengeance and conscience cannot be arranged according to the conventions. Hamlet feels the claims of both with all the power of his intelligent and passionate imagination.

In the prayer scene Hamlet's words follow the pattern of the theme of poison. They are part of the intricate web of political intrigue. His actions, as he lowers his sword and refrains from stabbing an unarmed and unsuspecting opponent, follow the theme of military honour and the pattern of the duel. Behind the words of all of the characters the audience can sense an expanding universe of motive. It was, I believe, in tribute to this creation of a collective unconscious in the play that Alfred Adler wrote:

> There is only one case in which killing can be justified, and that is in self-defence, when our own life or the life of another person is in danger. No one has brought this problem more clearly under the purview of humanity than Shakespeare has done in *Hamlet*, although this has not been understood.[1]

The audience, however, are not left merely to theorize about the conscious and unconscious motives of the characters. The speculative world of the soliloquies is realized by the dramatist in vivid action upon the stage. The way in which this is achieved becomes clear in the seventh and last of the soliloquies.

On the way to England under the unofficial guard of Rosencrantz and Guildenstern Hamlet meets the army of Fortinbras on its way to war in Poland. This army, which the audience had first heard of in Horatio's speech on the battlements, now takes concrete shape and marches across the stage with drum and colours. It is a brilliant visual effect which confronts Hamlet and the audience with the conventional wisdom and the traditional sentiments about honour and glory, the call of duty and danger.

Hamlet measures himself against this standard of behaviour and again finds himself wanting in all the manly virtues. He is even disgusted by his own intellect (4 iv 32:2743 Q 26):

[1] Alfred Adler, *Social Interest*, 1938, 106.

Hamlet   How all occasions do inform against me,
And spur my dull revenge! What is a man,
If the chief good and market of his time
Be but to sleep and feed? A beast, no more!
Sure he that made us with such large discourse,
Looking before and after, gave us not
That capability and godlike reason
To fust in us unus'd. Now, whether it be
Bestial oblivion, or some craven scruple
Of thinking too precisely on th'event—
A thought which, quartered, hath but one part wisdom
And ever three parts coward—I do not know
Why yet I live to say 'This thing's to do',
Sith I have cause, and will, and strength, and means
To do't.

Hamlet here asserts that there are two possible explanations of his inaction.

He is suffering either from 'bestial oblivion'—since the memory of his father should otherwise have swept him to his revenge—or he is prevented from acting by 'some craven scruple'. This is a repetition of the argument of the fourth soliloquy that 'conscience does make cowards of us all' (3 i 83:1737) although here conscience definitely means the power of thought. The assertion that thought is cowardly because it inhibits physical action is now explicitly reinforced by a comparison with the army of Fortinbras (4 iv 46:2743 Q 40):

Hamlet   Examples gross as earth exhort me:
Witness this army, of such mass and charge,
Led by a delicate and tender prince,
Whose spirit, with divine ambition puff'd
Makes mouths at the invisible event,
Exposing what is mortal and unsure
To all that fortune, death, and danger, dare,
Even for an egg-shell.

The soldier who risks his life for an 'egg-shell' is comparable to the actor who wept 'for nothing' (2 ii 550:1597). The actor and the soldier are figures through whom Hamlet is able to act out his own fantasy of passion. The basis of his comparison is that, given his situation, they would unquestionably perform the act of revenge. From this Hamlet concludes that he is a coward who is inferior to both the actor and the soldier.

The audience watch Hamlet make the same transition in the action of the play that he makes in thought in the soliloquies. He acts a part in a scene of his own devising which turns out to be a powerful and aggressive attack upon the King. He is forced to defend his life in the deadly encounter of the 'play' with foils. Hamlet, in other words, is successful as an actor or a soldier. His self-contempt is based upon the fact that he has not hurled himself into the passionate act of revenge. The very fantasy figures that he has created, however, help to suggest that Hamlet's interpretation of his own role is here mistaken.

The actor and the soldier do not simply occur in the soliloquies. They appear on the stage in the person of the First Player or in the character of Fortinbras. The war, and the performance, which are the central images of the soliloquies are also the major physical images of the stage performance. These images from Hamlet's conscious mind walk the stage in order to make clear to the audience the nature of Hamlet's unconscious wishes and desires.

Throughout the soliloquies Hamlet has assumed that 'remembrance' and 'revenge' are identical terms. The actual contradiction of emotional tone between the soliloquies of 'conscience' and 'remembrance' and the soliloquies of will suggests that the desire to remember is not compatible with the compulsion to revenge.

Hamlet must remember the soldierly figure of the Ghost who was both Hyperion the sun-king and a loving husband. In order to revenge that memory he must play the part of a murderer who strikes down his victim in secret. The difficulty of Hamlet's situation is that in order to fulfil the command that seems to come from his father he must act in a way which makes him resemble his uncle Claudius.

He is prevented from acting in this way by his memory, his conscience, and the operation of chance which he ascribes to the guidance of providence. In the balance of Hamlet's consciousness the dramatist counterpoises remembrance and revenge. In failing to act as a secret murderer Hamlet remembers his father more accurately than if he had plunged into the bloody part that he believes is required of him. For the role of avenger Hamlet substitutes, first, the part of an actor who uses words as his weapons; next, a soldier who is unexpectedly skilled in the art of single combat.

This change is effected by the inner-play. The performance of *The Murder of Gonzago* transforms Hamlet from an actor unsure of his part into a soldier with an assured duty to perform. The attack upon the

King has made the duel of wit and words a deadly contest of 'mighty opposites' (5 ii 62:3565). Since it has become a duel Hamlet is content, like the soldiers, to depend upon his skill but leave the outcome to chance or providence. The final development of his own consciousness, therefore, is an abandonment of his ceaseless questioning and an acceptance of his role.

Hamlet's interpretation of the soldier's role, however, is contrasted with the attitude of the Norwegian captain. As a member of an army on its way to battle the captain gives a matter-of-fact account of the grim reality behind the façade of the Polish adventure. Fortinbras fights as the 'natural' expression of his aggressive but 'honourable' intentions. Hamlet takes up the sword only when his own weapons of words have provoked his opponents into violence. The images created in the soliloquies of bitter self-reproach make it clear that within the terms of poison, play, and duel—which is the state of Denmark and the condition of the theatre of the world—Claudius is opposed by a man who, whatever his faults, does have a sufficient command of the necessary arts of actor, politician, and soldier to enable him to 'win at the odds' (5 ii 203:3660).

The soliloquies cease because the consciousness of Hamlet expands in the last two meditations to fill the whole play. The graveyard scene and the duel scene are the logical outcome of the performance of *The Murder of Gonzago*. They raise again the early questions of the play. They are concerned with remembrance and the final oblivion of death, with conscience and the desire to retaliate in revenge. They re-examine, and allow the audience to redefine, the traditional heroic values of honour, duty, courage, and action.

The last meditation, spoken to Horatio immediately before the poisoned duel, is almost a return to the questioning rhythms of 'To be or not to be' (5 ii 211:3668):

Hamlet   Not a whit, we defy augury: there is a special
                providence in the fall of a sparrow. If it be now, 'tis not
                to come; if it be not to come, it will be now; if it be
                not now, yet it will come—the readiness is all.

The self-denigration of 'Thus conscience does make cowards of us all' (3 i 83:1737) has been replaced by the self-reliance of 'the readiness is all'.

Since the exact reasons for this change are 'unconscious' on Hamlet's part they cannot be discovered simply by inspecting the soliloquies and meditations. They can be found in the performance of those servants of the fantasy and imagination, the actors. The inner-play dominates the thought and action of the central scenes of *Hamlet* for good dramatic reasons. The recitation by the First Player suggests to Hamlet the presentation of 'something like the murder of my father' (2 ii 591:1635). This inner-play does more than confirm his suspicions and 'catch the conscience of the King' (2 ii 601:1645). The recited account of the fall of Troy, the advice which Hamlet gives to the Players, and the argument of the inner-play itself all contribute to the great central debate carried on in the soliloquies and meditations of Hamlet.

If, in *Hamlet*, the great instrument of awareness is the centre of consciousness created in Hamlet's divided mind, then the great instrument of conscience is the inner-play. *The Murder of Gonzago* expresses in exact dramatic form the considerations of conscience which cannot be completely dramatized in the soliloquies.

Chapter 4

POISON IN JEST
the Play Scene

The Murder of Gonzago is a vitally important part of the action of *Hamlet*. The passionate account of the fall of Troy recited by the First Player suggests to Hamlet this theatrical method of unmasking the King. The performance provides apparent proof that Claudius is both a murderer and a villain. The incidents of the court play which confirm the King's guilt also corroborate his own aroused suspicions of Hamlet. Unable to forget his dead brother while his nephew keeps his memory so dangerously alive, Claudius determines to consign Hamlet to oblivion. This attempt makes the inner-play a turning point in the story. The King's effort to achieve security completes his own exposure and costs him his life.

The arrival of the tragedians of the city has, therefore, far-reaching consequences for the plot of the play. They do more than advance the story. They present in concrete terms that metaphor of the theatre— the idea of the play—which has been present in the language since Hamlet's first appearance upon the stage. Shakespeare's use of his own theatre as one of the major symbols of *Hamlet* has attracted a great deal of serious critical attention.[1] What is remarkable about this symbolism is not that it describes Hamlet's situation in theatrical terms. It

[1] See John Dover Wilson, *What Happens in Hamlet*, 1935; Harley Granville-Barker, *Prefaces to Shakespeare: Third Series*, 1937; Francis Fergusson, *The Idea of a Theatre*, 1949; Anne Righter, *Shakespeare and the Idea of the Play*, 1962; Charles R. Forker, 'Shakespeare's Theatrical Symbolism and Its Function in *Hamlet*'.

is that it offers the spectators a much clearer view of the main issues of the play than that possessed by the characters.

Shakespeare's employment of the inner-play is a brilliant adaptation of an old technical device which adds a new dimension to the argument of the play. It performs a double function as an incident in the story and a controlling force in the dramatic plot. It is designed by Hamlet to make the King and Queen convict themselves of murder. The King's reaction exposes the corrupt social and sexual fabric of his court. Based upon murder, it can only be maintained by murder. The inner-play contains an implied threat that these past crimes will in the future be most thoroughly revenged. The artistic triumph is to make this promised act of vengeance as much the subject of the Players' theatrical illusion as the performed murder.

Hamlet treats the 'dream of passion' (2 ii 545:1592) spoken by the First Player, or the 'false fire' (3 ii 260:2137) of the court play, as illusions which should spur him on to the necessary reality of killing the King. Since they do not have this effect it has often been assumed that they are merely incidental to the revenge plot. In the action of the court play, however, together with the First Player's speech and Hamlet's advice to the actors, Shakespeare presents the great questions of *Hamlet* in visual and theatrical images which supplement and clarify the logical difficulties, semantic confusions, and contradictory emotions revealed in the soliloquies. The illusion of the theatre is thus used within the play to concentrate the attention of the audience upon the reality of the problems faced by its fictional characters.

The Players and their performance are essential to the audience's perception and understanding of *Hamlet*. After *The Murder of Gonzago* the play's problems no longer exist only in the mind of Hamlet. They have become part of the experience of the audience. The way in which the audience is allowed to form its own perception of events instead of merely relying upon the reports of the characters is perhaps the supreme triumph of the dramatist's art in *Hamlet*.

It is evident that Hamlet uses the speech and theatrical images of the court play to show Claudius his own past, make him understand his present situation, and inform him of the close pursuit of future vengeance. It is thus a form of what James J. Gibson has called 'mediated perception':

The process by which an individual becomes aware of what exists

Shakespeare Quarterly, xiv (1964), 215–29; M. C. Bradbrook, *Shakespeare the Craftsman*, 1969.

and what goes on around him is perception. The process by which a human individual is *made* aware of things outside his immediate environment is one stage higher. It is mediated perception. It involves the action of another person besides the perceiver. A man or a child can, as we say, *be told* about things, or *be taught*, or *be given to understand*, or *be informed*, or *be shown*. Speech, that triumph of the human species, is the earliest and perhaps the principal vehicle for this indirect apprehension. But speech symbols have their limitations, and a powerful supplement to speech was acquired in the discovery of image making.[1]

The Murder of Gonzago, as performed in the context of the court, is an image which contains information that is perceived in different ways by Hamlet, by Claudius, and by the audience in the theatre.

The King and Hamlet receive more information from the inner-play than the rest of the court. So far as the courtiers are concerned it is 'the image of a murder done in Vienna' (3 ii 233:2106). They cannot see the relationship between this image and a murder committed at Elsinore. Similarly the Prince and King themselves make use of only a fraction of the information presented by the Players. The King interprets the inner-play in the light of his own most immediate concerns. Hamlet seizes upon one episode from the First Player's speech, the grief of Hecuba, and develops from that his third soliloquy. These details are, of course, of supreme importance for the characters and for the play. It should not be forgotten, however, that an audience in the theatre has listened to the whole of the actor's recitation and the speeches of the Player King and Queen before observing the reactions of the main characters.

It is plain that there is a direct relationship between the form of the inner-play and the Ghost's account of the murder of King Hamlet. The connection between them and Aeneas' tale to Dido or the advice to the actors is not so immediately obvious. It will be argued that this obliquity is part of a carefully calculated dramatic effect. It seems probable that the progression, from an account of a murder at Elsinore, to the story of the revenge of Pyrrhus at Troy, to the image of a murder done in Vienna which includes the threat of final vengeance at Elsinore, is not accidental. It is designed to have a profound effect upon the audience.

It is not necessary to assume that an audience has retained all of the

[1] James J. Gibson, *The Senses Considered as Perceptual Systems*, 1966 (U.K. 1968), 234.

details of these events for comparison and analysis. The perception of the audience is not based upon memory but upon their capacity to distinguish what Gibson calls 'invariant information'. In an important passage Gibson argues that:

> It should now be clear that the brain does not have to integrate successive visual sensations in immediate memory. There is no necessary reason to suppose that the fixations have to be retained. The invariance of perception with varying samples of overlapping stimulation may be accounted for by invariant information and by an attunement of the whole retino-neuro-muscular system to invariant information. The development of this attunement, or the education of attention, depends on past experience but not on the *storage* of past experiences.[1]

It is not essential to accept the thesis that the senses act as perceptual systems hunting for information in the environment to see that something very close to the 'education of attention' is proceeding in *Hamlet*.

The varying events described in the play's language or represented in visual imagery upon the stage all differ in marked fashion from each other. It is not really possible to say that the vengeance of Pyrrhus is parallel to the act of revenge which the Ghost has commanded Hamlet to perform. The Player King is not an exact parallel to King Hamlet. Although the actions of the poisoner Lucianus resemble the method of murder used by Claudius, his role is sinisterly ambiguous since he is described by Hamlet as 'nephew to the King' (3 ii 238:2112). The murder at Elsinore, the destruction of Troy, the murder in Vienna, and the threatened revenge at Elsinore all have one thing in common. From their shifting perceptions of time, place, and circumstance the audience are being educated to attend to the invariant fact of murder.

The theatrical imagery, therefore, provides more than an interesting comparison of information about the theatre. Just as Hamlet uses the inner-play to give Claudius a 'mediated perception' of his own crime, so Shakespeare uses the Players and their performance to offer to his audience a 'mediated perception' of murder and consequently a greater understanding of the issues that are involved if Hamlet does kill the King. It is in this sense that it is possible to call the court play the great instrument of conscience in *Hamlet*. It awakens the King's memory and forces him to bring himself to trial before the bar of his own conscience. It illuminates Hamlet's own conception of his role. It asks

[1] Ibid., 262.

the audience to experience, understand, and judge the nature of both crime and punishment.

The play scene is one of a crucial series of scenes in which Shakespeare develops the plot in rapid and decisive fashion. The court of Denmark assembles four times on the stage in the course of the play. The council scene, the play scene, the burial of Ophelia, and the duel are all ceremonial occasions which reflect the past and continuing life of the court. Each ceremony has an unalterable effect upon the psychology of every character who takes part.

Upon the court's first appearance the courtiers bend their wills to serve Claudius. He directs their attention to the future and the affairs of the new reign. Only Hamlet remembers the past. The play scene awakens the King's memory, even against his will. Hamlet demonstrates that the loyal service of the court is unknowing complicity in crime. He directs the attention of the King and the audience to the promised revenge. The King's new understanding of his own situation causes him to arrange the final 'play' with foils.

The method chosen to obliterate Hamlet is ironically designed to allow Laertes to avenge the memory of his dead father and sister. This duel becomes a fatal exercise of the will which provides Hamlet with the opportunity for his own revenge. As *Hamlet* ends Fortinbras arrives from the Polish wars to claim 'some rights of memory' (5 ii 381:3885) in the kingdom. Horatio prepares to deliver the true report of events which will also be the rites of memory for the Prince of Denmark.

The court expresses, and influences, the memory, understanding, and will of all of the characters. This does not mean that the entire play should be interpreted as an exercise in Augustinian theology. The description of the powers of the soul is based upon classical precedent and, as used for example in the *Phaedrus*, is itself a highly dramatic way of describing certain observable operations of the human mind. Shakespeare makes use of this traditionally dramatic psychology to illustrate clearly the acute struggle raging within the minds of his characters on stage.

The First Player's recitation of Aeneas' tale to Dido is an important event in the creation of this dramatic psychology. The speech follows the play's basic pattern of murder and revenge and, like the inner-play, it emphasizes their similarity. The argument about revenge is repeated in the play scene, prayer scene, and closet scene. The action of revenge is advanced in the play scene, the scenes of conspiracy between Claudius and Laertes, and the graveyard scene. By the time the duel scene is reached the argument and action have fused and the 'argument' of the play is complete.

Aeneas describes the death of King Priam during the sack of Troy. Pyrrhus, who kills him, is the son of Achilles. He had joined the Greek army before Troy to avenge his father and fulfil the prophecy of Calchas—that Troy would never be taken without his help. Priam's death is therefore a successful act of vengeance. The horror of it, however, causes even Pyrrhus to pause in its commission (2 ii 474: 1521):

> *First Player* So, as a painted tyrant, Pyrrhus stood
> And, like a neutral to his will and matter,
> Did nothing.

The situation, and the language and imagery, of this speech are repeated in the prayer and closet scenes.

The speech describes a battlefield, and Fortune and War, expressed in the imagery of the classical gods, are its governing concepts. The sword of Pyrrhus falls with all the force of the hammers of the Cyclops forging the armour of Mars. It can withstand any number of the slings or arrows of war since it is 'forg'd for proof eterne' (2 ii 484: 1530). Mars can neither be conquered nor subdued—except by the power of Venus, goddess of love and pity. According to the speech, the death of Priam should have been sufficient to awaken the pity of the Gods; make them break the wheel of Fortune (2 ii 490:1536):

> *First Player* And bowl the round nave down the hill of heaven
> As low as to the fiends.

At the very least it ought to cause 'the burning eyes of heaven' (2 ii 511:1558) to weep. Pity touches neither the gods nor Pyrrhus. It is the First Player who changes colour and is forced to break off his speech in tears.

The fall of Troy is part of the classical and heroic past. In the imagery of the play it is associated with the Olympian gods whom Hamlet so frequently uses as a contrast for the cowardly present. Hyperion the sun-king, Niobe, and Hercules are used to describe the transition from the golden world in which his father was alive to the prison of the present. Pyrrhus is clearly a son who finds no difficulty in accepting the heroic role of avenging his father's death. He is untouched by the pity which throws the actor out of his part. The comparison and contrast between Hamlet and the First Player is emphasized on Shakespeare's stage by the probability that Burbage is playing Hamlet and the First Player is made up to look like Burbage.[1] Hamlet blames himself for not sharing the Player's passion. Like the Player, however, Hamlet is torn between the part that he has to perform, the pitiless avenger, and the pity which is shown perhaps most clearly in his mother's closet and in the graveyard.

The First Player, therefore, acts as a mirror for Hamlet in the same way that the inner-play will act as a mirror for the corrupt court of Claudius. The resemblance between the Players and the actors is not, however, the only reason for associating the fall of Troy with the past, and the future, history of the Kingdom of Denmark. The presence of Pyrrhus covered in blood amid the flaming ruins of the city marks the end of a story. It had begun on the slopes of Mount Ida when Priam's son Paris acted as judge in the contest of beauty between Athena/ Minerva, goddess of wisdom, Hera/Juno, wife of the ruler of heaven and goddess of majesty, and Aphrodite/Venus, goddess of beauty. Promised the love of Helen, Paris awarded the prize of the apple to Aphrodite/Venus. This choice of love and passion above wisdom and majesty led to the long siege and final destruction of Troy.

The Judgment of Paris became a symbol or allegory for the Renaissance of the choice which faces any prince or ruler. As Edgar Wind explains:

> To compliment a prince on his universality by comparing his judgement to that of Paris became a fixed formula of Renaissance euphuism. In Lyly's *Euphues and his England* (1580), Peele's *Arraignment of Paris* (1584), Sabie's *Pan's Pipe* (1595), to name only a few, the same compliment was addressed to Queen Elizabeth. It was carried to extremes in an allegorical portrait at Hampton Court in which the Queen puts the three goddesses to shame because, as the inscription fulsomely asserts, she combines in herself the gifts which they possess only separately.[2]

The comparison was more serious than compliment. Marsilio Ficino urged it upon Lorenzo de' Medici when he wrote to him pointing out that to pursue wisdom, or power, or pleasure at the expense of the others is wrong or even blasphemous.

---

[1] M. C. Bradbrook, *Shakespeare the Craftsman*, 1969, 129 f.: 'The first player naturally is Burbage, and he confronts the real Burbage (who is of course playing Hamlet) made up with the small pointed beard familiar from the Dulwich portrait. "What!" asks the original, commenting on the unexpected addition to his understudy's countenance, "thy face is valenced since I saw thee last; com'st thou to beard me in Denmark?" '

[2] Edgar Wind, *Pagan Mysteries in the Renaissance*, 1967, 82.

The joint rulers of the kingdom of Denmark, Claudius and Gertrude, have made the same error of judgment as Paris. They have preferred the life of passion to wisdom and majesty. The crash of the burning city round Pyrrhus is the inevitable consequence of the rape of fair Helen. The lust of the King and Queen threatens to turn Denmark into a waste land of shame whose destruction lights up the figure of revenge. Hamlet's choice of Aeneas' tale to Dido for recitation was not a random selection on the part of the dramatist.

Shakespeare had already used the story of Troy's destruction in *The Rape of Lucrece* as a symbol of the spreading consequences of lust. Awaiting the arrival of her husband Collatine in order to redeem her honour by committing suicide in his presence, Lucrece spends the interval contemplating a painting of the destruction of Troy which includes Pyrrhus killing Priam before Hecuba's eyes. Lucrece identifies 'one man's lust' as the entire cause of this destruction (*The Rape of Lucrece*, 1471):

'Show me the strumpet that began this stir,
That with my nails her beauty I may tear.
Thy heat of lust, fond Paris, did incur
This load of wrath that burning Troy doth bear.
Thy eye kindled the fire that burneth here;
    And here in Troy, for trespass of thine eye,
    The sire, the son, the dame, and daughter die.

'Why should the private pleasure of some one
Become the public plague of many moe?
Let sin, alone committed, light alone
Upon his head that hath transgressed so;
Let guiltless souls be freed from guilty woe.
    For one's offence why should so many fall,
    To plague a private sin in general?

'Lo, here weeps Hecuba, here Priam dies,
Here manly Hector faints, here Troilus sounds;
Here friend by friend in bloody channel lies,
And friend to friend gives unadvised wounds,
And one man's lust these many lives confounds.
    Had doting Priam check'd his son's desire,
    Troy had been bright with fame, and not with fire.

The Player's speech describes the results of an act of ungoverned passion. One of the natural consequences of the Judgment of Paris is the emergence of the black figure of Pyrrhus from the wooden horse— a supreme symbol of the fortune of war—to cover himself in the blood of Ilium's destruction and avenge his father. The passion of revenge overtakes the passion of lust. Hamlet seizes upon that part of the speech that most exactly expresses his own position. In order to curb the uncontrolled lust of the King, Hamlet desires to deliver himself up to the powerful passion of vengeance. He assumes that only lack of passion has prevented him from acting like the actor who describes Pyrrhus.

The emotions involved are thus extremely complex. The Player's speech is an oblique dramatization of past events. It is also a terrifying forecast for the future. Yet it is not Pyrrhus that Hamlet desires to imitate but the actor, and he has paused for pity. The vision of Troy in *Hamlet* is not so simple as the vision of Troy seen by Lucrece. In *The Rape of Lucrece* the crime of Paris is followed by the inevitable vengeance which is regarded almost as part of the original act. In *Hamlet* Pyrrhus pauses and in that pause becomes an agent responsible for the massacre which he then executes.

A similar complication is dramatized in the prayer scene. Claudius pauses in the double business of trying to repent and yet keep his crown. He ends by accepting the responsibility for his crime and its consequences by continuing with his course of murder. Hamlet stands behind him with drawn sword but, like a 'painted tyrant' (2 ii 474: 1521), does nothing. The damnation soliloquy, however, is a full acceptance of responsibility for the act of vengeance. Both attitudes make the characters resemble the hell-bent figure of Pyrrhus. Neither seems to leave much room for the human pity which broke off the actor's speech.

Between these two representations of roused vengeance lie the nunnery scene, the advice to the actors, and the play scene. All are connected with the idea of unmasking an individual's real character or thoughts by means of play. The nunnery scene is aimed at Hamlet's own antic disposition. The advice to the actors arises naturally out of Hamlet's need to insert a speech in his 'dream of passion' (2 ii 545: 1592) in order to turn it into nightmare for the King.

The speech sums up an important part of Renaissance critical theory, but it is more than a piece of literary criticism. In this context it cannot simply be read as Shakespeare's own views of acting or even as a specific criticism of an actor's performance. The audience are bound to extend Hamlet's words to the Players to the actor playing Hamlet. The questions considered—how to express passion in a way which remains 'natural'—have direct relevance to Hamlet's own chosen role as a character within a play. It is significant that he should warn the Players against overdoing the acting of Termagant between the recitation of the vengeance of Pyrrhus and the enactment of the crime of Lucianus.

It is one of the paradoxes of the art of acting that the extremes of human emotion can only be fully expressed in the way described (3 ii 5:1852):

Hamlet   Nor do not saw the air too much with your hand, thus, but use all gently; for in the very torrent, tempest, and, as I may say, whirlwind of your passion, you must acquire and beget a temperance that may give it smoothness. O, it offends me to the soul to hear a robustious periwig-pated fellow tear a passion to tatters, to very rags, to split the ears of the groundlings, who, for the most part, are capable of nothing but inexplicable dumb shows and noise. I would have such a fellow whipp'd for o'erdoing Termagant; it out-herods Herod. Pray you avoid it.

Both of Hamlet's examples of excess come from the mystery cycles. Termagant is a fictitious god of violent disposition who was supposedly worshipped by Mohammedans. Herod's part included the massacre of the innocents.

This is evidently advice that applies to the characters as well as to the Players. In the graveyard scene Hamlet becomes enraged by the theatrical rant of Laertes over Ophelia's body. Yet in the third soliloquy he had suggested that an actor with his 'cue for passion' (2 ii 554:1601) would 'drown the stage with tears' (2 ii 555:1602). The whirlwind of passion threatens to carry men beyond what is 'natural' in life as well as in art. It is this double use of 'nature' which is central to the second part of Hamlet's discussion of the art of acting.

The player is advised (3 ii 16:1864):

Hamlet   Be not too tame neither, but let your own discretion be your tutor. Suit the action to the word, the word to the action; with this special observance, that you o'erstep not the modesty of nature; for anything so o'erdone is from the purpose of playing, whose end, both at the first and now, was and is to hold, as 'twere, the mirror up to nature; to show virtue her own feature, scorn her own image, and the very age and body of the time his form and pressure.

He must not 'o'erstep the modesty of nature' in his representation. Yet *The Murder of Gonzago* holds a mirror up to the nature of the court and reveals that it is engaged in such 'unnatural' activities as murder. The use of the term 'mirror' in literature contemporary with *Hamlet* indicates that it implied not merely a reflection or copy but an image of the truth. In this case the actors, although they do not know it, are destined to prove that Claudius, in reaching his throne, stepped beyond 'the modesty of nature'.

After the inner-play, on his way to his mother's closet, Hamlet shows himself aware of the possibility that his own part may carry him beyond the bounds of nature. He reminds himself that he must not kill his mother. The pattern of playing, however, has conveyed more information than Hamlet is conscious of to the audience. It has suggested that the part which Hamlet is determined to play, the part of the avenger of blood, is 'o'erdone' and unnatural.

It is this capacity for conveying information to the audience in rapid and economic fashion which makes the 'play-within-a-play' so popular a device with the Elizabethan and Jacobean dramatists. In Thomas Kyd's influential *Spanish Tragedy*, for example, the play presented at court fulfils three important functions. It provides a realistic opportunity for revenge. It is only in 'play' that the avengers can approach their victims with swords in their hands. Secondly, it permits the characters to 'rehearse' or repeat an ironic parody of their former roles in the 'real' action. It thus gives the audience an ironic advantage over the intended victims and prepares for the fatal ending to their parts. Finally it is an emblematic representation of that 'poetic justice' which makes the conduct of the avengers excusable and even warrantable.

The device is repeated by so many dramatists using so many different theatrical combinations that the critic is tempted to treat it as a mere genre effect—whose use depends as much upon custom and stage tradition as upon the inner dramatic logic of a particular play. It is, however, possible to argue that the enormous power of such late examples of this effect as the double masque of murderers in *The Revenger's Tragedy* or the spectacularly reciprocating murderous masque of *Women Beware Women* demonstrates the necessity of the metaphor of 'playing' in this kind of situation. The way in which the masque of murderers repeats the avengers' dance in *The Revenger's*

Tragedy makes an important dramatic point whose moral implications are essential to the play. A full explanation of this point would have required extended treatment that could only with difficulty be made 'dramatic'. Some of the difficulties of that treatment may be observed in George Chapman's *The Revenge of Bussy D'Ambois*.

Shakespeare's use of this traditional device is strikingly original. It is used to provoke questions of 'justice' and moral interpretation. These questions are raised in the First Player's passionate speech. They are examined in Hamlet's third and fourth soliloquies and in the advice to the Players. They are finally presented in action within the frame-work of two meditations on the musical harmony of the human spirit. The passionate debate raised by the questions has frequently distracted critical attention from the art of their presentation.

The Murder of Gonzago, therefore, acts as a mirror for the whole court, including Hamlet. This strange theatrical entertainment with its unexpected dumb show and interrupted action has the capacity for allowing the audience to look 'before and after' (4 iv 37:2743 Q 31). It sums up the action that is past and provides a forecast or commentary on the action that is yet to come. It is the great point of balance in the play.

Hamlet has designed its production to recall a series of past incidents to the King's mind. Claudius alone can recognize the details which he has rigorously excluded from his own imagination. The rhetoric of oblivion turns out to have been more than a mask for hypocrisy. It was essential to the mental stability of Claudius. Once he has allowed him-self to examine his past crime he is irrevocably changed. Thought leads to remorse and almost drives him to repentance. In these circumstances it is hardly surprising that the King has no natural memory of these disturbing events. Hamlet uses the court performance to provide him with an artificial memory.

The inner-play is thus a mnemonic aid or memory system of a kind familiar to the Renaissance.[1] It acts as a stimulus for the consciousness and conscience of Claudius in the same way that Hamlet's 'word' (1 v 110:795) is used to remember the Ghost and his command. The words spoken by the Players, and the action and gestures which they use to make them expressive,[2] combine to make the court play a literal and technical 'theatre of memory' for the King.

The art of memory is an ethical as well as a rhetorical device. In

---

[1] Frances A. Yates, *The Art of Memory*, 1966.
[2] Frances A. Yates, 'The Stage in Robert Fludd's Memory System', *Shakespeare Studies*, iii (1967), ed. J. Leeds Barroll, 138–66.

De Inventione Cicero had defined the four parts of virtue as Prudence, Justice, Fortitude, and Temperance. Prudence is the knowledge of 'what is good, what is bad, and what is neither good nor bad'. It is composed of three parts: memory, intelligence, and foresight. It is, as Dr Frances Yates has argued, 'through Cicero's definitions of the virtues in this work that the artificial memory became in the Middle Ages a part of the cardinal virtue of Prudence'.[1] Aquinas quotes Cicero's definition of Prudence in his *Summa*[2] and uses it to prove that memory is a part of Prudence. The artificial memory has become a valuable aid in the soul's progress towards salvation.

If it is accepted that the inner-play is a memory system and that memory is a part of prudence, it becomes clearer why it is both a picture of the past and a possible prediction of the future. Intelligence and foresight, the other parts of prudence, deal with the present and the future. The virtue of prudence therefore implies a concern with the three parts of time. In this sense the inner-play portrays the hideous past which has made the intolerable present and determined the inevitably disastrous future. The operation of intelligence and foresight, however, ought to allow the characters, in Hamlet's words to his mother, to 'repent what's past; avoid what is to come' (3 iv 150:2533). At its lowest level the court play is an example of prudence on Hamlet's part since it was wise to test the veracity of the Ghost. Claudius would show good judgment if the memory presented in show caused him to have the foresight to repent. The power of this memory system, however, is more than prudential.

The philosophers of the Renaissance developed the classical and medieval memory systems and transformed them into a hermetic and occult art. In the work of magicians such as Henricus Cornelius Agrippa the memory images became associated with astral magic. Both Marsilio Ficino and Giordano Bruno use this combination for their own purposes. Frances Yates has argued that an understanding of this magical use of memory is fundamental to any appreciation of these most artistically influential of the Renaissance philosophers:

> The Hermetic experience of reflecting the universe in the mind is, I believe, at the root of Renaissance magic memory, in which the classical mnemonic with places and images is now understood, or applied, as a method of achieving this experience by imprinting archetypal, or magically activated, images on the memory. By using

[1] Frances A. Yates, *The Art of Memory*, 1966, 20–1, 70 ff.
[2] Thomas Aquinas, *Summa Theologiae*, II, II, Quaestio 49.

magical or talismanic images as memory-images, the Magus hoped to acquire universal knowledge, and also powers, obtaining through the magical organization of the imagination a magically powerful personality, tuned in, as it were, to the powers of the cosmos.[1]

Bruno's views on magical images and their relationship to the harmony of the universe are important, for example, in *De gli eroici furori*. The first dialogue in the second part of that work begins with a discussion of the harmony of the universe and the 'great year' of the world. It then proceeds to a discussion of a major emblem of prudence:

Maricondo	Whatever may be our circumstances, the present afflicts us more than the past does, and both present and past together please us less than the future can; for we always hold the future in expectation and hope, as you can see very well represented by this emblem borrowed from ancient Egypt. The Egyptians have left us a particular statue in which three heads rose from the same bust; one of a wolf who looked behind him, the other of a lion who looked to one side, and the third of a dog who looked ahead, in order to indicate that things of the past afflict us by the memory of them, but not as much as things of the present torment us in fact, while the future always promises better things. Accordingly this emblem contains a wolf who howls, a lion who roars and a dog who laughs.
Cesarino	What does the motto written above it express?
Maricondo	Notice that over the wolf is the word, *Iam*; over the lion, *Modo*, and over the dog, *Praeterea*, words which represent the three parts of Time.[2]

Bruno is describing the image of the god in the great temple of Serapis at Alexandria and some of the details are possibly borrowed from the account in Macrobius, *Saturnalia*, 1. 20. It is a recurring emblem in the Renaissance and one of the most instructive examples is a picture in the National Gallery, London, ascribed to Titian but which Edgar Wind believes is more probably the work of Cesare Vecelli.[3]

[1] Frances A. Yates, *Giordano Bruno and the Hermetic Tradition*, 1964, 191–2.
[2] P. E. Memmo Jr, *Giordano Bruno's The Heroic Frenzies: A Translation with Introduction and Notes*, 1964, 179–80.
[3] Edgar Wind, *Pagan Mysteries in the Renaissance*, 1967, 259–62.

(see pl. 3.) Here the three animal heads of Serapis are surmounted by three human heads which are joined together in the same fashion. Wind argues that the three human heads represent prudence while the animal heads, representing the three parts of time, portray the virtue of good counsel. This virtue is distinct from prudence since it can only be acquired with old age. In the *De Inventione* Cicero had defined virtue in Stoic terms. The Renaissance image of prudence, looking before and after, is not less Stoic. Wind has argued that the human heads, associated with the parts of time, suggest what Augustine called 'a vestige of the Trinity'. The combination of this image with the triple head of the Egyptian god warns the onlooker that virtue, subject to the slow torment of time, must still be judged by eternal standards. In terms of such standards, human life, however prudent, must become a test to destruction.

It is not suggested that Shakespeare had been studying the head of Serapis before he wrote *Hamlet*. In the inner-play, however, he has constructed an intricate memory image which is certainly closely associated with the operation of prudence and the passage of time. Its effect upon the King is similar to one of the psychological consequences attributed by Bruno to such an image—'it behoves one who has sought a kingdom and now possesses it to feel the fear of losing it'.[1] The actors who arrive at Elsinore upon their enforced travel vanish from the play as soon as their function is performed. Their theatrical illusion is framed by Hamlet's two meditations on the musical harmony and mystery of the human spirit. The inner-play is a weapon aimed at that mystery in Claudius. It also acts as a flare which illumines it in Hamlet. The 'mystery' play performed by the actors is a major part of the dramatic harmony of *Hamlet*. That fiction is concerned with the harmony of an individual mind and its relation to the state of Denmark and the universe which surrounds it. Art's 'mediated perception' of human problems can alter men's lives.

The audience are left in no doubt that they are watching a dramatic realization of the past. Talking to Ophelia before the entrance of the actors, Hamlet breaks out in a bitter attack upon his mother. Ophelia, and the courtiers, must treat this as a manifestation of grief, melancholia, or madness. It is a clear direction from the dramatist to both his actors and his audience to observe the element of time (3 ii 117: 1975):

Ophelia   You are merry, my lord.

[1] P. E. Memmo Jr, *Giordano Bruno's The Heroic Frenzies: A Translation with Introduction and Notes*, 1964, 181.

Hamlet	Who, I?
Ophelia	Ay, my lord.
Hamlet	O God, your only jig-maker! What should a man do but be merry? For look you how cheerfully my mother looks, and my father died within's two hours.
Ophelia	Nay, 'tis twice two months, my lord.

Hamlet, in his first soliloquy, speaks of his father as having been dead for two months. His mother's marriage had taken place one month after the funeral. It is now 'twice two months' since the King's death but to Hamlet, in both jest and earnest, it seems like 'two hours'. It is possible that a comparison is intended with the 'two hours' traffic' (*Romeo and Juliet*, Prologue 12) of a stage performance. There can be no doubt that the present action will make his death an immediate experience for Claudius.

Hamlet associates this shift in time with the theatricality of traditional festival (3 ii 125:1984):

Hamlet	O heavens! die two months ago and not forgotten yet? Then there's hope a great man's memory may outlive his life half a year; but by'r lady, 'a must build churches, then; or else shall 'a suffer not thinking on, with the hobby horse, whose epitaph is 'For O, for O, the hobby horse is forgot'.

A great man can only insure his memory by building a church in which prayers may be said for his soul. The church thus acts as a memory system. God, however, to whom such prayers must be addressed, is also a jig-maker and all the world may be the dance of festival as well as a stage. Hamlet uses the players to jog the memory of the court and upset its current merry-making. Instead of a church, Hamlet has built a play to his father's memory and forced the entire court to attend it. As he speaks the epitaph for the hobby horse, the dumb show enters.

By the late 1590s the dumb show, although still favoured by some writers of popular drama, was treated by the leading dramatists as an old-fashioned device. It has been suggested that Shakespeare used it to indicate that *The Murder of Gonzago* was an old-fashioned play. It is strange, if that was his purpose, that he should have chosen to write so unusual and atypical a dumb show. Such a device normally acts as an easily interpreted emblem of the following play.

The show before the first act of *Gorboduc*, for example, presents 'six wild men clothed in leaves' who are unable to break a bundle of sticks tied together. Once they have been untied the men break them easily. A more complex example occurs before the third act of *Locrine*, E 3 r:

> *Enter Ate as before. The dumb show. A crocodile*
> *sitting on a river's bank, and a little snake stinging*
> *it. Then let both of them fall into the water.*

The traditional dumb show does not mime the complete action of the following play or scene.

It is, however, exactly this function that the dumb show in *Hamlet* performs. The stage directions in the Quarto of 1604/5 and the 1623 Folio differ in detail but their essence is the same. They show a King and Queen passionately in love, the King's murder by a 'fellow' who pours poison into his ear, and the wooing and winning of the Queen by the poisoner. Shakespeare indicates clearly to his actors that this is part of his own dramatic design by making Hamlet complain in an aside of the Players' indiscretion. The actors are called upon to show unusual skill and dexterity in presenting this unique episode[1] as an act without words.

The dumb show has created a critical problem. It is asked why the King, who rises at the sight of the poisoning in the spoken play, is not affected by the dumb show. It is sometimes suggested that he does not see it. Yet the most obvious way to ensure that he does not see it is to cut it entirely. It is hardly necessary if its function is to inform the audience of the plot of the inner-play. They have already been told that it will resemble the murder of Hamlet's father. It exists, however, not to create difficulties for the actors but to help them affect the emotions of the audience.

The actor playing Claudius will not be in too great difficulty if he treats the double action as a demonstration of the art of memory. Actions alone are not enough to stir the King's conscience. It requires the words of the Players and Hamlet's ironic commentary upon them to cause an alarming awareness to seep from the unconscious to the conscious mind of the King. The most important feature of the dumb show, for actors and audience, is that it should be performed in silence.

Shakespeare turns to this pictorial and visual presentation of events because he requires an effect which language cannot perform. The dumb show comes close to being a neutral presentation of the facts for

[1] Dieter Mehl, *The Elizabethan Dumb Show*, 1965, 113.

the benefit of the audience. This neutral record is necessary because, as A. J. Ayer has pointed out:

> There is no sharp dividing line between the description of facts and their interpretation; even at the level of common sense our ordinary language will be found to carry a considerable load of theory.

Consequently:

> no record of the facts can be free from all interpretation. One's account of what actually happens is governed by one's idea of what is possible.[1]

It is a fairly easy matter to determine that one has been an eye-witness of one man killing another. To say that one has seen a murder is more complex. The killing may be accidental or justifiable homicide. The difference between them depends upon a number of perceptions which, once they are described in language, inevitably carry a large burden of theory and interpretation. There is no character on or off the stage, from the Ghost to the King, who can provide an impartial account of the crime of Claudius. The dumb show provides the audience with their own eye-witness of the actual event which they can then interpret for themselves.

Once in possession of this nearly neutral record, the audience can observe its interpretation by Hamlet and the Players in the spoken play. Hamlet is testing the Ghost's story. The King's violent reaction reveals that he believes he has seen the murder of his brother. The interpretations of Claudius, and of Hamlet, coincide. The effect of the dumb show is thus to put the facts beyond dramatic dispute. The original murder has not only been described: it has been dramatized and witnessed.

The record is particularly necessary because the conversation between the Player King and Queen carries a special load of theory. It is more than an attack on Gertrude's second marriage. It is an accusation of murder. The protestations of the Player Queen are a bitter parody of the doctrine of remembrance. Her arguments (3 ii 174:2047):

Player Queen In second husband let me be accurst!
      None wed the second but who kill'd the first

and

      The instances that second marriage move
      Are base respects of thrift, but none of love.

[1] A. J. Ayer, *Philosophy and Language*, 1960, 18, 26.

> A second time I kill my husband dead,
> When second husband kisses me in bed

could be a terrible expression of passion indicating that she is in league with the poisoner. Hamlet clearly believes that his mother was, and is, the poisoner's accomplice. Gertrude's lack of comprehension should indicate to the audience that she is not aware, until the closet scene, that her first husband was murdered by her second.

Hamlet's comment 'That's wormwood, wormwood' (3 ii 176: 2049) makes explicit his own double interpretation of the play. It is an allusion to the bitter herb regarded as a cure for worms in the ear or in the womb.[1] These words are, as Hamlet later suggests to Rosencrantz and Guildenstern, the beginning of a bitter cure for Denmark. Hamlet regards Claudius as the source of corruption, of the 'politic worms' (4 iii 21:2686) which feed upon the body-politic and the dead bodies of the characters. He poisoned the ear of the King, abused the general 'ear' of Denmark, and has wormed his way into the Queen's confidence, belly and womb by persuading her to commit incest and adultery. 'Wormwood' links the Queen in Hamlet's mind with the original 'juice of cursed hebona in a vial' (1 v 62:747). The Player Queen's words appear to be those of comfort and remembrance. In fact they are the very poison of death and oblivion for the Player King. Yet, as spoken within the inner-play, they are also the wormwood which will purge the state of the effect of that original murder.

Expecting his mother to be as much moved as the King, Hamlet turns to her to ensure that she has understood what she has seen and heard (3 ii 224:2097):

Hamlet   Madam, how like you this play?

Queen   The lady doth protest too much, methinks.

Hamlet   O, but she'll keep her word.

Gertrude's criticism is accurate, but her words contain a double interpretation. The lady's protestations may be excessive because they are unreasonable. They may also, and it is in this sense that the phrase has passed into common usage, be excessive because they conceal some guilty complicity. Hamlet's reply is equally ambiguous. He seems to suggest that the Player Queen will keep the promises which Gertrude has so flagrantly broken. It then becomes clear that she keeps her word by embracing the man who killed her husband. This is evidently Hamlet's view of Gertrude.

[1] Dorothy C. Hockey, 'Wormwood, Wormwood!', *English Language Notes*, iii (1965), 174–7.

The Player King responds to his wife's passionate assertions of undying love with the reminder that human emotions which are not prudently grounded in the memory are inevitably short and shallow (3 ii 181:2054):

Player King I do believe you think what now you speak;
But what we do determine oft we break.
Purpose is but the slave to memory,
Of violent birth, but poor validity;
Which now, the fruit unripe, sticks on the tree;
But fall unshaken when they mellow be.

If purpose is the slave of memory, memory itself is subject to time. Forgetfulness and oblivion are the natural course of events and human intentions ripen and rot like fruit.

In these circumstances human purpose and passion can only be very uncertain guides to action:

What to ourselves in passion we propose,
The passion ending, doth the purpose lose.
The violence of either grief or joy
Their own enactures with themselves destroy.
Where joy most revels grief doth most lament;
Grief joys, joy grieves, on slender accident.

Grief or joy appear to wear the same twisted mask as they wore in the first court scene showing 'an auspicious and a dropping eye' (1 ii 11:189).

The speeches of the Player King and Queen reopen the argument between memory and oblivion. They carry it a stage further. In the view of the Player King, human love is no more reliable a passion than grief or joy. Fortune or chance is stronger than any of them:

This world is not for aye; nor 'tis not strange
That even our loves should with our fortunes change;
For 'tis a question left us yet to prove,
Whether love lead fortune or else fortune love.
The great man down, you mark his favourite flies;
The poor advanc'd makes friends of enemies.

Although the question is said to be 'left to prove', all of the examples are in fortune's favour. The supremacy of time and fortune are thus urged against the extravagant terms of eternal remembrance used by the Player Queen.

Humanity is totally subject to chance because it has no way of realizing its feeble intentions and transitory passions in action:

But, orderly to end where I begun,
Our wills and fates do so contrary run
That our devices still are overthrown;
Our thoughts are ours, their ends none of our own.

This acceptance of the limitations of human effort does not negate the effects of human passion. The Player King's view of mutability will receive support from the entry of the man who murders him. It may, however, permit a certain charity to be extended in particular cases. The Ghost seems to intend to extend this charity to Gertrude, as the Player King extends it to his Queen. The very uncertainty of fortune becomes an argument for charity.

The actual words of the inner-play, therefore, continue the debate between Hamlet and Claudius about whether it is more 'natural' to remember or to forget. The Player King appears to subscribe to an extended form of the rhetoric of oblivion. He dramatizes one of the great questions of the play. That human life is subject to death and decay is evident. Difficulty arises when an individual has to accept this mutability as inevitable in his own particular case. Tension always exists between the general rules and their particular application.

Claudius makes no attempt to apply his general theories of human conduct to his own affairs. The rhetoric of oblivion is designed to discourage passions which he would find personally inconvenient. The King has, in fact, no sense of the dominance of chance and fortune expressed by the Player King. The symbols of chance and occasion imply that, as Pyrrhus was the natural consequence of the crime of Paris, as the Player Queen's love could change with the King's fortune, so an inevitable and implacable vengeance waits on the crime of Claudius.

The entire career of Claudius is an attempt to control fortune and mitigate the effects of chance. It is a perpetual search for security. He regards human weakness as something to be exploited in order to narrow the odds against him. The inner play makes his destruction certain because it ensures that he cannot take his own advice and forget the dead. Remembrance causes him to seek the salvation of his life and crown in the wager on the 'play' with foils. Here too he attempts to control the odds by the dangerous deception of the poisoned sword and the poisoned cup. These very resources require a fatal reliance on his own good luck and fortune which overthrows his devices and leads to the end of his own death.

The Player King's apparently undeniable assertion that fortune is a power superior to memory is thus contained in a performance which is itself an instrument of memory, love and conscience. Like the grave-yard scene it is an acknowledgment of time's triumph in a play which is an enduring record of Shakespeare's own memory and under-standing. By the end of the play Hamlet defies augury and commits himself to the special providence which lies beyond fortune. *Hamlet* itself defeats the power of time by continuing to speak across the cen-turies of the passion of human love. The argument is central to the play, to the sonnets, and to the life of the artist. The inevitability of death may warrant an acceptance of the failure of human love. That very acceptance is itself exercise in charity and understanding. It negates that view of the world which only recognizes 'remembrance of ourselves' (1 ii 7:185). To believe that love may falter is not to accept the ruthless passion of total self-regard.

This passion is now dramatized by the black figure of Lucianus who walks on as the poisoner in the play. It is clear that he is there to enact the crime of Claudius—and yet he is identified by Hamlet in terms which make him a living and explicit threat to the real Claudius. The King has intervened in the conversation between Gertrude and Hamlet in order to protect his wife from humiliation by her tactless and per-haps insane son. At this moment the court play ceases to be an investi-gation of Gertrude's marriage and becomes a direct and aggressive attack mounted by Hamlet against the King (3 ii 227:2100):

King	Have you heard the argument? Is there no offence in't?
Hamlet	No, no; they do but jest, poison in jest; no offence i'th'world.
King	What do you call the play?
Hamlet	*The Mouse-trap.* Marry, how? Tropically. This play is the image of a murder done in Vienna: Gonzago is the Duke's name; his wife, Baptista. You shall see anon. 'Tis a knavish piece of work; but what of that? Your Majesty, and we that have free souls, it touches us not. Let the galled jade wince, our withers are unwrung.

Enter Lucianus

This is one Lucianus, nephew to the King.

The King uses the word 'offence' for the second time in the play since Hamlet punned on its meaning to Horatio at 1 v 136:830. The word will occur with increasing frequency in the prayer and closet scenes. Hamlet's puns are frequently designed by the dramatist to aid the memory of the audience. The exchange draws attention to the fact that the argument of the inner-play contains a good deal of both kinds of 'offence' for Claudius.

The courtly commonplace of 'Your Majesty, and we that have free souls' is turned into a deadly distinction between those with free souls, who are not touched by the play, and the King—who will shortly be touched to the quick. The Players may, without offence, poison one another in jest: but the offence which lies between Hamlet and Claudius is no jesting matter.

The audience are aware that the play is called *The Murder of Gonzago*. Shakespeare stirs their memory by making Hamlet name the Duke and his wife. Hamlet also calls the play *The Mouse-trap* and explains the title as a trope or figure of speech. There is an implied pun on trope and trap since 'Marry trap' was 'the jeer used to a plotter whose own plot had recoiled on himself'.[1] The figurative language of the court play does act as a trap for the King. The speech is typical of Hamlet's language to his opponents. It appears to be figurative, the courtiers consider it either mad or irrelevant—and Hamlet intends it to be taken literally. He calls his play *The Mouse-trap* because he has just cast Claudius for the major role of the mouse.

The entire action of *Hamlet* may be viewed as a series of traps and stratagems. At the same time that Hamlet is trying to 'tent' or test Claudius, the King is making serious efforts to discover the cause of Hamlet's disaffection. For this purpose he sent for Rosencrantz and Guildenstern and agreed to test the 'mad for love' hypothesis of Polonius. As the King sits at the inner-play he has failed in two attempts to penetrate the heart of Hamlet's 'mystery'. He has two more—the closet scene and the projected voyage to England—in preparation. The performance solves his problem at the same time that it exposes him and leaves him for a moment defence-less.

The second stratagem of Polonius continues to function although it is no longer necessary. It is ironic that Polonius, the most indefatigable setter of traps in the play, should fall victim to one of his own devising. When the mouse-trap snaps shut it kills Polonius instead of the King. Having failed to understand the play, he can have no idea of how dangerous his mission in Gertrude's closet will be. The penalty of that ignorance is death.

[1] M. C. Bradbrook, *Shakespeare the Craftsman*, 1969, 133.

In death he accomplishes better service for the King than he performed alive. Claudius now has a plausible excuse for removing Hamlet from the court. He makes it an opportunity for two murderous attempts upon his life. This death serves as a trap which draws all the other characters into the grave. The immediate result of *The Mousetrap*, therefore, is a new series of traps which dominate the second half of *Hamlet*. The inner-play is both a 'murder' and a 'trap' which requires two titles because it is both a representation of past events and a prediction of future possibilities.

It is this involvement of the inner-play with the three parts of time which explains the presence of the dumb show. The story of *Hamlet* began with the murder of a King by his brother. The story will end when Hamlet has avenged his father and killed Claudius. *The Murder of Gonzago* begins with the killing of a King in wordless action. It is abruptly interrupted at the moment when a man identified as the King's nephew is pouring poison into his ear. The double performance of the act of poison suggests not only the murder which is past but the murder that is yet to come—the predicted killing of the King by his nephew.

The inner-play presents the act of murder as first a matter of memory and then an expression of will. It is a representation of Hamlet's desire and will to revenge himself upon the King. In dramatizing that desire it also raises acute questions about the nature of revenge. The play holds a mirror up to Hamlet as well as the King.

The actor who plays Lucianus has, at his first entry, to improvise suitably villainous faces while the court finish their conversation. The only thanks he receives for this courtesy is a criticism of his acting and what appears to be a gratuitous prompt from Hamlet (3 ii 247:2121):

Hamlet	Begin, murderer; pox, leave thy damnable faces and begin. Come; the croaking raven doth bellow for revenge.

This line is not repeated by Lucianus and does not form part of the inner-play. It is a quotation, or misquotation, from *The True Tragedie of Richard the Third*, a play in the repertory of the Queen's Men which had been published in an evidently mutilated text in 1594.

This play has been treated as a 'source' for *Richard III*. It is equally possible, and perhaps rather more probable, that the play was written in imitation of Shakespeare's success and that the text we possess is a version memorially reconstructed by the actors for touring or for publication.[1] In that case Shakespeare would derive considerable professional amusement from Hamlet's own memorial error.

The lines, however, exist to inform the audience rather than amuse Shakespeare. They are another indication of the ambiguous function of Lucianus. Hamlet mocks at this figure with its grotesque face and he scorns the high style horror of the tragedy of blood. Yet his own language at the end of the scene, 'Now could I drink hot blood' (3 ii 380:2261) parallels the language he has formerly parodied.

The Players, like the head of Serapis, have three incompatible faces. The inner-play itself is presented before the court in what amounts to three sections—divided by the conversation of the court audience. The dumb show presents the events of four months past, and the actors are unmistakably King Hamlet, Gertrude, and Claudius. The Player King and Queen engage in an argument about fortune, memory, and oblivion which is the immediate and present concern of the court. The entry of Lucianus lets slip the black desire for future destruction that exists just below the smiling surface of the court.

It is evident, therefore, that Lucianus is Claudius. It is even possible that he is meant to be made up as a double image of the King, as the First Player is the image of the actor who plays Hamlet. The King admits the identification—and yet he treats the performance, correctly, as a clear threat to his own life. Like Lucianus, Claudius has poisoned a King. For that crime he will have to reckon with his nephew—and on the stage a nephew bends over to poison a sleeping King. In the future predicted by the inner-play it seems possible that Hamlet's role may be to play the part of Lucianus.

Lucianus is only one of a series of figures in the play whose conduct is passionate, revengeful, murderous, and ambiguous. He has been anticipated by Pyrrhus who is both murderer and avenger. He will be succeeded by Laertes pursuing a similar poisonous and revengeful course of action as a result of the inner-play. Pyrrhus perhaps resembles Hamlet. Lucianus certainly resembles Claudius. Although Hamlet is not Lucianus, the fifth and sixth soliloquies—the soliloquies of will and blood—make it clear that he fully intends to play the part of Lucianus. The inner-play demonstrates that if Hamlet does know his course and

[1] G. Bullough (ed.), *Narrative and Dramatic Sources of Shakespeare*, iii, 1960, 237–9; G. B. Churchill, '*Richard the Third* up to Shakespeare', *Palaestra*, x (1900); Leo Kirshbaum, 'A Census of Bad Quartos', *Review of English Studies*, xiv (1938), 20–43; E. A. J. Honigmann, 'Shakespeare's Lost Source Plays', *Modern Language Review*, xlix (1954), 305; E. A. J. Honigmann (ed.), *King John* (New Arden edition), 1959, lv.

act like a traditional avenger then he will be playing a part that has already been filled by Claudius. The parallel figures reveal to the audience the kind of man that Hamlet will have to become if he fulfils his chosen task.

In this way the inner-play offers the audience a perception of the moral dilemma which creates the problem of *Hamlet*. It appears that in order to achieve the revenge that he most deeply desires Hamlet must become like Claudius, the man he most detests and loathes. It is clear, therefore, that Hamlet is in danger of making the same kind of error of judgment as Claudius. Faced with the choice of the active, contemplative, or passionate life implicit in the Judgment of Paris, he will have selected a life of unbridled passion. Such a decision would inevitably transform him into passion's slave—just as Laertes and Claudius become the slaves and eventually the victims of their desire to avenge themselves on Hamlet.

The importance of the speeches of the Player King now become evident. If they did not exist it would be easy to read the inner-play as a condemnation of passion—a usual, easy, and useless moral commonplace. The importance of the symbolism created by the Players is that it is as fatal to reject passion as it is to ignore wisdom and power. The Player King accepts, as Hamlet will have to learn to accept, the great role played by passion in human affairs. One of the consequences of such an acceptance is the commitment beyond chance and fortune.

The impossible choice between wisdom, power, and passion is the same question that is dramatized in the soliloquies of memory, understanding, and will. The soliloquies are Hamlet's attempts to find some way in which he can 'suit the action to the word, the word to the action' (3 ii 17:1865). The inner-play now dramatizes this heart of Hamlet's mystery for the audience. It is an act of remembrance which is intended as the prelude to an act of revenge. It is a demonstration of the power of memory and conscience presented by a man who feels that his duty is to play the passionate part of Lucianus at the same time that he admires, above all else, the balanced blood and judgment of Horatio. The play scene dramatizes the exact way in which remembrance is, for Hamlet, incompatible with revenge.

When Hamlet comes upon the King at prayer the demands of his chosen role as an avenger of blood make him spare a man whom he believes to be in a state of grace. The King's prayer is the result of the awakening of his conscience and understanding by the inner-play. The power of the play as an instrument of conscience thus defeats its use as a weapon of passion. The King's gain in self-knowledge, however, is defeated by his own will. He is determined, at all costs, to maintain his false position as King. The pursuit of this passion delivers him up to the very vengeance proposed by Hamlet. It is the King, and not Hamlet, who is engaged in a secret murder at that moment of vengeance.

The play scene decisively changes Hamlet's role. He becomes convinced that he must act as an avenger at the very instant that the inner-play has put the possibility of that revenge-murder for ever beyond him. He is instead committed to a secret battle for his own life. In presenting *The Murder of Gonzago* Hamlet used the weapons of words to unmask Claudius. His success in forcing the King to betray himself transforms his own part to that of a soldier—a change which is clearly marked in the soliloquies and by the appearance of the army of Fortinbras.

It is hardly surprising that Hamlet should feel and express such passionate hatred for the King. If he were not capable of such intensity he would be duller than the weed on the wharf of Lethe, the river of forgetfulness. It is not necessarily weakness which makes him express this will in words rather than deeds. Successful secret aggression, although generally admired, is not always the most admirable of human qualities. The triple nature of the inner-play makes it at one and the same time the great image of hatred and murder and the great instrument of conscience within *Hamlet*. In the person of Lucianus it dramatizes what M. C. Bradbrook has called 'the compelling power of that part of ourselves which we do not desire to meet'.[1]

The stage play is thus used within a stage play as a magnificent symbol of the power of perception and understanding. Speech and physical action are used to achieve a double purpose. It forces Claudius to understand himself, and that self-knowledge destroys him. It reveals to the audience the extent to which Hamlet does not understand himself or his own actions. Aware of a compulsion to avenge his dead father, he is not aware that this desire, so far as it requires him to play the role of Lucianus, is opposed by his memory and understanding.

Just as Hamlet rehearses the roles of actor, avenger, and soldier in soliloquy, so the Players give the audience a 'mediated perception' of what Hamlet would have to be like in order to kill the King. Since Hamlet is not Lucianus, and the soliloquies have made it clear that he is unlikely to become Lucianus, it can hardly surprise the audience that when the 'real' opportunity occurs Hamlet pauses for thought before

[1] M. C. Bradbrook, 'Shakespeare's Primitive Art', *Proceedings of the British Academy*, li (1965), 216–34.

striking a man in the ritual position of submission and repentance.

Claudius destroys himself because he misinterprets the information contained in the inner-play. He sees two of his deepest fears realized upon the stage. The Players enact his own past, which he had thought dead and safely buried. In their performance he thinks he also sees the act which he fears may be the consequence of that past—his own murder by his nephew. Both interpretations are explicit in the prayer scene. He attempts to repent and atone for the past—and yet he has already taken energetic measures to protect himself from any future consequences. Determined to prevent the translation of his fears into fact, he selects the one method which can turn them into reality. This selection is due to his own misunderstanding of the drama that he has watched. He acts upon his fears for the future, and neglects the account of the past. In the poisoned duel the past finally overtakes him and the King dies by his own poison.

The inner-play's counterpoint of action and speech, silent deeds and their varied interpretation, is a vital principle of organization in the play. The dumb show is used as a recurring oracular forecast of a developing pattern of disaster. The first appearance of the Ghost is a dumb show. Ophelia describes to her father how Hamlet appeared to her in her closet in distraught dumb show. This silent action is a consequence of the Ghost's appearance and both lead on to the performance of the court play. The results of its dumb show of murder continue through the prayer and closet scenes to the end of the play. That end, however, is anticipated by a final dumb show. In the graveyard Hamlet casts down the skull of Yorick, the King's Jester and master of the spoken word, and advises him that his last joke must take the form of the grinning dumb show of death.

The skull is another reminder of the inevitability of death and the triumph of chance and fortune. It is the last act of the 'poison in jest' of the court play and the poison in 'play' of the court entertainment. As the action of *Hamlet* moves towards its final silence through the graveyard, Shakespeare raises some of the most profound questions of the play.

The grave has been dug because of the death of Ophelia. It is difficult to overestimate her importance in the structure of the entire play. During the play scene Hamlet has been sitting at her feet commenting upon the performance of both Players and courtiers. Her presence at that dream of passion further complicates the intricate psychology of *Hamlet*.

Chapter 5

THE POWER OF BEAUTY
Hamlet and Ophelia

After the play, the killing begins. The first death among the characters is not the revenge-killing predicted in the inner-play's double image of death. It is, however, a logical although unforeseen development of that action. From a dramatic point of view the play scene has built up so much tension that some kind of release of passion on the stage is essential. The mouse-trap therefore snaps shut. Only when it has done so is it discovered that it has killed a 'wretched, rash, intruding fool' (3 iv 31:2413) instead of the hoped for 'rat' (3 iv 23:2404).

With the death of Polonius the plot of *Hamlet* assumes a new and violent velocity. The sudden sword-thrust through the arras of Gertrude's closet transforms Hamlet from a man who has been training himself to perform the role of avenger into a homicide who falls victim to a pursuing and implacable vengeance. This sudden metamorphosis may be 'accidental' as far as Hamlet's own intentions are concerned, but it represents a clear and deliberate choice on the part of the dramatist which has decisive consequences for the orientation of the entire play.

Its dramatic purpose is clear. The theme of violence, and the reaction and response to violence, is suddenly viewed in a different perspective. The use of Pyrrhus and Lucianus allows Shakespeare to demonstrate the kind of man who would be capable of killing the King without thinking about it. The death of Polonius allows Shakespeare to investigate what might have happened if Hamlet had killed the King without thinking about it.

The way in which Laertes and Ophelia react to their father's death with the full capacity of their passionate natures supplies the answer. The chain of disaster and sudden death would continue. Shakespeare makes Hamlet use a comparison from painting in order to draw the audience's attention to this change in perspective (5 ii 75:3579):

Hamlet   But I am very sorry, good Horatio,
          That to Laertes I forgot myself;
          For by the image of my cause I see
          The portraiture of his.

It is not only the stage play which holds a mirror up to nature. Individuals, or even their pictures, may serve the same purpose.

Hamlet actually describes Laertes as a mirror in conversation with Osric before the 'play' with foils (5 ii 112:3610 Q 6):

Hamlet   Sir, his definement suffers no perdition in you; though
          I know, to divide him inventorially would dozy
          th'arithmetic of memory, and yet but yaw neither in
          respect of his quick sail. But, in the verity of extolment,
          I take him to be a soul of great article, and his infusion
          of such dearth and rareness as, to make true diction of
          him, his semblable is his mirror, and who else would
          trace him, his umbrage, nothing more.

According to this ironic account, the only person capable of acting as a 'mirror' or model for the qualities of Laertes is his own reflection seen in a glass. Anyone who attempts to use Laertes as a 'mirror' and to model himself upon him will achieve only the distinction of becoming like his shadow, not his reflection.

Osric's praise of Laertes as the perfect gentleman thus provokes the reply that his perfection is beyond imitation. Laertes, however, is also the 'mirror' of the perfect avenger. Hamlet feels that he ought to imitate this part, but has not done so. The different perspective with which Hamlet's cause is painted or reflected in Laertes casts new light on it for the audience.

The imagery of painting and reflection thus draws attention to the new system that is being introduced into the great series of reflecting 'mirrors' which forms the play of Hamlet. In this fashion Hamlet reverses roles with Claudius, and becomes a pursued killer, without actually playing the part of Lucianus. The graveyard scene and the duel scene are both the direct outcome of the death of Polonius. The conduct of Ophelia and Laertes shapes the second half of the play.

This repetition of the revenge theme alters the balance of the action. The fate of Polonius and his family is inextricably linked with the court of Denmark. The story of how that family is overwhelmed by disaster is also a history of the court's destruction. The grief of Ophelia and the anger of Laertes are contrasted with Hamlet's conduct. These comparisons do more than suggest other answers to the questions asked at the beginning of the play. They change the nature of the questions.

Ophelia and Laertes actually pursue the courses of action considered by Hamlet in soliloquy. Laertes chooses to be a violent avenger of blood. Ophelia follows a different course which leads her 'not to be' (3 i 56:1710). After the death of her father Ophelia suffers from what the King calls 'the poison of deep grief' (4 v 73:2813). This drives her to madness and the despair which so poisons her memory, understanding, and will that it leads to her death. This death may be accidental or suicidal. In both cases it has strong overtones of self-destruction.

Laertes, enraged at the death of his father, is plunged into a deep and equally poisonous grief by the madness and sudden end of his sister. Intent upon vengeance, Laertes is soon involved in the 'madness' of the King's plot against Hamlet. This leads to his own independent proposal for the use of poison upon his unbated rapier—a suggestion that leads to his own destruction and the death of the King.

Hamlet is subject to exactly the same passions as Ophelia and Laertes. Grief, hate, madness, revenge, and self-destruction are the great themes of the soliloquies. Ophelia and Laertes are both ignorant of the murder of King Hamlet. Their conduct thus provides what appears to be independent testimony about the central situation. The King may exhort Hamlet to accept his father's death as 'natural'. He does not expect Laertes or Ophelia to respond to the killing of Polonius in a calm or reasonable fashion.

The way in which Laertes and Ophelia plunge passionately to murder and self-destruction allows the audience to measure the force of the passions which Hamlet is struggling to control. The aggressive and passionate feelings of ambition, revenge, and self-destruction are all 'natural' reactions. Only Hamlet attempts to control these passions by an uncommon awareness, consciousness, and intelligence. This control is not lightly acquired. The sudden reversal of roles in which Hamlet becomes a killer turned prey for a new and vengeful hunter allows Shakespeare to examine these involved emotions and passions on a psychological as well as a physical level.

The idea that the hunter is also hunted in his turn may be safely traced back to mankind's earliest experiences. The Renaissance, however, was particularly interested in the psychological development of the idea expressed in Ovid's *Metamorphoses*, iii. The hunter Acteon, who lost his way in the forest and saw Diana naked, was changed into a stag by the goddess and pursued and killed by his own hounds.

The medieval and Renaissance commentators who had moralized Ovid in a tradition which stretches from John of Garland's *Integumenta* (*c.* 1234) through the French *Ovide Moralisé* and the work of Petrus Berchorius to George Sandys's *Ovid's Metamorphosis, Englished Mythologiz'd and Represented in Figures* (1632) had frequently interpreted Acteon as a man pursued and destroyed by the hounds of his own passion. An engraving of Acteon is used as an emblem of *Voluptas aerumnosa* in Geoffrey Whitney's *A Choice of Emblems* (1586).

That Shakespeare was perfectly familiar with such an idea is clearly demonstrated by the opening of *Twelfth Night* (1 i 16:20):

Curio	Will you go hunt, my lord?

Duke	What, Curio?

Curio	The hart.

Duke	Why, so I do, the noblest that I have.
	O, when mine eyes did see Olivia first,
	Methought she purg'd the air of pestilence!
	That instant was I turn'd into a hart
	And my desires, like fell and cruel hounds,
	E'er since pursue me.

When Fortinbras surveys the corpses on the stage at the end of *Hamlet* he compares the sight to a display of game at the end of an unusually savage day's hunting (5 ii 356:3857):

Fortinbras	This quarry cries on havoc. O proud death,
	What feast is toward in thine eternal cell
	That thou so many princes at a shot
	So bloodily hast struck?

'Havoc' is a battle-cry indicating that no quarter or mercy should be shown to the enemy. Hunting which results in havoc leads to indiscriminate slaughter and thus oversteps the written and unwritten laws which govern the pursuit of game. Death is a cruel sportsman.

Such a 'quarry' has unquestionably been produced by the principal characters. They have released wild passions which have, in the end, 'hounded' them all to death. The lust and ambition of Claudius have driven him on to seize the crown. That seizure automatically marks him as the victim of a pursuing vengeance. Yet this vengeance is itself a passion which brings further pursuit and destruction in its wake.

The search for vengeance in *Hamlet* is frequently referred to in terms of hunting. This imagery is most closely associated with the presentation of the inner-play. When Rosencrantz and Guildenstern first report the actors' arrival they use an image from falconry to describe the children's companies whose popularity in the city has forced the actors to go on tour (2 ii 335:1387). Hamlet, in calling immediately for a speech, says: 'We'll e'en to it like French falconers, fly at anything we see' (2 ii 423:1474).

By the end of *The Murder of Gonzago* the image of the hunt has become a symbol of Hamlet's success and triumph in hunting and hounding the King (3 ii 265:2143):

Hamlet   Why, let the strucken deer go weep,
                    The hart ungalled play;
                    For some must watch, while some must sleep;
                    Thus runs the world away.

Hamlet is aware, however, that the very success of his device may make the King hunt him with more urgent determination. When Rosencrantz and Guildenstern arrive to summon him to his mother's closet Hamlet treats them as stealthy hunters trying to keep downwind from their prey: 'Why do you go about to recover the wind of me, as if you would drive me into a toil?' (3 ii 337:2216).

This image of Rosencrantz and Guildenstern as the King's hunters or dogs is realized in physical action after the death of Polonius when Hamlet escapes from his guards with the cry of 'Hide fox, and all after' (4 ii 30:2659). The inner-play acts as a trap which forces the King out of cover and exposes him to the hounds of his own passions. The death of Polonius means that he can also use Rosencrantz and Guildenstern, and after them Laertes, to run down and kill Hamlet. The inner-play is an image of the destructive passions that it releases in its audience.

Within the context of tragedy it is evident that many dramatists used the theme of an avenger entirely consumed and then destroyed by his own passion for revenge. Shakespeare's use of this theme illuminates new, and unexpected, aspects of the moral and psychological questions which are the fundamental basis of *Hamlet*. Claudius, in his search for security, makes use of Laertes's passion for vengeance. Ironically he thus places in Hamlet's hands, at the most suitable occasion, the perfect instrument of vengeance. There could be no clearer demonstration of the 'dream of passion' (2 ii 545:1592) pursued by the King. It is evident that the dramatic justification for the existence of Polonius is the manner of his death.

It is clear that Hamlet shares many of the passions which destroy the King and Laertes. It is easy, therefore, to assume that all passion is condemned by the play and that its moral is as commonplace as the one which Arthur Brooke prefaced to his version of *The Tragical Historye of Romeus and Juliet* (1562):

> The glorious triumphe of the continent man upon the lustes of wanton fleshe, incourageth men to honest restraynt of wyld affections, the shamefull and wretched endes of such, as have yelded their libertie thrall to fowle desires, teache men to witholde themselves from the hedlong fall of loose dishonestie.[1]

As in *Romeo and Juliet*, Shakespeare's examination of the problem is psychologically more complex and morally more profound and charitable than the simple opposition between reason and passion so well loved by authors in the tradition of *A Mirror for Magistrates*. The passion for which Romeo and Juliet sacrifice themselves cannot be dismissed as evil or even described as an undesirable development in the strife-torn and hate-ridden city of Verona. The reason which would condemn these lovers would be an instrument of little service to humanity.

The world of Elsinore is infinitely darker and more terrible than Verona. In it the torch of human passion is carried by a pair of lovers whose history is even more 'star-cross'd' (*Romeo and Juliet*, Prologue 6) than that of Romeo and Juliet. Their love blazes in the language of the play with a sexuality as fierce and open as that which displays Hero naked to Leander in Marlowe's *Hero and Leander*. Shakespeare had read, or re-read, *Hero and Leander* while writing *Romeo and Juliet*. That play is filled with clear and deliberate verbal echoes of Marlowe's poem. The knowledge gained in writing *Romeo and Juliet* is now developed in the severer harmonies of *Hamlet*. The great love scene between Hamlet and Ophelia, however, is not performed on a balcony or in a bedroom. It takes place in the graveyard, when Ophelia is already beyond the reach of human love.

[1] G. Bullough (ed.), *Narrative and Dramatic Sources of Shakespeare*, i, 1957, 284.

It is in the graveyard, and in a burst of passion, that Hamlet discovers one of the truths which has eluded him throughout the play. The imagery of hunting is concerned with the traps which are set in order to obtain information. This hunt, however, is also a search for truth on the part of the characters. Polonius expresses this when he describes the trap that he has set for Hamlet in the nunnery scene (2 ii 156:1188):

Polonius   If circumstances lead me, I will find
            Where truth is hid, though it were hid indeed
            Within the centre.

Truth, for the audience as well as for Polonius, proves to have an unexpected centre.

The truth about Denmark is that the present King murdered his brother to obtain his crown and queen. This act of love is a hunt of murderous passion in which the King and most of the court are finally pulled down and killed. The search for power and love becomes a chase in which death is the only victor—an unseen hunter whose presence is only recognized when it is too late. The search for justice and revenge relentlessly pursued by Laertes makes him, in turn, a marked victim of the hunt of death. The closer that Polonius comes to discovering the 'truth' about Denmark, the nearer he is to death.

The discovery that the King is a murderer creates the problems of the play. The certain proof supplied by the inner-play does not solve the problem of *Hamlet*. The question remains, how does one deal with such a man without becoming like him? The death of Polonius, and the conduct of Laertes, make it clear that the hunt of death will never cease so long as one vengeance pursues another. The only power which can break this chain of murder is the passion of love—love which could be expressed even at this stage, as Claudius knows and reveals in the prayer scene, by repentance for the wrong he has done his brother and renunciation of the love and power gained by his crime.

It was, however, the passion of love which first drove Claudius and Gertrude to prefer the life of passion above that of wisdom and majesty. The passion which destroys the court of Denmark has the same fundamental root as the only passion that can save the state of Denmark. The play contains other mysteries, and is concerned with other truths, than the fact that Claudius murdered his brother. The conflict is not therefore simply a conflict between reason and passion. That would be a 'poor concussion of positives on one side with negatives on the other'.[1] The conflict is the different ways in which the

[1] Henry James, *The Art of the Novel: Critical Prefaces by Henry James*, ed. R. P. Blackmur, 1934, 132, quoted on page 7.

same fundamental passions, based upon man's aggressive, sexual, and compassionate nature, develop in the individual. It is clear that Giordano Bruno's image of the twin peaks of Parnassus[1] is an attempt to come to some kind of psychological understanding of the competing and apparently contradictory passions which meet in the name of love.

It must be emphasized again that while it is possible, and I believe that it is probable, that Shakespeare had read Bruno's *De gli eroici furori*, no part of this critical argument depends upon that hypothetical assumption. It is not possible to explain *Hamlet* as a dramatization of the philosophy of Bruno. They were both, however, great artists using the traditional symbolism of the Renaissance to describe and dramatize certain observable aspects of human psychology. The correspondence of their imagery—the battle within the soul, the Judgment of Paris, the hunt of passion, and the image of prudence—makes a comparison both interesting and instructive for the critic.

In this context, therefore, Bruno's treatment of the traditional figure of Acteon is particularly interesting. He does not regard him as simply the victim of his own passions. Instead he is a seeker after truth. It is not possible, in Bruno's view, for the human soul on this earth to attain a complete knowledge and understanding of the divine harmony and perfection of the universe. This harmony he symbolizes by Apollo, god of the sun. Diana, chaste huntress and goddess of the moon, then becomes the symbol of the power and beauty of the universe that may, after long search in the dark forest, finally be seen and comprehended by the human intellect.

In the Second Dialogue of the second part of *De gli eroici furori* Bruno writes:

> I say very few are the Acteons to whom destiny gives the power to contemplate Diana naked, and the power to become so enamoured of the beautiful harmony of the body of nature, so fallen beneath the gaze of these two lights of the dual splendour of goodness and beauty, that they are transformed into deer, inasmuch as they are no longer the hunters but the hunted.[2]

In this context the dogs which pursue Acteon are not simply the lusts of the flesh which destroy him. They are a desire and passion for a divine harmony which make him indifferent to the 'thousand natural shocks/That flesh is heir to' (3 i 62–3:1716–17):

[1] Quoted on page 65.
[2] P. E. Memmo Jr, *Giordano Bruno's The Heroic Frenzies: A Translation with Introduction and Notes*, 1964, 225–6, cf. 123.

The result is that the dogs, as thoughts bent upon divine things, devour this Acteon and make him dead to the vulgar, to the multitude, free him from the snares of the perturbing senses and the fleshly prison of matter, so that he no longer sees his Diana as through a glass or a window, but having thrown down the earthly walls, he sees a complete view of the whole horizon.[1]

This Diana is 'the being and truth of intelligible nature, in which is infused the sun and the splendour of a superior nature'. The man who has fallen in love with this Diana may truly be said to be possessed by the 'heroic frenzy' of Bruno's title. The pursuit of this kind of passion is the beginning of wisdom.

It is not necessary to make Hamlet an inhabitant of Bruno's world of Pythagorean symbols and Platonic forms in order to realize that he is a man torn by conflicting passions. Bruno claimed to solve problems which Shakespeare was content to dramatize. Hamlet's love and memory of his father spur him on to revenge his death. That very act of revenge would transform him into a beast like Claudius who is bound to be destroyed by the ungoverned force of his own unleashed passions. The only method of escape is to penetrate further into the forest in order to catch a glimpse of the goodness and beauty of the naked Diana and be devoured by the dogs of love instead of the dogs of war. In order to be an avenger it is necessary to stifle such passions. Hamlet, however, catches more than a glimpse of them beside Ophelia's grave. The power and passion of human love is not dead within him, although he has failed to recognize it until that point in the play. It is, in its fashion, a heroic frenzy. It cannot save Hamlet, or lead him to the state of divine contemplation which is the goal of Bruno's search, but it does introduce a new element which has profound implications for the psychology of the whole play.

Shakespeare, therefore, uses the death of Polonius as the starting-point for a dramatization of passions which cut deep into the roots of man's social and sexual existence. The Judgment of Paris and the act of love are seen as having political as well as sexual consequences. The complex symbolism of the play makes it a carefully created and controlled fictional or dream structure which invites the audience to abandon their orthodox moral, political, and sexual certainties in order to become aware of depths of instinctual feeling which are only now being barely sounded and charted by our psychology. It is

[1] P. E. Memmo Jr, *Giordano Bruno's The Heroic Frenzies: A Translation with Introduction and Notes*, 1964, 225–6, cf. 123.

impossible to explain *Hamlet* by the metaphysics of Giordano Bruno or by the metaphysics of Sigmund Freud because the play advances beyond their principles. It is an organized system of perception for obtaining information about human psychology.

The character of Ophelia is essential to Shakespeare's dramatization of human passion in *Hamlet*. It is not surprising that her scenes carry a burden of dramatic consequence out of all proportion to their length. It is evident that the dramatist has succeeded in making them dramatically effective by filling them with intense and almost unendurable tragic emotions. Like Hamlet, Ophelia is a character whose troubled mind and consciousness have encouraged critics to seek for 'real' or 'historical' explanations of her conduct. The measure of Shakespeare's success is the way a critical 'mythology' has grown round Ophelia.

It is extremely important to see that the dramatic character of Ophelia gathers myth and metaphysical speculation for the same reason as the dramatic character of Hamlet. Both are active centres of consciousness which mirror, and help to interpret, the events of the play for the audience. Ophelia's mind is not, perhaps, as 'finely aware and richly responsible' a consciousness as Hamlet's.[1] It is a much more sensitive instrument than the minds of Laertes, Polonius, Gertrude, or even Claudius. It creates an extremely concentrated effect because it is concerned only with the passion of human love—having had its understanding in all other directions carefully limited by the dramatist.

The consciousness is necessary because, as Henry James pointed out in the preface to *The Tragic Muse*:

> No character in a play (any play not a mere monologue) has, for the right expression of the thing, a *usurping* consciousness; the consciousness of others is exhibited exactly in the same way as that of the 'hero'; the prodigious consciousness of Hamlet, the most capacious and most crowded, the moral presence the most asserted, in the whole range of fiction, only takes its turn with that of the other agents of the story, no matter how occasional these may be. It is left in other words to answer for itself equally with theirs.[2]

This observation is not entirely accurate. The play is clearly designed to express the consciousness of Hamlet in a way that is denied to many of the other characters. The obvious discrepancy between the aware-

[1] Henry James, *The Art of the Novel: Critical Prefaces by Henry James*, ed. R. P. Blackmur, 1934, 62, quoted on page 61.
[2] Ibid., 90.

ness of Hamlet and the dramatic ignorance of the other characters is consciously exploited for comic effect by Tom Stoppard in his play *Rosencrantz and Guildenstern Are Dead.* It is true, however, that the minds of the other characters are used in the great central scenes to help provide a searching examination of Hamlet's own role in the play. Ophelia is the most highly developed, and the most important, of these reflecting minds.

When Hamlet appears to Ophelia in her closet with his doublet unbraced, no hat upon his head, his stockings ungartered and a look (2 i 83:979):

Ophelia   As if he had been loosed out of hell
             To speak of horrors,

he is behaving in the traditional fashion of distraught lovers. Ophelia and Polonius interpret this conduct as the effect of disappointment in love. The nunnery scene is devised as a 'show' to convince the King of this interpretation. It fails in this purpose because Polonius has mis-interpreted Hamlet's actions. The audience has had the benefit of the Ghost's information. It will therefore be able to interpret Hamlet's conduct, more correctly, as Hamlet's farewell to love in order to con-centrate upon his task of revenge. He is clearing his memory, as he had sworn to do in the second soliloquy, of 'all trivial fond records' (1 v 99:784).

Hamlet does not take his leave of Ophelia in this way simply because she might prove a mild distraction during the task of revenge. He believes, and this belief can be demonstrated from the imagery of the play, that to yield to his love for Ophelia would be to enter the fickle hopeless world of passionate love for a woman in which his mother and uncle wallow as if in a pigsty. It would be to commit the same Judgment of Paris and prefer passion above wisdom and power. Hamlet therefore sees Ophelia as a threat to his memory, his dedication to the task of revenge, and to his whole existence. Only when she is dead does he recognize that this view was wholly and disastrously mistaken.

Hamlet is shown as being called upon to make the traditional 'choice of life' that is familiar from the literature and painting of the Middle Ages and the Renaissance. The symbolism of this choice of life is similar to the Judgment of Paris but it is not identical with it. It may be illustrated by a consideration of two paintings by Raphael, *The Dream of Scipio* in the National Gallery, London, and its companion piece, *The Three Graces*, in the Musée Condé, Chantilly. (See pl. 2.) In his account of these paintings in *Pagan Mysteries in the Renaissance*, Edgar Wind draws attention to a number of recurring patterns in Classical and Renaissance imagery. These patterns are, I believe, applicable to the study of *Hamlet*, although they are not necessarily a complete and sufficient explanation of Shakespeare's imagery.

In *The Dream of Scipio*:

> The young hero lies at the foot of a laurel tree, apparently dreaming of his fame. Two women approach him. The sterner one presents him with a sword and a book, the more gracious offers a flower. These three attributes—book, sword and flower—signify the three powers in the soul of man: intelligence, strength, and sensibility, or (as Plato called them) mind, courage, and desire. In the Platonic scheme of the 'tripartite life', two gifts, the intellectual and moral, are of the spirit while the third gift (the flower) is of the senses. Together they constitute a complete man, but as they mingle in different proportions they produce different characters and dispositions.[1]

It is evident that the imagery of the book, the sword, and the flower is of great significance in the structure of *Hamlet*. It represents the choice between *contemplativa*, *activa*, and *voluptaria*, or the pursuit of wisdom, power, and pleasure. It has already been argued that the fall of Troy symbolizes the choice of Gertrude and Claudius as the Judgment of Paris, and that the soliloquies operate in terms of memory, understanding, and will—the Augustinian powers of the soul. These are now seen to be part of a larger series of images which present to the audience the choice of life open to the characters throughout the play.

Hamlet had attempted to follow the contemplative life when he sought to return to the University of Wittenberg. He is called to the active life of revenge by the Ghost. He attempts to follow the passionate life of hatred for the King at the same time that he rejects the passionate life of his love for Ophelia. It is clear that he has failed to understand the true nature of the passionate life of the senses. This is evidently also the situation of Claudius, Laertes, and Gertrude, for they fail to understand the flowers and herbs of healing and grace offered to them by Ophelia in the scenes of her madness.

Hamlet is twice presented as reading a book during the play. He may also be carrying one at the beginning of the nunnery scene. There

[1] Edgar Wind, *Pagan Mysteries in the Renaissance*, 1967, 81.

he finds Ophelia, apparently the picture of chaste contemplation, reading a book which has been handed to her by her father to use as a stage property in the 'show' devised for the King. In exhorting her to retire to a nunnery Hamlet is suggesting that she devote herself solely to a life of contemplation—a life that he would have preferred to follow if the King had not kept him at Elsinore.

The sword of the active life is carried by the armed figure of the dead King. The famous duel fought with Fortinbras is a paradigm of the active life of a King and a ruler. This example is kept alive in the play by the example of young Fortinbras and the presence of his army. Both Laertes and Hamlet become involved in the active life when they meet with rapiers in their hands. One of these rapiers is poisoned and it becomes plain that Claudius, too, leads an active existence, although his chosen activity is murder. The poisoned chalice is a powerful symbol of that union of action and contemplative cunning.

Ophelia carries the flower of the passionate life. The language of flowers is, in a very important sense, the language of passion in the play. The flowers may be rosemary or rue, the herbs of grace, which Ophelia carries in her scenes of madness. They may be the 'mixture rank, of midnight weeds collected' (3 ii 251:2127) referred to by Lucianus and used by Claudius to poison his brother. The flowers of passion may be herbs of health, or weeds which threaten to poison the entire kingdom of Denmark. What is instructive is that Polonius and Laertes regard Hamlet as the major threat to the fair flower of Ophelia's passion.

They are unaware of Hamlet's own fierce rejection of the passion of love and the life of the senses—a rejection which causes him to treat Ophelia as if she were a bawd or a whore. Only in the graveyard does Hamlet recognize his love for Ophelia—a passion that is proclaimed in defiance of memory and understanding since it is an expression of love for a now senseless corpse. Only once he has embraced the passionate life of human love is Hamlet's union of the active, contemplative, and passionate lives complete. Only then is he ready to purge the court and kingdom of Denmark of the festering misuse of passion which threatens to poison it. It is essential to recognize that Claudius's and Gertrude's abuse of love is not intended as a condemnation of all desire. The flower is a necessary addition to the book and the sword.

Shakespeare uses only one brief scene to establish Ophelia before he calls upon her to perform some of the most difficult and important acting in the play. It is vital that all the actors should be aware of the purpose and fundamental nature of this scene. It is too often scurried through in order to permit suitable pauses and dramatic effects in the scene with the Ghost. The company must understand that there can be no *Hamlet* without Ophelia and that this scene establishes the reflecting consciousness used in the nunnery, play, and graveyard scenes.

It establishes an atmosphere of acute sexual anxiety. Ophelia has only spoken one half-line in the play when her brother starts to reprove her for recklessly exposing herself to Hamlet's advances (1 iii 5:467):

> *Laertes*   For Hamlet, and the trifling of his favour,
> Hold it a fashion and a toy in blood,
> A violet in the youth of primy nature,
> Forward not permanent, sweet not lasting,
> The perfume and suppliance of a minute;
> No more.

The violet is an image which links the play's sexuality to the graveyard. Ophelia is unable to offer her brother violets on his return from France since 'they wither'd all when my father died' (4 v 181:2936). Laertes hopes that violets may spring from her dead body.

The scene uses the complete range of the play's imagery of poison, play, and duel in order to impress upon Ophelia the danger of her sexual situation and to inform the audience of a passion that might otherwise pass unregarded. It is a passion which has important consequences for the play. Laertes begins by offering Ophelia reasons of state. If the safety, or perhaps, as the Folio reads, sanctity, of Denmark depends upon Hamlet's choice of a future queen, so the sanity and health of Ophelia depend upon her ability to realize that Hamlet's 'will' in these matters is not his own. She must accordingly treat any protestations of love as dangerous to her honour and perhaps poisonous to life itself (1 iii 29:492):

> *Laertes*   Then weigh what loss your honour may sustain,
> If with too credent ear you list his songs,
> Or lose your heart, or your chaste treasure open
> To his unmast'red importunity.
> Fear it, Ophelia, fear it, my dear sister;
> And keep you in the rear of your affection,
> Out of the shot and danger of desire.
> The chariest maid is prodigal enough
> If she unmask her beauty to the moon.
> Virtue itself scapes not calumnious strokes;
> The canker galls the infants of the spring

> Too oft before their buttons be disclos'd
> And in the morn and liquid dew of youth
> Contagious blastments are most imminent.

If Ophelia 'weighs' Hamlet's greatness she must realize he is not
master of his 'will'. She should then proceed to 'weigh' the danger she
will incur if she permits him to master her 'will'. Will is a common
expression for sexual desire. It is not certain that it carries the explicit
sexual sense of Sonnet 135 here, but the implications of 'your chaste
treasure open' are clear enough. Hamlet must approach that area
through her ear and her heart. Ophelia must therefore be wary of the
engagement that takes place in her own mind and urges her to yield
these parts to her enemy. She must keep 'in the rear' of her own
passions and therefore 'out of the shot and danger of desire'.

The duel or military engagement between the lovers now turns into
a masque or play. The end of a masque occurs when the dancers unmask. The end of the play of love is near when the lovers unmask by
removing their clothes. Laertes warns Ophelia that maids must unmask
when the moon is their only audience.

Roses are 'the infants of the spring'—or at least the phrase describes
them in *Love's Labour's Lost*, 1 i 101:110—and Laertes later calls
Ophelia 'rose of May' (4 v 154:2910). The flower imagery, however,
carries a submerged metaphor of sexual passion. The dew of Ophelia's
youth would certainly be blasted if, as a result of opening her chaste
treasure to Hamlet, she should canker the rose of her chastity by giving
birth to a real infant of the spring. The details of the story found in
the *Danish History* of Saxo Grammaticus are thus reversed. The young
woman was there used by the King as a device to entrap Amleth. Laertes
and Polonius are anxious to protect Ophelia from the cunning trap
for her chastity laid by the Prince—a trap which they think would
poison their honour and her life.

Ophelia accepts this advice with a certain amount of irony—an irony
which expresses her character but also runs deeper than her present
consciousness in the language of the play. Shakespeare is preparing the
mind of his audience for later dramatic effects (1 iii 45:508):

Ophelia I shall the effect of this good lesson keep
     As watchman to my heart. But, good my brother,
     Do not, as some ungracious pastors do,
     Show me the steep and thorny way to heaven,
     Whiles, like a puff'd and reckless libertine,

> Himself the primrose path of dalliance treads
> And recks not his own rede.

The guard set by Ophelia on her heart may find the real enemy within. The guard upon the battlements will find themselves in that situation in the next scene.

It will shortly be evident—from the Polonius–Reynaldo scene—that Polonius does expect Laertes to tread the path of dalliance at least as far as the Paris brothels. Both Polonius and Laertes prove 'ungracious' as shepherds to Ophelia. It is ironic that Laertes should attack the Priest in the graveyard for not following the rule of Christian charity. 'The primrose path' is the road to hell. The entire family are in danger of taking it. Polonius follows it as a servant of the King whose whole power is based upon such dalliance. Laertes follows it gladly when he returns to avenge his father. In the graveyard the Priest indicates that he regards Ophelia's death as no more than a passport to hell. Ophelia sees more dangers in the situation than are visible to her father and brother.

The entry of Polonius develops both the imagery and the action. His speech of good advice is a traditional, and therefore 'memorable', genre which can be traced to a variety of possible sources. The 'wise father' tradition continues from David's advice to Solomon through Erasmus's version of Isocrates' *Letter to Demonicus* to the versions usually cited as sources—Lord Burghley's ten precepts to his son and Euphues' advice to Philautus in John Lyly's *Euphues* (1578). Yet, as Doris V. Falk[1] has pointed out, the great difference is that all of these fathers begin by offering their sons spiritual advice. Polonius gives only the prudential maxims of the practised politician.

Like Claudius, Polonius is both rhetorician and politician. An actor must cause his audience to nod wisely at the conventional wisdom of (I iii 78:543):

Polonius This above all—to thine own self be true
     And it must follow as the night the day,
     Thou canst not then be false to any man

and yet cause them to doubt the context in which this advice is given. The passions of remembrance and love are hardly to be controlled by this fashion of self-regard. Polonius now makes it impossible for Ophelia to trust her own judgment, and therefore be true to herself, in the terrible transactions of the heart.

[1] Doris V. Falk, 'Proverbs and the Polonius Destiny', *Shakespeare Quarterly*, xviii (1967), 23–36.

Polonius believes that Hamlet intends to deceive Ophelia. For every one of her statements about love, Polonius has a different, and discreditable, interpretation.

Polonius picks up Ophelia's phrase, 'many tenders of his affection to me' (I ii 99–100:565–6) and, in heavy sarcastic fashion, develops its meaning of 'offer for contract'. In the metamorphoses which follow Hamlet first seeks to pass counterfeit money and offers 'tenders' which 'are not sterling' (I iii 107:573). He then becomes a man whose vows are a snare and a delusion set simply as 'springes to catch woodcocks' (I iii 115:581). Hamlet next becomes the general of a besieging army, a Machiavellian tactician who calls for a parley in order to obtain the unconditional surrender of the opposing forces. Finally he appears as an actor dressed in false clothes to utter fictitious vows (I iii 126:592):

Polonius   In few, Ophelia,
Do not believe his vows; for they are brokers,
Not of that dye which their investments show
But mere implorators of unholy suits,
Breathing like sanctified and pious bonds,
The better to beguile.

Hamlet's vows are 'brokers'—or go-betweens—who do not possess the capital, or the powers, shown in their documents and are therefore engaged in the business of fraud. Polonius is still elaborating the 'offer for contract' sense of Ophelia's original choice of 'tender'. One such possible contract suggested by Hamlet's vows is 'a contract of eternal bond of love' (*Twelfth Night*, 5 i 150:2318). The bonds of such a ceremony would be 'pious bonds' and if they breathe it is because they represent the vows spoken in the marriage service.

Hamlet's vows are 'mere implorators of unholy suits' because they use the colour of the robes worn at the ceremony of marriage to give a semblance of propriety to their own fraudulent purpose—which is presumably to obtain Ophelia's 'chaste treasure'. Ophelia would be a fool to listen to Hamlet and would expose her father as a fool for not looking after his daughter. Like the good advice of Laertes, the tedious but bitter jokes of Polonius contain a buried metaphor. If Ophelia really took Hamlet's 'tenders for true pay' she might literally 'think' herself 'a baby' and 'tender' or give birth to a 'fool' or child. An unwanted pregnancy would be a grave consequence for Ophelia.

The irony of the situation is that it is their failure to believe Hamlet's vows which makes fools of them all. The Priest regards the ceremony at the graveyard as 'unholy' and would never have performed it unless the King had acted as 'broker'. The part that Polonius imagines Hamlet to be playing—a cunning false-seemer gratifying his lust by fraud and guile—is an accurate picture of the King of Denmark.

Polonius attempts to make Ophelia forget Hamlet in his own version of the rhetoric of oblivion. Polonius and Laertes, unaware of the poisoning of King Hamlet, identify the Prince as the source of poison. He is a threat to Ophelia's chastity and his madness endangers the stability of the entire kingdom. This initial mistake renders their triangle of affection fatal. It leads to the graveyard and the oblivion of death.

This scene indicates both the difficulty, and the immense opportunity, of the part of Ophelia. Although her reply to her brother is spirited, Ophelia's behaviour is sober, steadfast, and apparently demure. Yet in the language of the other characters she appears as an active and exciting participant in the submerged inner life of the court. The solemn warnings of her brother and father contain a strong libidinous undercurrent of sexuality. They regard her as a girl of vibrant personality who must restrain and 'understand' herself in order not to ally herself with her lover. Both speeches picture Ophelia as seduced, made pregnant, and abandoned by Hamlet.

When Hamlet encounters her in the nunnery and play scenes his language is so overtly sexual that it might be considered obscene or insulting. It is fairly evident that, at this stage of the action, Hamlet views Ophelia as he considers his mother—a passionate voluptuary whose flagrant sexuality is a poisonous and destroying force. The image of poison which Polonius and Laertes see in Hamlet, he sees in Gertrude and Ophelia. Yet his choice of language, and the very violence of his reaction, show that he is far from immune to such poison. The fantasy picture of Ophelia created by Polonius, Laertes, and Hamlet reveals their own most deeply rooted fears and acute sexual anxieties.

Their description of Ophelia is not entirely fantasy. The scenes of madness reveal, beyond all reasonable doubt, a strong-willed and passionately sexual nature which breaks out violently in thought and deed once the restraints of reason have been removed. In her songs Ophelia describes herself as seduced, made pregnant, and abandoned.

It is, therefore, hardly surprising that a character who is so variously described should cause some difference of critical opinion. It is not simply a historical accident, nor is it solely a matter of individual predilection, that Ophelia should appear to some critics as demure and to others as depraved. There are outspoken confident moral judgments, such as Rebecca West's decisive opinion that 'the truth is that Ophelia was a disreputable young woman: not scandalously so, but still disreputable'.[1] The continuing debate about such textual cruces as 'pious bonds' (1 iii 130:596), emended by Theobald to 'pious bawds' with no apparent textual justification, or the argument whether 'nunnery' (3 i 121:1776) means 'a community of nuns' or 'a brothel' are equally all part of a passionate argument about the nature of Ophelia's character.

Since this ambiguity is not accidental, but derives from the ways in which Shakespeare has made the other characters describe her, it is hardly surprising that critics who are also psychologists should assume that Ophelia and Gertrude are different, and perhaps incompatible, aspects of the same female figure. It would be correct to say that at certain stages of the play Hamlet's attitude to Ophelia is governed by his love–hate relationship with his mother. To treat Ophelia simply as a mother-substitute, however, is to over-simplify and distort the imagery which expresses the play's unusually complex psychology.

If it is possible to categorize Ophelia beyond doubt as an injured innocent, or a sly slut, or even a 'disreputable young woman', then the moral problems of the play can be simplified. Conventional attitudes can be adopted to events which, if taken seriously, must arouse in the audience a terror and a pity at the tragic possibilities of human existence which are not easily allayed by any soothing or reassuring system of metaphysics. The desire to simplify Ophelia and resolve her into components which can be classified in terms of current critical, moral, or psychological orthodoxies, is the same kind of critical simplification which attached the puritanical title of *Sacred and Profane Love* to Titian's masterpiece in the Gallery Borghese at Rome. (See pl. 4.)

The paintings of Titian contain visual imagery which is as provocative, and as divisive, as the imagery of Renaissance drama. Like that drama, they make demands upon the intellect and emotions of the spectator rather than offering him comfortable reassurance. The Renaissance handled its visual imagery in exactly the same way that Picasso has claimed he treats his:

> When I paint, I always try to give an image people are not expecting and beyond that, one they reject. That's what interests me. It's in this sense that I mean I always try to be subversive. That is, I give a man an image of himself whose elements are collected from among the usual ways of seeing things in traditional painting

1 Rebecca West, *The Court and the Castle*, 1958, 17.

and then reassembled in a fashion that is unexpected and disturbing enough to make it impossible for him to escape the questions it raises.[1]

It is now being claimed that Shakespeare's imagery in treating Ophelia is remarkably similar to Titian's painting. Both are unexpected and disturbing enough to make it impossible for the spectator to escape the questions raised.

Titian's painting shows two women, one clothed, the other naked except for a loin-cloth and a red cloak over one shoulder. Between them is a fountain, carved with various figures, in which Cupid appears to dip his hand. The figures carved on the fountain are scenes of chastisement. 'A man is being scourged, a woman dragged by the hair, and an unbridled horse is led away by the mane'.[2] Edgar Wind argues that these symbols on the fountain of love 'show how animal passion must be chastened and bridled'.[3]

It is possible that the figures on the fountain link the chastisement of love to the chastisement of Fortune. The woman with the flying forelock may be the figure of *Fortuna*. An unbridled horse is also listed in Cartari's *Le Imagini . . . de i dei de gli antichi* as a symbol of fortune. Wind then argues that:

If the reliefs on the fountain thus demonstrate that animal passion has been exorcized, it would follow that the water in the fountain of love is pure, although it is gently stirred by Amor; and it follows further that the two women conversing at the fountain in the presence of the god are both representatives of a love above the 'profane', their dialogue rising to those *casti misteri amorosi di Platone* which allow for two forms of chastened love, *Amore celeste e umano*. Human Love, while beautifully adorned, is the more restrained of the two because she knows her adornments to be vicarious, whereas Celestial Love, who is unadorned, is the more passionate and ardent, holding in her hand a vase from which a flame rises. Between the two, Amor is seen setting the water of the fountain in motion, an idyllic version of the 'spirit moving over the face of the waters', which changes chastity into love. As the movement of the group is from left to right, the three figures again illustrate the progression from *Pulchritudo* through *Amor* to *Voluptas*, with Amor playing his traditional part as a mediating or converting power. The theme of the picture is therefore exactly what the untutored eye has often suspected—an initiation of Beauty into Love.[4]

[1] Françoise Gilot, *Life With Picasso*, 1965, 64.
[2] Edgar Wind, *Pagan Mysteries in the Renaissance*, 1967, 141–51.
[3] Ibid.
[4] Ibid.

The figures on the fountain make it clear that although one may 'fall in love' it requires intense effort and arduous application to reach the kind of love symbolized by the two women. The elements of the painting are part of the long attempt made by the Classical, Medieval, and Renaissance artists and philosophers to reconcile virtue with pleasure. Raphael's *Dream of Scipio* and the choice of life which must embrace wisdom, power, and pleasure is part of this tradition. So is the companion painting of *The Three Graces*. Wind believes that this painting was originally placed back to back with *The Dream of Scipio*, like the obverse and reverse of a medal.

The three graces are Chastity, Beauty, and Pleasure. They are naked, except for Chastity who has a light loin-cloth, and they are joined together in the rhythm of an eternal dance. The different qualities of these three female figures together make up the feminine principle which is also the power of pleasure or love. Just as each man must strive, in his choice of life, to be a union of wisdom, power, and pleasure, so every woman must be a combination of chastity, beauty, and passion. A woman is therefore three women, since she possesses the graces within her, and the different balance or harmony that they adopt in their dance of the spirit determines her character.

Since the three graces are also the power of pleasure they also form part of the character of every man. It is disastrous to ignore the graces and it may be equally disastrous to neglect any one of them. They must all be pursued if the individual is to acquire within his own soul the harmony of the dance which is also in tune with the music of the spheres and the divine order of the world. It is not enough to be wise, or powerful, or to be in love. It is insufficient to be as chaste as ice, or simply beautiful, or entirely devoted to pleasure. A man or woman is called to be a complete union of opposites.[1]

Wind draws attention to the extreme importance of the balance of the group in Raphael's painting:

Not quite so abstemious as Chastity, nor so liberally adorned as Pleasure, Beauty holds the balance between them, being chaste and pleasurable in one. She touches Chastity's shoulder as she turns towards Pleasure; and so subtle is the distribution of weights that,

[1] The Platonic concept of such a union of opposites has had a long and important influence in European thought. Its development by Montaigne, Pascal, Proust, and Sainte-Beuve is applied to *Hamlet* by Peter Alexander in *Hamlet: Father and Son*, 1955.

although the group retains its classical symmetry, the emphasis is decidedly to the right.[1]

This distribution of weight creates a mathematical union of scale and proportion with its companion painting. In *The Dream of Scipio* the ratio of gifts is two to one against pleasure. In *The Three Graces* the ratio of grace is two to one in pleasure's favour:

> In offering these gifts of love, the Graces counterbalance the demands of Scipio's heroic dream. Instead of two gifts of the spirit and one of the senses, they bring two delectable gifts and one of restraint. While the hero is advised to adopt a rule of action by which he subordinates his pleasure to his duties, he is here invited to soften these severities and allow virtue to come to fruition in joy. The discipline of Scipio is only one side of the picture; the other is his affectionate liberality. *Virtus* and *Amor* belong together.[2]

In the nunnery scene when Hamlet meets Ophelia he has just finished an agonizing attempt to harmonize the conflicting passions in his own soul. 'To be or not to be' (3 i 56:1710) demonstrates his difficulties in pursuing an active, a contemplative, or a passionate life. When he looks up from this desperate debate Hamlet sees the figure of a solitary girl reading a book. She appears to be the symbol of quiet and chaste contemplation. The language which Hamlet addresses to Ophelia in the nunnery scene is founded on the image of the three graces.

Ophelia's first action is to deny the power of the book of contemplation which she holds in her hand. She breaks the power of memory by offering to return to Hamlet the remembrances of their mutual love. To Hamlet this repudiation of memory makes Ophelia, like his mother, the figure of *Voluptas*—but a figure of passion who is not subject to the chastening of love or the chastening of fortune. Hamlet sees an engrossing and forgetful lust which makes women lower than beasts. Gertrude has broken the harmony of the graces by her hasty marriage. Hamlet now denies that grace can ever have existed in the female sex. He identifies Ophelia as unrestrained and lustful passion. It is hardly surprising that she is unable to understand him.

The terms used by Hamlet in this exchange, 'honesty', 'beauty', and a 'bawd', are the names of the three graces—except that the grace of pleasure or passion is identified as the whore of lust (3 i 103:1758):

[1] Edgar Wind, *Pagan Mysteries in the Renaissance*, 1967, 81–96.
[2] Ibid.

Hamlet	Ha, ha! Are you honest?
Ophelia	My lord?
Hamlet	Are you fair?
Ophelia	What means your lordship?
Hamlet	That if you be honest and fair, your honesty should admit no discourse to your beauty.
Ophelia	Could beauty, my lord, have better commerce than with honesty?
Hamlet	Ay truly; for the power of beauty will sooner transform honesty from what it is to a bawd than the force of honesty can translate beauty into his likeness. This was sometime a paradox, but now the time gives it proof.

Hamlet warns Ophelia that the dance of the graces is a progression to lust rather than passion. Any contact between 'honesty' or *Castitas* and 'beauty' or *Pulchritudo* must transform honesty into a bawd. Hamlet believes that this result is the inevitable outcome of the 'discourse' of beauty and honesty since 'the time gives it proof' in the conduct of his mother.

From this belief there follows the conclusion that he is himself tainted with this lust—since he is by birth a prisoner of the nature that he must have inherited from the whore his mother (3 i 118:1772):

Hamlet	You should not have believ'd me; for virtue cannot so inoculate our old stock but we shall relish of it. I loved you not.
Ophelia	I was the more deceived.

Since all women are symbolized by the solitary figure of *Voluptas*, mankind is entirely corrupted by the disease of lust. Marriage and the birth of children are thus a biological confidence trick in which a union formed without love or faith breeds 'sinners' who are in turn condemned to a wanton progress to oblivion.

The only way of breaking this endless wheel of misfortune is to stop the process of human reproduction. This can only be accomplished if women in general, and Ophelia, become the figure of *Castitas* and abjure marriage by retiring from the world to a nunnery. It is important to realize that Hamlet's attack is not directed at women alone. Hamlet regards himself as equally vicious and corrupt (2 i 124:1779):

Hamlet   I am very proud, revengeful, ambitious; with more
offences at my beck than I have thoughts to put them in,
imagination to give them shape, or time to act them
in. What should such fellows as I do crawling between
earth and heaven? We are arrant knaves, all; believe
none of us. Go thy ways to a nunnery.

Marriage is for fools. The doors should be shut upon her father that
'he may play the fool nowhere but in's own house' (3 i 132:1787).
Ophelia should take care to marry a fool since no married woman can
escape calumny and wise men are aware that women make them
'monsters'.

'Monsters' in this sense probably means men with horns or cuckolds.
Since all marriage vows are contracted between a fool and a whore
Hamlet now embarks upon his bitter and extraordinary attack upon
the whorish art of painting the face (3 i 142:1798):

Hamlet   I have heard of your paintings too, well enough; God
hath given you one face, and you make yourselves
another. You jig and amble, and you lisp, and nickname
God's creatures, and make your wantonness your
gnorance.

As a description of Ophelia this is irrelevant 'madness'. There is
little doubt that the figure with the painted face, the provocative walk,
and the transformation of God's handiwork is the traditional and
powerful image of *Voluptas* in her less reputable guise of fleshly lust.
The image is particularly powerful in this context since the audience
are aware that Ophelia is acting as a front or 'face' for the King.[1]
Claudius has just used the image of a harlot's painted face to describe
his own conduct (3 i 50:1702):

King   How smart a lash that speech doth give my conscience!
The harlot's cheek, beautied with plast'ring art,
Is not more ugly to the thing that helps it
Than is my deed to my most painted word.
O heavy burden!

Hamlet's attack is an attack upon the court, and it is at least in part
accurate.

The double sense of 'nunnery' is thus extremely important for the
rising tension of the scene. Since Hamlet is exhorting Ophelia to

[1] Helen Gardner, 'Lawful Espials', *Modern Language Review*, xxxiii (1938), 345–55;
D. J. Palmer, 'Stage Spectators in *Hamlet*', *English Studies*, xlvii (1966), 423–30.

assume the attributes of *Castitas* it must mean 'a community or body of nuns'. Since, however, he also sees her as the painted figure of *Voluptas* it seems probable that 'nunnery' could also be a blasphemous euphemism for a brothel. In making use of Ophelia to protect his lust, Claudius, and Polonius are treating her like a prostitute. This implication is sustained by the way in which Polonius has offered to 'loose my daughter to him' (2 ii 161:1196), while Hamlet identifies Polonius as a 'fishmonger' (2 ii 173:1211) who may also be a brothel-keeper. The King of Denmark has turned the whole court into a brothel or stews by making the royal bed 'a couch for luxury and damned incest' (1 v 83:768).

Hamlet's generalizations about the nature of *Voluptas* are correct. He has rightly detected the satyr's face leering behind the painted harlot's mask of court ceremony. He is wrong, however, when he imagines that Ophelia is a particularly vicious part of this false show. This error, created by the terrible pressure of the passions which divide Hamlet, makes him appear a madman to Ophelia.

Her description of the Prince allows Shakespeare, like Raphael, to link the symbolism of the choice of life to the dance of the three graces (3 i 150:1806):

Ophelia   O, what a noble mind is here o'erthrown!
            The courtier's, soldier's, scholar's, eye, tongue, sword;
            Th'expectancy and rose of the fair state,
            The glass of fashion and the mould of form,
            Th'observed of all observers—quite, quite down!

Hamlet's union of the active, contemplative and passionate life had seemed to Ophelia best expressed in his vows of love. It is this harmony which she now believes has been shattered (3 i 155:1811):

Ophelia   And I, of ladies most deject and wretched,
            That suck'd the honey of his music vows,
            Now see that noble and most sovereign reason,
            Like sweet bells jangled, out of time and harsh;
            That unmatch'd form and feature of blown youth
            Blasted with ecstasy.

Ophelia's conclusion is, in part, accurate. It is unbalanced of Hamlet to assume that all women must be figures of vice and agents of corruption. Her judgment of Hamlet, however, is as mistaken as his view of her. In Denmark the harmony of the initiation of beauty into love, the harmony which informs Titian's painting of *Amor–Pulchritudo–Voluptas* and which should be the basis of the affection between Ophelia and Hamlet, has been destroyed by Claudius and Gertrude. The fierce rejection of Ophelia is a symptom of the damage done to the balance of Hamlet's affections by his mother's marriage. This very revulsion is also an indication of the intensity of the inner struggle which will eventually restore harmony to Denmark.

Ophelia's supreme importance in the play is that she reminds the audience, and eventually Hamlet, that sexual passion may be the mediating force which turns beauty into a passionate but higher love, as well as the unrestrained and degrading power which corrupts Gertrude and Claudius. The chastening of love and the chastening of fortune endured by these lovers is so severe that it destroys them both. The passion of love, however, which Hamlet at last comes to recognize in the graveyard is the only power which can prevent him from becoming, like Pyrrhus, Lucianus, Claudius, or Laertes, another black, blood-splashed figure of unrestrained and murderous passion.

Ophelia cannot know that the reason for Hamlet's bitter attack is that 'the time is out of joint' (I v 189:885), and therefore his words sound 'like sweet bells jangled, out of time and harsh'. The time has been lost because the sovereign of Denmark has abandoned the harmony of reason in favour of the pleasures to be gained by murder and incest. It is not Hamlet, but the court, which has really gone mad. It is this murderous passion of lust, this hidden figure of *Voluptas* behind the arras, which turns the meeting of Hamlet and Ophelia, which should have been a triumph ceremony[1] of the mutual remembrance of their love, into a bitter scene of forgetfulness, mutual incomprehension, and misdirected aggression.

In the nunnery scene Shakespeare makes the hardest demand that any dramatist can make of his principal actor. He asks him to lose the sympathy of the audience. This is different from asking him to play the part of a villain. The actor who plays Richard III or Iago is in no danger of being asked to sacrifice his emotional control over the audience. He can control the audience's sympathies and direct in what way they should be out of sympathy with the character.

The actor playing Hamlet is asked to abandon his claim upon the audience in favour of Ophelia. An actor playing Hamlet should be on his guard against mitigating the obviously mistaken cruelty of the nunnery scene.[2] Hamlet is cruel to Ophelia in order that Shakespeare

[1] Konrad Lorenz, *On Aggression*, Bantam Books, 1967, 169 ff.
[2] Carol J. Carlisle, in 'Hamlet's "Cruelty" in the Nunnery Scene: The Actors' Views' (*Shakespeare Quarterly*, xviii (1967), 129–40), gives an interesting account

may be kind to his audience. The audience reacts against Hamlet when he misjudges so totally the character of the girl he loves. This reaction may be traced and proved in detail in the history of Hamlet criticism. This natural audience reaction is part of Shakespeare's calculated demonstration that love and kindness are potent forces in human affairs even in the dark labyrinth of Elsinore. Ophelia's love, her madness, and even her death are an indication that a passionate female sexuality may exist as an intrinsic part of the three graces. Upon an acceptance of that harmony depends the safety and health of the individual and the state. Hamlet and Ophelia form part of Shakespeare's case for the dramatic defence of humanity.

The nunnery scene is one of forgetfulness and 'purposes mistook' (5 ii 376:3879). The play scene, in which Ophelia also plays an important part, is a memory device designed to recall a love that has been forgotten. It is concerned with dalliance and sexual play and shows how the 'primrose path' (1 iii 50:513) leads to the murder of a King. The themes of love and death, which will dominate the imagery of the graveyard, are already present in *The Murder of Gonzago*.

The mirror which Hamlet holds up to the court contains, it has already been suggested, a rather different reflection from the mirror that it holds up to the audience. The 'dream of passion' (2 ii 545:1592) is only complete once the audience have taken account of Hamlet's comments upon the action. He is sitting at Ophelia's feet in the position traditionally adopted by young lovers in public. His words are concerned with the act that young lovers usually perform in private. They are of such an unexampled sexual frankness that they have provoked a general reaction of critical shock and an unusual, if uneasy, editorial silence.

Hamlet's language of bitter bawdry has often been condemned. This condemnation, and the pall of editorial self-censorship, suggest that these words must have a very powerful effect upon an audience capable of understanding them. Hamlet's openly sexual suggestions to Ophelia are in marked contrast to the combination of fair words and foul deeds by which the King has removed all impediments to his own marriage of untrue minds. If his soothing hypocrisy seems a 'normal' reaction then that is an interesting commentary upon our own sexual situation.

The sexual imagery of the three exchanges between Hamlet and Ophelia during the performance of the inner-play is neither random

of the way in which many famous actors have tried to retain the audience's sympathy by romanticizing the action at this point.

nor accidental. It is again based upon the image of the three graces and it develops a pattern of fantasy action that contrasts with the murderous passion being presented by the Players. It is an important expression of Hamlet's conscious and unconscious wishes and desires. It provides a possible forecast for the future of the characters that is very different from the prediction which follows from the appearance of the black figure of Lucianus.

The word games between Hamlet and Ophelia start when Hamlet rejects his mother's invitation to sit beside her. He prefers to sit beside Ophelia in order to observe the reactions of the King and Queen. The language also expresses another, and more intimate, level of action (3 ii 108:1966):

Hamlet	Lady, shall I lie in your lap?
Ophelia	No, my lord.
Hamlet	I mean, my head upon your lap.
Ophelia	Ay, my lord.
Hamlet	Do you think I meant country matters?
Ophelia	I think nothing, my lord.
Hamlet	That's a fair thought to lie between maid's legs.
Ophelia	What is, my lord?
Hamlet	Nothing.

The 'country matters' that are performed in a lady's lap may be fairly assumed to be the same as the act about to be enjoyed by the 'country copulatives' in *As You Like It* 5 iii 54:2632. If Ophelia thinks 'nothing' about such an act Hamlet suggests that she may be so chaste that she has no 'thing' or sexual organ between her legs. That Shakespeare intended the pun on 'no thing' is perhaps indicated by the fact that he makes Hamlet use it again of the King at 4 ii 29:2657. Hamlet explains to Rosencrantz and Guildenstern that the King is a 'thing' of 'no thing'—although the implications are here political as well as sexual.

It seems beyond doubt that 'country matters' contains a deliberate pun on 'cunt'. This kind of pun is a method of sexual aggression and may well represent the siege to Ophelia's chastity feared by Polonius and Laertes. It is an expression of a desire that is never fulfilled in the play. The bed on which such an act might have been performed becomes the bridal bed of the grave where Ophelia is claimed as the bride of death.

Gertrude makes the bed-grave comparison explicit in her farewell speech (5 i 238:3436):

Gertrude   I hop'd thou shouldst have been my Hamlet's wife:
I thought thy bride-bed to have deck'd, sweet maid,
And not have strew'd thy grave.

It was, however, the 'country matters' engaged in by Gertrude with Claudius which led to the 'maimed rites' (5 i 213:3408) of Ophelia's incomplete burial service. Even the unwilling Priest has to allow her 'her virgin crants, her maiden strewments' (5 i 225–6:3421–2). Hamlet's suggestion that she has no 'thing' between her legs is supported by this more sombre imagery. Ophelia does possess the grace of *Castitas*.

The argument is carried a stage further when Ophelia is puzzled by the dumb show and asks Hamlet for enlightenment. Hamlet changes the meaning of the word 'show' and suggests that Ophelia might herself become a performer who could unmask for the benefit of the actor playing the Prologue (3 ii 138:2010):

Ophelia   Will 'a tell us what this show meant?

Hamlet   Ay, or any show that you will show him. Be not you asham'd to show, he'll not shame to tell you what it means.

Ophelia   You are naught, you are naught. I'll mark the play.

In his original warning to Ophelia, Laertes had advised her to 'unmask' her beauty only to the moon. It is this sense of unmasking or 'show' that Hamlet puns upon here. He does not actually suggest that Ophelia should perform a strip-show in order to reveal her naked beauty to the actor, but the metaphor of a strip-show is buried in his words. The actor will not be ashamed to tell Ophelia the meaning of any 'show' she is not ashamed to show him. She would, of course, be ashamed to show him her unmasked beauty and Hamlet is very well aware of the fact.

The pun is a further aggressive sexual advance based upon the fact that Ophelia has obeyed the caution of her father and brother and hardly showed herself to Hamlet, let alone unmasked her beauty for him. Ophelia turns the obscene joke aside, but is evidently aware of its meaning, when she describes Hamlet as 'naught'. It is a clear sexual

recognition, for the benefit of the audience, of the beauty that lies
hidden from view beneath Ophelia's clothes.

This recognition is supremely important. The inner-play is concerned with exposing the ugliness that the court has kept hidden from
view. Hamlet regards this hidden ugliness as the real truth about the
world. He describes the Prologue as being as brief 'as woman's love'
(3 ii 149:2022). The sexuality of Ophelia is a deliberate challenge to
this corrupt view of the world and its passions. Hamlet has now
admitted that he is sitting at the feet of a girl who combines *Castitas*
and *Pulchritudo*. He can still only imagine *Voluptas* as a degrading
passion. His last exchange with Ophelia suggests that this is a tragic
mistake.

Hamlet is engaged in explaining the entry of Lucianus to the King
when Ophelia interrupts him (3 ii 239:2113):

Ophelia   You are as good as a chorus, my lord.

Hamlet   I could interpret between you and your love, if I could
        see the puppets dallying.

Ophelia   You are keen, my lord, you are keen.

Hamlet   It would cost you a groaning to take off mine edge.

Ophelia   Still better, and worse.

Hamlet   So you mis-take your husbands.—Begin murderer; pox,
        leave thy damnable faces and begin.

The dallying of puppets is an action that might logically follow from
the kind of show that Ophelia was invited to perform for the actor.

An interpreter is an actor who gives words to the dumb show
performed by puppets. Their use is shown in Ben Jonson's *Bartholomew
Fair* (5 iii 75):

Cokes   These be players minors indeed. Do you call these
            players?

Leatherhead They are actors, sir, and as good as any, none disprais'd,
            for dumb shows: indeed I am the mouth of them all.

Hamlet would interpret to Ophelia the actions of the 'puppets' as they
performed the dalliance of love. These 'puppets' may be intended to
be more flesh than wood since Hamlet himself clearly intends to take
part in the show. It will cost Ophelia the 'groaning' of losing her
virginity to take off the 'edge' of his wit or sexual appetite.

Ophelia regards this display of wit as both 'better', or wittier, and 'worse' or even more indecent than his other suggestions. In these three exchanges Hamlet has established that she is a virgin, has suggested that she ought to remove her clothes and display her beauty, and now deliberately proposes that she might engage in the kind of passionate act which might result in the mis-take of a husband. The sexual puns and innuendoes thus lead Ophelia from *Castitas* through *Pulchritudo* to *Voluptas*. Beauty is thus initiated into Passion by Love and the harmony of the graces is completed at the level of an obscene joke.

Hamlet still clearly regards Ophelia as the kind of figure of sensual passion who makes all marriage a mis-take. In the world presented by the inner-play chastity can only be turned into a bawd by beauty. This interpretation of the world is supported by the presence on stage of the Player Queen and Gertrude. It is contradicted by the presence of Ophelia.

It has already been argued that Shakespeare controls the time scheme of *Hamlet* by dramatizing the past, present and future of his characters during the 'eternal present' of the court performance. The inner-play is an image of passionate sexual love as well as a representation of murder. It is, therefore, important that it is as much an assault upon the Queen's betrayal of her love as an accusation levelled at the King.

The inner-play presents the golden world of the past, filled with the protestations of a Queen in love and moderated only by the Player King's belief that even love is subject to time and fortune. The Player Queen's protestations move even Gertrude to unfavourable criticism. The false vows of the inner-play are uttered in the presence of the woman whose own marriage vows were not proof against the assault of Claudius. He won her by appearing as the 'implorator' of the unholy suit of incest disguised as the 'sanctified and pious bonds' (1 iii 130:596) of a royal marriage.

As *The Murder of Gonzago* shows how the marriage that existed in the past became a 'primrose path of dalliance' (1 iii 50:513), so the interaction of the play and its royal spectators demonstrates how love was turned by poison into murderous lust. The entry of the 'Fellow' in the dumb show and of Lucianus in the spoken play show how the King's death shattered the remembrance of love. The past has become the present union of lust and murderous will that dare not remember how it came into existence.

As Claudius and Gertrude watch the play they are watching the growth of their own poisonous love and the birth of their incestuous marriage. They are themselves the things 'rank and gross in nature' (I ii 136:320) which now possess the 'unweeded garden' (I ii 135:319) of the present. According to the inner-play, the world of love inevitably becomes the world of lust. All human passion is either a false and hypocritical show or else an appetite that degrades men below the level of beasts. As Hamlet sits with his eyes riveted to the King's face he represents a threat of the further operation of murderous passion in the future.

The inner-play presents a prediction, or what Jan Kott calls a forecast,[1] for the future. This prediction is fulfilled in the play but it is brought about in an unexpected fashion which has not been predicted by the action of *The Murder of Gonzago*. Hamlet desires to play the part of Lucianus but does not perform it. Similarly, although Ophelia is cast for the part of *Voluptas*, in common with Gertrude and the Player Queen, she is finally destroyed because of her obsessive remembrance and love for her father rather than by an oblivious pleasure in the present. Behind the obscene jests of man's sexuality lies a grave reality. Ophelia really possesses a balance and harmony of the graces in which her beauty might have become the reality of a passionate love. This harmony is shattered by the tragic conditions of Elsinore.

At this point in the action the stage picture is of supreme importance. The three pairs of lovers on the stage present the audience with the choice of love and the comparison of the different depths and capacity for human passion that is so familiar in Shakespearean comedy. The inner-play of *A Midsummer Night's Dream* or the 'show' of manhood adopted by Viola in *Twelfth Night* reveal an infinite variety within the harmony of love. The inner-play in *Hamlet* serves a similar function.

The marriage that is past, the marriage that is present, and the possible marriage that might exist in the future are present in the actors taking the parts of Players and the Characters of their stage audience. King Hamlet and Gertrude are presented by the Players in Duke Gonzago and Baptista. Claudius and Gertrude exhibit their own misalliance. The only hope for Denmark appears to lie in the future consummation of the marriage of Hamlet and Ophelia. That future, however, has already been mortgaged to pay the debts of the past.

In *Twelfth Night* the Clown, Feste, sings of the way a journey should end (*Twelfth Night* 2 iii 41:742):

Clown   Trip no further, pretty sweeting;

[1] Jan Kott, 'Hamlet and Orestes', *Publications of the Modern Language Association of America*, lxxxii (1967), 303–13.

> Journeys end in lovers meeting
> Every wise man's son doth know.

Journey's end for Hamlet is near when he returns to Elsinore from the voyage to England. Once he arrives he hears a love-song which is also sung by a Clown. This Clown, however, is also a gravemaker and the meeting which Hamlet at last recognizes as a lovers' meeting is also an encounter with death at the edge of a grave.

The proof of the sterility and horror of the court of Denmark is that it had no place for the passionate life of love and remembrance symbolized by Ophelia and her flowers. In this world of madness the only soil suitable for the 'rose of May' (4 v 154:2910) is the earth which covers her dead body. The flowers which the Queen drops into her grave mark the defeat of love and the end of hope in the play. The graveyard scene is one of the most tragic in the play because the characters are burying the future.

The graveyard scene, which is also the scene of Hamlet's final declaration of the passionate sexual love which has blazed through his supposed obscenities, is a dramatic and logical consequence of the death of Polonius. It thus repeats, in interesting fashion, one of the patterns of *Romeo and Juliet*. Romeo, provoked by the death of Mercutio, kills Juliet's cousin Tybalt in a duel. Hamlet, provoked by his father's murder, kills Ophelia's father Polonius in a fashion that is certainly mistaken but which may still be culpable.

One of the most tragic and passionate scenes in *Romeo and Juliet* is the scene in which Juliet hears of Tybalt's death from her Nurse. Her instant reaction is hate and assent to the conventional wisdom of grief and revenge expressed by the Nurse. Slowly at first, and then more strongly, she rejects hatred and starts to fight her way back to her love for Romeo across the gulf of blood and despair that threatens to divide them. Passionate love here re-creates itself by an act of remembrance and dedicates itself to a new understanding.

This leap of intelligence and love is not possible in *Hamlet*. Juliet requires all the arguments of her reason to assist the passion of her love for Romeo against the rising tide of hate. Ophelia's reason has been shattered by the death of Polonius and in madness she can find no relief except death. Juliet has the firm knowledge of a love expressed in a recent marriage with which to face the furies released by Tybalt's death. Ophelia has no more than a love expressed before the play began and since apparently denied in the bitterness of the nunnery and play scenes. The conditions which permitted the leap of love and faith in Verona do not obtain in Elsinore.

The severed and mutilated passion of Hamlet and Ophelia, darkened by all the bitterness of misunderstanding and the language of obscenity, still dignifies the power and possibility of sexual passionate human love. The consummated union of Gertrude and Claudius degrades it. The hope which the play offers its spectators is a dance of the three graces—a vision of a passionate life directed by the operation of memory and the forces of intelligence. The agony of the graveyard is the knowledge of an insupportable loss.

Chapter 6

THE KING'S JESTER
the Graveyard

In Shakespearean comedy the competing claims of the contemplative, the active, and the passionate life are usually reconciled in the harmony of marriage—one of the supreme examples of Pleasure reconciled to Virtue. The tragedy of *Hamlet* begins at a point where this harmony has been broken. Hamlet's problem is not merely to restore the harmony of the kingdom of Denmark: it is to restore the dance of the graces in his own imagination. Instead of the three figures of the graces he can, when he thinks of women, only see the unrestrained figure of *Voluptas*. This serious misunderstanding of the nature of human passion can be extremely dangerous. To destroy the harmonious concord of the graces may annihilate the human mind and plunge the individual into insanity or death.

Hamlet's most effective attack upon the figure of *Voluptas* is the way in which he forces his mother to see herself as the personification of lust. Hamlet is attempting to repeat, in different terms, the theatre of memory which had transfixed the King. The play, prayer, and closet scenes are, as we have argued, turning points in the play. In these scenes the King's view of the court—a cheerful orgy of good sense mingled with covert sensuality which is marred only by the mad melancholy of the Prince—begins to yield to Hamlet's view of a world reeking of decay presided over by a drunken satyr whose presence blasts and infects the entire kingdom with a disease that proves fatal to those who serve his will.

The King has recognized Hamlet's view of Denmark in the inner-play. He found it terrifying and, even while acknowledging its truth in prayer, he acts to close his mind to that knowledge. Gertrude catches a glimpse of this horror as her son forces her to compare the portraits of the two men who have been her husband. Hamlet's words act as daggers which rip at her peace and remind her how far she has failed to live up to the ideals that should have informed her marriage. Hamlet uses his imagination as a mirror in which Gertrude sees a reflection of herself which she knows to be true but finds unbearable.

In trying to expose his mother's soul to her own horrified gaze Hamlet is showing his mother a true picture. Such a passionate attack upon passion, however, endangers the harmony of the graces within Hamlet's mind. As he proceeds to his mother's closet after the play scene, Hamlet, in the fifth soliloquy, utters words which are charged with a threat more terrible than the figures of Pyrrhus or Lucianus (3 ii 383:2264):

Hamlet O heart, lose not thy nature; let not ever
    The soul of Nero enter this firm bosom.
    Let me be cruel, not unnatural:
    I will speak daggers to her, but use none.

The Queen, however, finds his behaviour so strange and incomprehensible (since she has understood none of the passion released in Hamlet by the success of the inner-play) that she believes she is about to be assaulted and perhaps murdered by a madman. Her cry for help kills Polonius.

The inner-play, therefore, dramatizes the power that unites Hamlet and Ophelia and the forces that separate them for ever. They are united by a mutual sexual passion which might grow to a mutual love. Hamlet is prevented from recognizing this love by his ignorant identification of Ophelia as *Voluptas*. The death of Polonius makes this mistake irreversible since it destroys Ophelia's reason. It is ironic that in the closet scene Hamlet begins to understand that his view of the rapacious nature of female sexuality is inadequate even as a description of his mother.

Hamlet's interview with his mother has been, of course, the subject of extended critical and psychological commentary. The scene is certainly charged with intense sexual passion. It is important, however, to examine its place in the careful pattern of Shakespeare's symbolic language and logic. Hamlet's relationship with his mother is of crucial importance. It would be a mistake to regard it as the hidden key which provides a complete solution to all the problems of the play.

It is evident that Hamlet's disgust at his mother's sexuality, and his positively prurient interest in the sweaty details of her copulation with Claudius, may represent a sense of failure and jealousy which is sexual and aggressive in origin. Jealousy is, as the Renaissance knew very well, often the inseparable companion and sign of love. Shakespeare would dramatize exactly these symptoms in *Othello*. In *De gli eroici furori* Giordano Bruno describes jealousy as 'the daughter of love' which nevertheless 'never ceases to disturb and poison everything found beautiful and good in love'.[1] The closet scene is unquestionably concerned with one of the aspects of love. In trying to convict his mother before the bar of her conscience, Hamlet awakens his own and avoids acting as the slave of passion.

In the two pictures, 'the counterfeit presentment of two brothers (3 iv 54:2438), Hamlet shows his mother a reflection of the living embodiment of lust—corrupt, blind, and without any of the saving graces of love or human affection. Hamlet's words rip off one by one the masks in which Gertrude has played the roles of wife, mother, and lover. He exposes an incestuous adultress whose passions have led her to murder her husband. Hamlet desires to torture this figure of *Voluptas*, if not to kill her. The image of active lust which he conjures up from his imagination nearly causes him to allow his own murderous passions to burst through all the bonds of love. The closet scene, and the pictures of the two kings, hold a mirror up to Hamlet which shows him close to matricide.

The imagery Hamlet uses in describing his father recalls the comparison between the two kings in the first soliloquy—'Hyperion to a satyr' (1 ii 140:324). This time the description of King Hamlet spans the whole pantheon of the Olympian gods (3 iv 55:2439):

> *Hamlet*   See what a grace was seated on this brow;
> Hyperion's curls; the front of Jove himself;
> An eye like Mars to threaten and command;
> A station like the herald Mercury
> New lighted on a heaven-kissing hill—
> A combination and a form indeed
> Where every god did seem to set his seal,
> To give the world assurance of a man.

[1] P. E. Memmo Jr, *Giordano Bruno's The Heroic Frenzies: A Translation with Introduction and Notes*, 1964, 90.

The choice of gods in this passage is not an arbitrary one. They are carefully selected for their qualities. The various powers of the Olympian gods unfold the character of the dead King and reveal the reasons that 'gave the world assurance of a man'.

The form of the speech is a traditional *descriptio*. Hamlet gives his mother a physical description of the details of a picture. At the same time, in comparing these features to the Olympian gods, he is delineating his father's character. This account of Hyperion the sun-king suggests that he possessed the majesty of Jove, the threatening aspect of Mars, and the swift balance of Mercury, messenger of the gods and the guider of souls, as he arrives on a 'heaven-kissing hill' to act as mediator between earth and heaven. In his son's eyes, King Hamlet was the sum of the divine qualities which govern the world from Olympus.

Gertrude has abandoned her place in this union of earth and heaven. Her choice of husbands involves two aspects of love. Each marriage has been a 'banquet of sense'. Married to King Hamlet she fed 'on this fair mountain' (3 iv 66:2450)—a banquet which might have been fit for the gods themselves. In her second marriage she is like a lost sheep strayed from the mountain to 'batten on this moor' (3 iv 67:2451). This banquet of sense is a feast of lust and sensuality. It comes to resemble the feeding of pigs wallowing in the 'nasty sty' (3 iv 94:2471) of the marriage bed.

Gertrude has failed to act as consort to the Olympian qualities of her husband. She is neither the moon, the counterpart of Hyperion, nor Juno goddess of majesty and wife of Jove, nor even Venus the goddess of love and beauty and the mistress of Mars. In the first court scene, therefore, when Claudius describes her as 'Th'imperial jointress to this warlike state' (1 ii 9:187) he is ironically mistaken. Instead of a fit consort for the true King of Denmark, Gertrude is a woman betrayed by the rebellious hell of passion into a state where 'reason pandars will' (3 iv 88:2463).

It is not sufficient to ascribe her choice to her sensuality. She cannot simply have yielded to her senses because, as Hamlet points out, Claudius is inferior to King Hamlet by every possible test of sensation. Her choice represents a horrible blind failure of the intellect and an atrophy of memory. The Judgment of Paris thus depends upon a failure of judgment which destroys more than the Olympian world of her marriage. It breaks the harmony of the graces within her own soul. Without judgment the dance of the graces becomes a whirl of passion which is literally hell-bent. As the daggers which Hamlet uses to his mother in speech become progressively sharper, he seems in danger of actually using a dagger to kill his mother. It is because Hamlet is approaching the centre of the whirlpool of passion that the Ghost reappears.

At this stage of the action, Hamlet has reversed the original command of the Ghost. He had sworn to avenge himself on Claudius, but not to taint his mind or contrive against his mother. She was to be left to her own conscience. In presenting the inner-play Hamlet caught the King's conscience. He has just left him wrestling with its terrible effects. He is now revenging himself upon his mother by tormenting her memory in an increasingly violent fashion. The Ghost appears to repeat the original command. Hamlet must remember. He must also revenge. This repetition emphasizes, although it does nothing to solve, the original problems of the play. It also, however, permits Shakespeare to develop the imagery of the harmony of the graces in a new and unexpected direction.

Gertrude does not see the Ghost. Despite Hamlet's assault upon her memory and understanding she does not acquire judgment until her last lines in the play. Although she accepts Hamlet's charges in the closet scene she is still prepared to throw her body between Claudius and the rebellious Laertes when he seems to threaten the life of the King. Yet she has not exposed her son's suspicions to her husband. At last, in the duel scene, she drinks from the cup intended for Hamlet and feels the prepared poison of Claudius working within her. She now knows that Hamlet's language in the closet scene was neither metaphor nor madness but a sober account of murderous fact. Her last words are a cry of warning to her son. These words are a measure of the victory won by Hamlet in the duel of wits and words that is the closet scene.

The Ghost's appearance is again dramatic rather than theological. It is not necessarily concerned with either assisting or preventing the salvation of Gertrude's soul. It does, however, permit both dramatist and actress to restore some dramatic dignity and sympathy to the character of Gertrude. The dignity is an essential element in the developing pattern of the play. The Ghost exhorts Hamlet to 'step between her and her fighting soul' (3 iv 113:2493), but it is Gertrude who attempts to comfort Hamlet in what she is now sure must be a fit of madness. Despite the savage attack that has been made upon her, despite the fact that she thinks she has been near death (and may have been closer to it in fact than she realizes), and despite the bitter self-knowledge of her own corruption, she reaches out in sympathy and natural affection to the violent troubled man who is also her son.

Hamlet's picture of his mother was not entirely accurate. The closet scene makes it clear that she was not an accomplice in her husband's murder. Nor is her identification as *Voluptas* the whole truth about her. It is not possible to act rationally on the assumption that she, or any other woman, can be so simply defined. Hamlet has unconsciously already given Claudius the opportunity to repent and ask pardon from heaven. He regards his mother as having committed an unforgivable sin. The Ghost shows no compassion for Claudius, but insists that Hamlet extend forgiveness and human charity to his mother. The memory of the golden Olympian world has not entirely vanished; Gertrude is not, like Claudius, totally committed to a murderous self-love.

It is interesting, and dramatically relevant, that she should describe the vision of the Ghost, which has probably saved her life, as 'madness'. Her diagnosis is similar to Ophelia's. It is equally incomplete. There are two separate and distinct states of mind which are described as 'madness' in *Hamlet*. Hamlet's vision and memory of his father appear to all the other characters to be either melancholy or madness. The events of the play, however, demonstrate that Hamlet's view of the court is correct and sane. The court is a sham, a false structure based upon the crime of murder and totally divorced from the real body-politic of Denmark.

It is the ungoverned passion which has led to murder that is the real 'madness' that afflicts Denmark. It is clear that, in this sense, Claudius is mad since he is determined that the killing shall never stop until he feels himself secure. It is evident that Hamlet is in danger of suffering from this kind of madness. In the nunnery scene, the prayer scene, and the closet scene, his passions are barely under control. He sees Ophelia, Claudius, and Gertrude as equally deformed by the passion of lust. This view is unbalanced and it nearly leads Hamlet to perform acts of murderous passion worthy of Lucianus or of Claudius. Yet Hamlet never fails in the course of the play to subject his passionate actions to the scrutiny of his understanding. When control is established, Hamlet draws back from such acts of frenzy. When Claudius regains control over his conscience in the prayer scene he seeks a method of fulfilling his consuming passion of self-regard.

There is, as Hamlet points out to his mother, only one way of escaping from the 'madness' of the ill effects of human passion (3 iv 150:2533):

Hamlet   Repent what's past; avoid what is to come;

And do not spread the compost on the weeds,
To make them ranker.

The fact that Gertrude cannot see the Ghost is, perhaps, an indication that the golden world of the past has gone beyond recall. Claudius is using the present to spread all the compost that he can find throughout the garden of Denmark. The guarantee, however, that the golden world did exist, and not only in Hamlet's infantile imagination, is the promise, however bitterly frustrated, that it could be re-created in the union of Hamlet and Ophelia.

Ophelia's sexuality is contrasted with Gertrude's in the same way that Hamlet's reactions are compared with those of Laertes and Fortinbras. In the nunnery and play scenes Hamlet judges Ophelia by the standards that he applies to his mother. The violence of this language betrays fear. This fear is justified since he evidently is his mother's son and has a violently sexual and passionate nature. In the closet scene he learns that his judgment of his mother must be tempered by the quality of mercy and charity. In the graveyard scene he finally recognizes the fierce blaze of his own passion for Ophelia. This is not a submerged expression of sexual desire for his mother. It is an indication that he has shaken off her influence from his mind and spirit. He is now able to accept, on his own terms, the claims of the life of passion. It comes too late for the enjoyment of pleasure since beauty must now be buried. Gertrude's fatal misuse of passion, and her ignorant delivery of her body to the oblivious lust of Claudius, has not, in the end, destroyed Hamlet's own capacity to love.

The scene between mother and son does not end in a grovelling repentance by Gertrude or in any formal forgiveness or reconciliation. The breach between them is not easily healed. It is freshly symbolized by the dead body which Hamlet has to drag from his mother's bedroom. It is a gulf which can only be bridged by understanding. In the closet scene Hamlet and Gertrude, through the intervention of the Ghost, begin to communicate across the river of her sexuality, which he fears, and the desert of his revulsion, which she has hardly understood. As the scene closes the audience should be in no doubt that they have witnessed a love scene. The strong bonds of family affection bind mother and son in what is still, despite the shadow of the past and the menace of the future, a dance of the graces.

Both have tried to break that harmony. In pursuing her sexual passion for Claudius, Gertrude has nearly fallen victim to her son's revengeful passion and desire for murder. The relationship which is now resumed between them is essentially sexual but not necessarily incestuous. It thus contrasts with Gertrude's relationship with Claudius which, necessarily incestuous to an Elizabethan audience, is also shown to lack certain of the fundamentals of a sexual union. It is a bond which Claudius does not value above his personal safety—as will be demonstrated in the duel scene. The existence of self-forgetfulness may be used, with some empirical support, to differentiate the bond of love from the egocentric passion of lust. Since Claudius is capable only of remembrance of himself, it is he, and not Hamlet, who is the emotional cripple in the play. In the closet scene the aggressive powers of the will threaten to destroy both Hamlet and Gertrude in an orgy of hatred whose roots reach deep into primitive sexual jealousy and possession. This will is restrained by the equally primitive, but fortunately in this case more powerful, powers of memory and the growth of an understanding which is also the power of conscience.

The play makes no claim that this delicate balance of the mind is easily maintained. The pressure and strain involved when a human mind has to attempt to reconcile the deepest and most intractable traits of which it is conscious—or unconscious—are not easy to endure. It is hardly an accident that within the play Hamlet contemplates madness and suicide, while Ophelia's mind is actually unbalanced in a fashion that contributes to her death. The competing claims of justice and mercy—the choice between the book, the sword, and the flower—are as difficult and as urgent a psychological problem in the twentieth century as they were in the seventeenth. The power of the play depends upon the accuracy and force with which these passions, dramatized upon the stage, make themselves felt in the minds of the audience.

Memory, which is of such importance for Hamlet, is clearly not a complete answer to the problem. It is her acute remembrance of her father which overwhelms Ophelia's reason. It is doubly ironic that even in madness she understands the true uses of the flower of passion better than most of the other members of the court. Ophelia gives the flowers of the true passionate life, the life that fits thoughts and remembrance in the harmony of rosemary and rue, to Claudius, Gertrude, and Laertes at the moment that the King is engaged in the task of dividing Laertes from his fair judgment and making him a beast capable of a passionate and treacherous revenge. In Ophelia's apparently mad exclamations, 'They say the owl was a baker's daughter' (4 v 40:2784) and 'O, how the wheel becomes it!' (4 v 168:2924), recent commentators have traced references to the abandonment of reason to lust (since the owl was the sacred bird of Minerva, goddess of wisdom, and the baker's daughter a prostitute)[1] and the emblem of Occasion with her wheel of opportunity.[2]

In reaching after what they regard as the perfect opportunity for revenge, Claudius and Laertes do turn wisdom into a bawd. Once Claudius has poisoned his mind, Laertes is prepared to poison his sword. The results are fatal for them all. The King, the Queen, and Laertes cannot understand Ophelia. They imagine that what she speaks is mere madness. They do not realize that this madness is much closer to sanity than the lunatic convolutions of their own deep plots of murder and sudden death. They allow the crimes of the past to overwhelm the only hope that existed of breaking the iron rule of chance and fortune. They deliver themselves up to fortune when they use occasion to make them the slaves of passion. Ophelia's song 'How should I your true love know' (4 v 23:2769) is one of the play's great questions.

The 'maimed rites' (5 i 213:3408) with which the representatives of church and state follow Ophelia to her grave bring more than her short, unhappy life to its close. When the King, the Queen, and the courtiers reach the edge of Ophelia's grave they have arrived at an important waymark on their own journey towards death. At this point in the play the images of disease and corruption which have been used to symbolize that 'something is rotten in the state of Denmark' (1 iv 90: 678) have ceased to be metaphorical. They have become literal references to the smell of putrefying human flesh.[3]

The black comedy of the Gravediggers, who take a macabre delight in their own worm's eye view of society, suddenly transfers the argument of the play from matters of love, honour, and responsibility to the question of survival. Like Claudius and Hamlet, the Gravediggers are concerned with the disposal of dead bodies. The court of Elsinore may be a battlefield of the soul. Shakespeare continually reminds his audience that such a battle may have real physical consequences. The Gravediggers remind the audience of the human consequences of battle. Such a reminder is necessary because the

[1] Robert Tracy, 'The Owl and the Baker's Daughter: A Note on *Hamlet* 4 iv 42–43', *Shakespeare Quarterly*, xvii (1966), 83–6.

[2] Doris V. Falk, 'Proverbs and the Polonius Destiny', *Shakespeare Quarterly*, xviii (1967), 23–36.

[3] R. D. Altick, in 'Hamlet and the Odour of Mortality' (*Shakespeare Quarterly*, v (1954), 167–76), draws attention to the importance of the physical smell of rot and decay in the imagery of the play.

unwelcome thoughts and experiences of man's mortality are easily repressed even in a century in which, as at Verdun in 1916, the smell of putrefaction was described as 'so disgusting that it almost gives a certain charm to the odour of gas shells'.[1]

Death is the end of the banquet of sense. The image of death as a feast or 'last supper' for worms is established in striking fashion during the search for the body of Polonius (4 iii 22:2686):

Hamlet   Your worm is your only emperor for diet: we fat all
           creatures else to fat us, and we fat ourselves for maggots;
           your fat king and your lean beggar is but variable
           service—two dishes, but to one table. That's the end.

The 'progress' of the King is seen as a journey 'through the guts of a beggar' (4 iii 31:2693) and the inevitable end of the human banquet of sense is, therefore, 'a certain convocation of politic worms' (4 iii 20: 2686). The Gravediggers perform the last service before such a banquet and their behaviour illustrates the place of the burial of the dead within the laws of nature and society.

Their language is a parody of the terms created by church and state to resolve the legal and spiritual problems of death. They are an important part of the debate about the nature of law and justice carried by the theme of the duel. Yet at the same time that the Clowns raise these great legal, moral, and political questions they make clear that the answers are 'academic'. The end of all action, and all responsibility, is symbolized by the skull which has shed the final mask of humanity and wears only the perpetual grin of death.

Hamlet's comments upon the skulls thrown up by the Clown have an almost choric quality. His imagination clothes the bare-boned death in flesh and the skull becomes Cain, 'that did the first murder' (5 i 77: 3269), or a politician, 'one that would circumvent God' (5 i 79:3271). The skull is then transformed into those twin pillars of society, a courtier and a lawyer, until Hamlet is assisted by the Clown to make the particular and positive identification of the skull of Yorick, the King's Jester. In form, Hamlet's meditation in the graveyard is a satire of the three estates which passes in review the history of mankind and reminds the audience that the pomp and circumstance of Caesar or Alexander ends in dust.

The Clowns themselves, crawling nearer to earth than heaven and yet enjoying wine and love songs and such admirable samples from death's jest book as their conundrum about the gallows-maker and the

[1] Alistair Horne, *The Price of Glory: Verdun 1916*, 1962, 175.

grave-maker, act as a necessary counterweight to the fact that, in *Hamlet*, only those who are prepared to imitate Cain seem likely to survive. As a patient politician Claudius has built 'stronger than a mason, a shipwright, or a carpenter' (5 i 50:3239). He is a grave-maker. The first grave that he made, however, failed to last till doomsday. Although he is unaware of the Ghost's appearance, Claudius has found himself forced to try to prepare a second grave—for Hamlet. As the graveyard scene ends, Claudius reminds Laertes of their agreed 'final solution' to the problem of *Hamlet* (5 i 288:3493):

King	Strengthen your patience in our last night's speech;
	We'll put the matter to the present push.—
	Good Gertrude, set some watch over your son.—
	This grave shall have a living monument.
	An hour of quiet shortly shall we see;
	Till then in patience our proceeding be.

This forecast of events is mistaken. The 'matter' which Claudius intends to press will make his own grave 'straight' as well as Hamlet's. The only quiet that Claudius will now know is the quiet of the grave.

The inevitability and swift approach of death is only part of the argument of the scene. As the Clown casts the skulls out of the grave he is re-opening an old argument. It is the debate between memory and oblivion started in the first court scene and most persuasively argued by the Queen (1 ii 72:252):

Queen	Thou know'st 'tis common—all that lives must die,
	Passing through nature to eternity.
Hamlet	Ay, madam, it is common.
Queen	If it be,
	Why seems it so particular with thee?

In the graveyard it is evident that Hamlet does know that 'all that lives must die'. The evidence for man's mortality assaults the senses. The process may be natural, but it is ugly as well as smelling sourly of decay.

The argument of the scene now imitates the argument of the play. It shifts abruptly from general considerations to a particular case. One of the most vital moments in the play is when Hamlet, examining the 'chap-fall'n' (5 i 185:3380) skull of Yorick, appears to accept that the end of all the playing, and all the painting, must be the last grave joke of death (5 i 186:3380):

Hamlet   Now get you to my lady's chamber, and tell her, let
her paint an inch thick, to this favour she must come;
make her laugh at that.

The actors who play the Gravediggers will have failed unless the audience have been laughing heartily at exactly that joke a minute before
these words are spoken. The skull holds a mirror up to the human
nature of the audience and shows them a death's head.

A few lines later the court carries in the body of Ophelia. There is
no need for the skull to go to 'my lady's chamber'. Ophelia is on her
way to the 'eternal cell' (5 ii 357:3858) of death which is also her
bridal bed. In attempting to garland a willow reflected in the 'glassy
stream' (4 vii 168:3159) Ophelia has found the 'weeping brook' (4 vii
176:3167) an entry to that 'undiscover'd country' (3 i 79:1733) which
had tormented Hamlet's imagination before the nunnery scene. In the
mirror of Hamlet's mind Ophelia then saw a reflection which she did
not understand. She thought that it was madness. It turns out to have
been the reflection of her own death. In the graveyard Hamlet sees
reflected in her dead face the failure of his love and the destruction of
his hopes as 'Th'expectancy and rose of the fair state' (3 i 152:1808).
What Henry James calls 'the prodigious consciousness of Hamlet' must
here become the consciousness of death. If the actors have done their
work well the chill of that terrible knowledge should induce, in the
theatre, the quiet of the grave.

This quiet is broken by the passion of Laertes and Hamlet. The
certainty of human mortality, and even the acceptance of the general
considerations set out so fully in Hamlet's conversation with the
Clown, cannot eliminate grief or pain. The loss of a unique and
irreplaceable human being is always unacceptable to those whose love
cannot yield to statistics. Death is an absolute condition that is the
natural end of mankind. Yet the death of any individual becomes a
particular case that alters irrevocably the balance of love and harmony
of spirit of those who knew the living being. The power of human
love compels them to cry out against the tragic operation of a general
and inescapable law. Ophelia carries with her to destruction a large
part of the play's treasure of human affection.

The graveyard scene thus proceeds by two stages. In the first Hamlet,
and the audience, are forced to admit the facts of mortality and contemplate the inevitable decay of the human body in the grave. The burial
of Ophelia then demonstrates, in a particular case, the total capitulation
of reason and the apparent defeat of love. Her death repeats the central

question of the soliloquies. If the human body must end 'stopping a bung-hole' (5 i 199:3392) does the harmony rung by the 'sweet bells' (3 i 158:1814) of the human reason have any significance?

This is the essential question of the play which has made 'To be or not to be' (3 i 56:1710) its most famous soliloquy and the skull its most memorable visual symbol. It receives only the answer of Hamlet's voice asking a further question (4 iv 36:2743 Q 30):

Hamlet   Sure he that made us with such large discourse,
                     Looking before and after, gave us not
                     That capability and godlike reason
                     To fust in us unus'd.

The opening of the graveyard scene makes it appear that the chief function of reason should be to reconcile man to his own dissolution.

This rational acceptance of mortality gives way to a passionate declaration of love. Laertes defies the natural law and catches his sister in his arms as if she still lived and breathed. He invokes the law of nations which holds men responsible and accountable for the consequences of their actions when he blames Hamlet for her death. At this moment Hamlet rejects the 'common' knowledge of death to proclaim his own love for Ophelia. Over her body, with the skulls at their feet, Hamlet and Laertes begin the struggle which will kill them both. Neither can win this contest of love, since the object of their affections is dead. The skulls still grinning on the stage remind the audience, as a *memento mori* should, that they have good reason to fear the dateless kingdom of death.

Hamlet and Laertes remind the audience that humanity is subject to other laws than the natural law of decay. The laws of love and affection bind human beings together and make possible the existence of society. Against the law of love, all have offended. There still exists a grace, whether in earth or heaven, which drives men and women to complete the pattern of human affection symbolized by Titian's painting of love or Raphael's harmony of the graces. The graveyard scene completes the pattern of the harmony of the graces in *Hamlet* and forces a new understanding upon the audience.

The search for a love of such heroic proportions that it can outlast death is not, perhaps, entirely rational. It is evident that death will gain its victory and that the final appeal of love may have to be made to heaven. Yet the bonds of love have obvious survival value for the human species. A belief in their power, despite the evidence of death, can hardly be called irrational. Hamlet's sudden recognition of his love

M

is a valid challenge to the eternal triumph of death. This perpetual search for the harmony of love, even at the edge of a grave in the murderous conditions of Elsinore, makes life both heroic and tragic.

In the graveyard Shakespeare achieves an intense dramatic balance between the themes of love and death. It is one of the most passionate scenes in the play. This combination of the imagery of love with the funereal trappings of death has rightly attracted the attention of psychologists as well as literary critics. In an article on 'The Graveyard Scene in *Hamlet*'[1] Norman J. Symons extended the Freud–Jones interpretation to account for Hamlet's 'strange behaviour' in the graveyard.

Symons examines the imagery used by both Hamlet and Laertes. His conclusion is that it represents 'a phallic contest between father and son'. The love which both so passionately proclaim for Ophelia is the result of their own unresolved conflicts with their parents. It is also possible to identify Hamlet's conflict more precisely. He treats Ophelia, and the grave in which she is buried, as substitutes for his mother. His violent behaviour in the graveyard is thus the discharge of his Oedipal passion for Gertrude.

It is probable that the imagery of Hamlet and Laertes is connected with their desire to assume their fathers' places in the world. The language of the graveyard scene, however, fits exactly into the symbolic Renaissance psychology expressed throughout the play in the emblems of the Judgment of Paris, the qualities of the Olympian gods, the battle of memory, understanding, and will within the soul, and the love dance of the three graces. These symbols, I believe, express more fully and exactly the sexual symbolism of the play than the 'simple' version of the Oedipus complex used by Symons to translate the scene into the orthodox symbolic equations of Freudian psychology. The traditional expressive symbols of Renaissance psychology are used by Shakespeare to present a complex and advanced series of psychological observations.

The passions represented are intricate and complex. Laertes, more like a lover than a brother, takes the body of his dead sister in his arms and calls upon the Gravediggers to cover them both (5 i 245: 3445):

Laertes   Now pile your dust upon the quick and dead,
                Till of this flat a mountain you have made
                T'o'ertop old Pelion or the skyish head
                Of blue Olympus.

[1] *International Journal of Psychoanalysis*, ix (1928), 96–119.

This extravagant gesture provokes Hamlet into coming forward to proclaim his own love for Ophelia.

He answers the passion of Laertes with a speech that he later describes as 'rant' (5 i 278:3481) or 'a tow'ring passion' (5 ii 80:3584). Shakespeare uses it to extend and develop in exact fashion the imagery of mountains used by Laertes (5 i 273:3476):

Hamlet   Be buried quick with her and so will I;
And, if thou prate of mountains, let them throw
Millions of acres on us till the ground,
Singeing his pate against the burning zone
Make Ossa like a wart.

It is certainly a remarkable coincidence that Hamlet's love for Ophelia should actually take his monument as far as 'the burning zone'—the sphere of the sun, who is also Hyperion and Hamlet's father. Symons is surely correct in refusing to treat this coincidence as accidental.

These two speeches are a careful restatement of the imagery of the Olympian gods used by Hamlet in the closet scene with his mother. Laertes proposes that the monument over the grave should be higher than Pelion or Olympus. Olympus is the home of the sky gods. Pelion is one of the mountains used by the generation of earth giants who attempted to scale heaven by piling Pelion on Ossa in order to drive Zeus, or Jove, from his throne. Hamlet asserts that his 'millions of acres' would reach the sun and make Ossa look like a wart. Hamlet pours scorn upon the passion of Laertes. He suggests, by his references to the drinking of 'eisel' or vinegar to induce melancholy and the eating of a crocodile in order to shed its hypocritical tears, that Laertes is merely indulging in an act—a 'show' of grief. He makes the same claim for his love for Ophelia that he made for his remembrance of his father—it represents 'that within which passes show' (1 ii 85:266).

The reappearance of this Olympian imagery is a sign of emotional development rather than emotional paralysis. Hamlet would now use the earth from the grave as a way of reaching his Olympian heaven. The road to the citadel of memory and understanding now lies through the passions of earth. Ophelia had always possessed an instinctual understanding of the life of passion from which Hamlet had tried to cut himself off. Laertes calls her 'a minist'ring angel' (5 i 235:3432) in defiance of the Priest. The imagery of the graces which has always been associated with Ophelia now suggests the possibility that she does possess the power or passion of heavenly love.

In accepting his love for Ophelia, therefore, Hamlet recognizes the true nature of *Voluptas*. He restores the emotional harmony and balance which had been shattered by his mother's marriage. The union of Hamlet and Ophelia would have combined the sword of the active life, the book of the contemplative life, and the flower of the passionate life. This combination would have been the initiation of beauty into passionate love. The resulting harmony would have allowed them to reach the sphere of the 'burning zone' and re-create the rule of Hyperion the sun-king.

Such a union of memory, understanding, and will would have restored health to the body-politic of Denmark. Instead of the poisonous rule of a satyr king and a thoughtless voluptuary a new generation would have succeeded in their own right to equal the Olympian achievements of the past. If there is such a specific emotional paralysis as an 'Oedipus complex' then *Hamlet*, like the *Oedipus Tyrannus* of Sophocles, is a demonstration of how a man may pick his way through the labyrinth of his own affections and overcome or escape such paralysis. Hamlet comes to terms with the aggressive and sexual complications inherent in the bond with both his parents and emerges free as an individual personality.

It is clear, whether the terminology used to describe them is theological, psychological, or biological, that such complications are the inalienable birthright of humanity. The development of the faculties of the body and the powers of the mind should enable an individual to create his own personal harmony. Anyone who succeeded in developing all of their potential capacities to the full would indeed be a 'paragon of animals' (2 ii 305:1354) who might with justice be compared to the Olympian gods. Individual growth, however, is inevitably always partial and incomplete. The very power of thought illumines the gap between man's capacities and his achievement.

This failure is often attributed to a discrepancy between the powers of the mind, dignified as 'reason', and the faculties of the body, debased as 'passion' or 'sensation'. The terms are inexact and endlessly misleading. It is essential to find some method of discussing the infinite variety of humanity. It is claimed that the tripartite imagery of *Hamlet* allows for a more complex and accurate approach to these psychological problems than the more usual separation of the soul from the body, the mind from the senses, or reason from passion.

The burial of Ophelia marks the acceptance of a power of love which can only be possessed by creatures whose brains are an essential part of their bodies. The concept of the three graces of the spirit was taken over from the Classical world by the philosophers of the

Renaissance because they felt it expressed an indissoluble union of mind, body, and spirit which forms part of the harmony of the law of nature and the grace of God.

In *Hamlet* the triple-faced passion of love is shown as both the cause, and the redemption, of much of the tragedy of human existence. Love can exist as an unbridled expression of the will which ends by poisoning the bonds of human affection and leads to murder or self-destruction. Combined with memory and understanding it forms the harmony of grace which is also the love of God. This love is infinite and can take account even of 'the fall of a sparrow' (5 ii 212:3669). Judged by this standard human love is necessarily limited and circumscribed.

It has been argued that the action of the play forces Hamlet to move from the contemplative life of a Wittenberg student, through the passionate life of an actor and presenter of plays, to the active life of a soldier engaged in a deadly but essential duty. The graveyard scene follows this pattern exactly. Hamlet contemplates the folly of all human pretensions as he examines the skulls. He is then forced to make his passionate declaration of love and, as a result, finds himself committed to active single combat with Laertes.

What distinguishes Hamlet from the other characters in the graveyard is not that he is virtuous while they are vicious. The attempt to cast up the moral accounts of the play is seldom a very profitable exercise. The difference is that Hamlet is conscious of the perpetual quest for balance and harmony in the human spirit in a way that escapes all of the other characters except Ophelia. It is the kind of search that Giordano Bruno called a heroic frenzy:

> The heroic frenzy, which our present discourse somewhat clarifies, differs from other more ignoble frenzies not as virtue differs from vice, but as vice practised in a divine way by a more divine subject differs from vice practised in a bestial way by a more bestial subject. Therefore, the difference is not according to the form of vice itself, but according to the subjects who practise it in different ways.[1]

Hamlet makes many mistakes, and his errors appear to have consequences as disastrous as the most ill-intentioned acts of the King. Hamlet, however, has never abandoned his belief in the power of thought and its ability to shape both conscience and consciousness.

The story of Hamlet and Ophelia is therefore a love story which is also, like *Romeo and Juliet*, an account of the growth of an under-

[1] P. E. Memmo Jr, *Giordano Bruno's The Heroic Frenzies: A Translation with Introduction and Notes*, 1964, 100.

standing which includes both consciousness and conscience. The working out of the pattern of the three graces is an education of the human mind, body, and spirit in the nature of love. This education is as closely associated with the passion of man's sexuality as it is with his intellect. This double sense of conscience and consciousness is essential to the argument of the sonnets. The union of understanding and passion is particularly well displayed in the ironic sexuality of Sonnet 151.

> Love is too young to know what conscience is;
> Yet who knows not conscience is born of love?
> Then, gentle cheater, urge not my amiss,
> Lest guilty of my faults thy sweet self prove.
> For thou betraying me, I do betray
> My nobler part to my gross body's treason;
> My soul doth tell my body that he may
> Triumph in love; flesh stays no farther reason,
> But, rising at thy name, doth point out thee
> As his triumphant prize. Proud of this pride,
> He is contented thy poor drudge to be,
> To stand in thy affairs, fall by thy side.
>   No want of conscience hold it that I call
>   Her 'love' for whose dear love I rise and fall.

The knowledge that is attained in the act of love is also the knowledge of good and evil. The growth of the male erection is also the growth of love and hence the origin of a spiritual power and understanding which allows its possessor the exercise of charity in human relationships. The triumph of the flesh is the triumph of conscience, although it is also treason and a betrayal of consciousness to passion.

The sonnets develop a charity which endures even after the loss of faith and the abandonment of all hope. It is this charity which Hamlet comes to show in the final duel. His refusal to accept as 'natural' the King's rhetoric of oblivion and death, and his acceptance of mortality in the graveyard, are both part of his recognition that the quality of a man's life depends upon the scope of his attention and an attitude of mind (5 ii 212:3669):

Hamlet   If it be now, 'tis not to come; if it be not to come, it
              will be now; if it be not now, yet it will come—the
              readiness is all.

Hamlet does not contain the triumphant assertions of the sonnets that art can make love shine bright in black ink and thus for ever defeat time. It does not require them. The entire play acts as a theatre of memory which stamps upon the mind of the audience an impression of Hamlet's consciousness. His intellect opposes to the arrows of fortune or the sea of troubles a series of insistent questions. They do not solve the riddle of the universe. They do define the nature of the man who asks them.

Shakespeare's pursuit of bewildering questions ends, not in oracular pronouncements, but in the clarity with which his dramatization of opposed passions mirrors, and helps to clarify, the confused and jarring elements within the minds and souls of its audience. *Hamlet*, like *The Murder of Gonzago*, offers an audience the possibility of recognizing themselves and their own problems, perhaps for the first time. If that opportunity is accepted, then *Hamlet* offers its spectators the possibility of following some of the threads that lead through the labyrinth of their own affections.

It is a brilliant dramatic effect which makes the way to an understanding of Hamlet's conscience lie through the beauty and bewildered consciousness of Ophelia. Death is not the main character in the graveyard scene. As Henry James wrote in the preface to *The Wings of the Dove*, commenting upon the difficulties he had experienced in making a dying girl the central character in the book:

> The way grew straight from the moment one recognized that the poet essentially *can't* be concerned with the act of dying. Let him deal with the sickest of the sick, it is still by the act of living that they appeal to him, and appeal the more as the conditions plot against them and prescribe the battle. The process of life gives way fighting, and often may so shine out on the lost ground as in no other connection.[1]

The art of tragedy is the creation of a lost ground upon which the conditions may plot against the characters and prescribe the battle.

The burial of Ophelia brings all of the characters in *Hamlet* into conflict on that final lost ground for humanity, a graveyard. The processes of life and love here shine out as at no other moment in the play. The very admission of death's extreme decrepitude is also an assertion of the value of human affection. The game of chance that men play with death can have only one ending (5 i 88:3281):

Hamlet   Did these bones cost no more the breeding but to play
               at loggats with them? Mine ache to think on't.

[1] Henry James, *The Art of the Novel: Critical Prefaces by Henry James*, ed. R. P. Blackmur, 1934, 289–90.

The search for harmony can only end in an unmusical silence (5 i 75: 3267):

Hamlet   That skull had a tongue in it, and could sing once.

The inevitable end of the game and the dusty end of the search do not prescribe the rule by which it was played, nor can they assign a value to the harmony of the song.

The Gravediggers' sardonic acceptance of death's triumph is paralleled by the courage and good humour with which Hamlet comes to accept the impossible odds offered to him by the King and Laertes. The characters make the play a pattern of poison, play, and duel. This pattern is a dance of death. The common theme of the dance of death is that life is a show in which all the human actors end by playing the same part. Even in the face of the silence of death, Hamlet asserts that it matters how the 'particular' part is played.

Chapter 7

POISON IN PLAY
the Duel Scene

Hamlet refers to his contest with Claudius as a duel on only one occasion. Rosencrantz and Guildenstern are not yet dead when Hamlet, telling Horatio of the King's plot against his life, speaks their ironic epitaph (5 ii 57:3560):

> *Hamlet*   Why, man, they did make love to this employment;
> They are not near my conscience; their defeat
> Does by their own insinuation grow:
> 'Tis dangerous when the baser nature comes
> Between the pass and fell incensed points
> Of mighty opposites.

The image of the duel, however, is one of the recurring patterns of the play. The first information that the audience hears about the court of Denmark is Horatio's account of the duel between King Hamlet and Fortinbras of Norway. The play's last scene is the duel between Laertes and Hamlet. Between these two points there rages a duel of wits and words, of traps and counter-stratagems, between Hamlet and Claudius.

It is comparatively easy for a dramatist to arrange a stage fight. It is more difficult to create a controlled fictional or dream structure in which the metallic slide and harsh tock of rapiers, opposed within the silent circle of the court, create a dissonance which is an important part of the play's imagery. As in the dumb show, the physical action on the stage fulfils a function which language alone cannot perform. The duel between Hamlet and Laertes is a necessary resolution to the theatrical situation. It is also the logical result of the limitless threat of coming violence which has filled the play from its first scene.

It is a spectacular visual representation of the unequal duel against impossible odds waged by Hamlet throughout the play. It is closely linked with the action of war and the imagery of military prowess which is so strong an element in the play. The play begins with an abrupt military challenge in an atmosphere of darkness and growing terror. It ends with a military funeral. The army of Fortinbras and the rebellion of Laertes are minor events compared with the continual references to siege warfare, cannon fire, and armed combat which fill the language of all the characters. The most important and the most characteristic feature of *Hamlet* is that it deals with a world at war.

The most important thing about the fight between Hamlet and Laertes is that it is not, in the strict sense, a duel. It is intended to be a fatal accident. What appears to be a gentlemanly exercise of skill—a wager upon a play or bout with foils—conceals a poisoned trap for Hamlet's life. It permits Laertes to achieve his private revenge for his father and his sister while serving the true interests of the state of Denmark—as those interests are interpreted by the King. He justifies the act by the need to protect himself and the state from a criminal who is masquerading as a dangerous lunatic. The King, however, has other buried reasons which he does not reveal to Laertes—among them the buried body of the murdered King of Denmark. The play with foils is therefore an exercise in chivalry, an act of vengeance, an attempted murder, and the last battle in the long war between Hamlet and Claudius.

The contest thus combines aspects of the three types of armed combat recognized by the Tudor lawyers and jurists. Since it is an episode in a concealed war between Hamlet and Claudius it is a fight between the champions of opposed armies—as the duel between King Hamlet and King Fortinbras was a combat of champions. It is intended as retribution for Hamlet's real and imagined crimes. It is therefore a judicial encounter or trial by battle. Thirdly it is an 'affair of honour' and therefore a duel.

These appeals to force were intended to settle quarrels or disputes which were outside the scope of the normal process of law without necessarily starting a vendetta, or involving an army in a battle, a state in a war. Claudius uses the play with foils for a rather different purpose. He desires to avoid any appeal to law. These reasons, which compel Claudius to arrange the poisoned duel, illustrate exactly the nature of the contest between himself and Hamlet. Having placed himself outside the law by murdering his brother, Claudius has to keep outside it while dealing with his nephew in case he, and not Hamlet, is revealed as the criminal in Denmark. Hamlet's problem is how to deal with a criminal who is also the King, and in command of the apparatus of law and order in the state.

Laertes raises a rebellion against the King in order to ensure that he revenges his father's death. Claudius meets this threat first by appealing to the divine right of kings, and next by persuading Laertes that Hamlet murdered Polonius as part of a plot against the King. He is then faced with a difficult question (4 vii 5 : 3012):

> Laertes   But tell me
> Why you proceeded not against these feats,
> So crimeful and so capital in nature,
> As by your safety, wisdom, all things else,
> You mainly were stirr'd up.

Claudius gives two reasons for not proceeding against Hamlet by due process of law. He is not prepared to offend Gertrude who 'lives almost by his looks' (4 vii 12 : 3020), and the common people of Denmark would never permit him to act against the Prince.

The King apologizes for these reasons. He is aware that to Laertes they may appear 'much unsinew'd' (4 vii 10 : 3018). This apology draws the attention of the audience to the very strong reasons that govern the King's conduct but which he is unable to explain to Laertes. If the situation described by Claudius actually existed in Denmark then his conduct would be politically disastrous. Not only does he prize his private passion for Gertrude above the law of his kingdom: he even admits that he is incapable of enforcing the law against the wishes of the 'general gender' (4 vii 18 : 3026). If the King, for personal consideration, refuses to apply the law, he creates exactly the conditions of anarchy in which the wild justice of private revenge must flourish.

Yet it has been established in the early scenes of the play that Claudius is a calculating, and generally successful, politician. If it is now his policy to encourage Laertes in an act of private revenge it is because he perceives in the passion of vengeance a perfect instrument for the execution of his own cold and murderous will. The inner-play has reminded the King of his past crime and convinced him of his present insecurity. The King uses Laertes as an agent acting outside the law because he recognizes that he is himself, despite his position as King of Denmark, an outlaw.

Faced with the rebellion of Laertes, Claudius finds it natural to use the language of legality to defend himself. Gertrude has thrown herself between the sword-arm of Laertes and her husband. Claudius indicates that he does not require her help (4 v 119:2867):

King	Let him go, Gertrude; do not fear our person:
	There's such divinity doth hedge a king
	That treason can but peep to what it would,
	Acts little of his will.

These conventional pieties, however, sit ill upon the tongue of a man who has himself broken through the hedge of that divinity to murder the King, his brother. Claudius acts his part as king by appealing to the law of God. It is an unwise refuge for a man who has committed the crime of Cain.

Despite this claim to the full God-given legal status of a king, Claudius has now to admit to Laertes that he is powerless to act against Hamlet within the law. The reasons that he gives to Laertes are transparent excuses for the true reason—which the audience already know. Claudius is not the lawful king of Denmark and his claim to divine sanction for his acts is totally false. Hamlet makes this point clear to the audience and to Rosencrantz and Guildenstern when they arrest him during the search for the body of Polonius. They cannot understand him, but the words are intended to catch the attention and the conscience of the audience (4 ii 25:2654):

Rosencrantz	My lord, you must tell us where the body is, and go with us to the King.
Hamlet	The body is with the King, but the King is not with the body. The King is a thing—
Guildenstern	A thing, my lord!
Hamlet	Of nothing. Bring me to him.

These words, as Jerah Johnson has pointed out, are a reference to the concept of the King's 'two bodies' developed in medieval and Tudor law. It is a clear indication that, in Hamlet's eyes, Claudius is not the King of Denmark.

Johnson quotes from the *Reports* of Edward Plowden who records the agreement reached by the crown lawyers at Serjeants Inn in 1561 that:

> the King has in him two Bodies, *viz.*, a Body natural, and a Body politic. His Body natural (if it be considered in itself) is a Body mortal, subject to all the infirmities that come by Nature or Accident, to the imbecility of Infancy or old Age, and to the like defects that happen to the natural Bodies of other people. But his Body politic is a Body that cannot be seen or handled, consisting of Policy and Government, and constituted for the Direction of the People, and the Management of the public weal, and this Body is utterly void of Infancy, and old Age, and other natural defects and Imbecilities, which the Body natural is subject to.[1]

It is not possible to separate the body-natural from the body-politic in the person of the king. When, however, the king dies, the jurists argued that there was a mystical transference of the body-politic to another living person. It is this theory which lies behind the traditional formula of succession: 'The King is dead. Long live the King!' It is the body-politic which is hedged with divinity and thus protects the body-natural. The entire state depends upon the health of this body-politic. Rosencrantz and Guildenstern believe that they are protecting it when they convey Hamlet to England. Claudius encourages Laertes to believe that it will also be served by his secret murder of private revenge.

Hamlet evidently takes a different view of these political realities. He argues that 'the body is with the King' since Claudius clearly possesses a body-natural, but 'the King is not with the body' because he neither possesses nor represents the body-politic of Denmark. He is a king of 'nothing'. This view has been fully presented in the extended comparison between the two Kings in the closet scene. Claudius is a 'king of shreds and patches' who has stolen the crown by murder and is in process of poisoning the whole body-politic of Denmark as he had poisoned the body-natural of its true King. Hamlet does not regard Claudius as in any sense the King of Denmark.

The court of Denmark differs in one vital respect from the court of

---

1 Jerah Johnson, 'The Concept of the "King's Two Bodies" in *Hamlet*', *Shakespeare Quarterly*, xviii (1967), 430–4. Johnson acknowledges that he is indebted to F. W. Maitland, *Selected Essays*, 1936, 104–6, and Ernst H. Kantorowicz, *The King's Two Bodies: A Study in Medieval Political Theology*, 1957.

Tudor England.[1] The Danish monarchy is described as an elective office. Shakespeare has gone to considerable trouble to establish this essential piece of information. Since Claudius has been duly elected he is not, in the strict sense, a usurper. If, however, he could be exposed as a murderer it is probable that 'the main voice of Denmark' (1 iii 28: 491) would condemn him. There are, therefore, two totally distinct views of the court in *Hamlet*. On the surface Claudius appears to be the legitimate King of Denmark and to command the loyalty of Polonius, Laertes, Rosencrantz, Guildenstern, and the rest of the court. It is perhaps significant that he does not appear to command the loyalty of the common people. Seen through the eyes of Hamlet, he is the satyr king who has eclipsed the true sun of majesty and represents nothing but himself.

The action of *Hamlet* shows the way in which Hamlet slowly forces the King to expose his guilt and proves his own view of the court correct. Hamlet's war against Claudius and the court is thus conducted from the 'seat' of his memory. From there he slowly undermines and exposes the King's position until Claudius is finally driven into the open where he is killed. Hamlet does not survive the battle, but Horatio is left to tell Fortinbras and Denmark 'how these things came about' (5 ii 372:3875). The buried secret of Claudius is also the poison or the ulcerous disease which has infected the entire body-politic of Denmark. Its excision is therefore a surgical as well as a military operation. The imagery of war, of disease, and of memory thus coalesce into the great pattern of poison, play, and duel which forms the structure of *Hamlet*.

The war between Hamlet and Claudius is necessarily secret and un-declared. It is a guerrilla war of the mind and spirit until it breaks out into the violent action of the last battle. This war is represented by three major patterns of military metaphor in the language of the play. There is the language of siege warfare in which the King and Hamlet appear as the rival generals of opposing forces engaged in underground and secret operations of mine and countermine. There is the language of artillery. The famous guns of Elsinore are discharged at intervals throughout the play on the King's command. Yet at the end of the play it is for Hamlet that Fortinbras orders them to fire a salute. Thirdly there is the language of single combat. This duel is first the combat of champions fought between King Hamlet and King Fortin-bras. It then becomes a duel of wits and words between Hamlet and

[1] E. A. J. Honigmann, 'The Politics of *Hamlet* and the World of the Play', in *Hamlet*, ed. J. R. Brown and B. Harris, 1963, 129–47.

Claudius. Finally it returns to the technical details of the fight with rapiers. Hamlet continually tries to provoke the King. Claudius always avoids the Prince by using a champion or substitute. Polonius, Ophelia, Gertrude, Rosencrantz, Guildenstern, and Laertes are all used as shields by the King. Only when they have all fallen is he left face to face with Hamlet. Even then his last words are a call for further help.

Claudius appears to start the war with an enormous advantage. He can call upon the full sanction of the law, majesty, and power of the kingdom of Denmark. It is clear, from his handling of the Norwegian crisis, that he is capable of using them with skill and determination. What defeats him is the knowledge which he, and Hamlet, possess. He knows that he is a murderer who is acting the part of a king. After the inner-play, he knows that Hamlet has somehow penetrated this disguise—or at least he acts upon that suspicion. It is essential to remove Hamlet, but impossible to do so with any show of legality. Claudius dare not risk another duel with words. He has been forced out of his part and can no longer 'suit the action to the word, the word to the action' (3 ii 17:1865). For all his skill as an actor, Claudius cannot finally perform the part of a king.

He is compelled to act as a politician and a poisoner. This means that Claudius can still use the apparatus of the state to further his own purpose, but he operates under a certain handicap. He is no longer a single secret murderer able to strike at his own unexpected time. That part remains vacant for Hamlet, if he cares to play it. Claudius has to work through others. Yet, if his courtiers knew the truth, it is doubtful if the King could count upon their support.

The King needs to find out how much Hamlet knows. Once it is clear that, whatever he knows, Hamlet is far too dangerous to live, Claudius has to find some way of eliminating him without arousing suspicion. The King's agents, consequently, never really know what they are looking for, or why Hamlet is such a threat to the present regime. They are therefore inefficient and the King is badly supplied with information. Since he gives his servants misleading information they are exposed to unnecessary and quite unexpected dangers. In the service of Claudius, the casualty rate is high. The King's need for secrecy forces him outside the power of his own law. The death of Polonius at last permits him to adopt the device of the play with foils. He is able to give Laertes clear and murderous directions. Unfortunately Claudius does not have complete control of the script.

Hamlet is in an equally difficult situation. He finds himself opposed by a man who can pervert all the instruments of legality and justice to his own secret and murderous ends. No appeal to justice seems possible, since the source of justice in Denmark is the conscience of the King. The most efficient weapon against such oppression is evidently sudden and secret murder. In choosing the weapon of words in a dramatic play to attack the conscience of the King, Hamlet is placing himself at serious risk. The King's reply to the poison in jest of *The Murder of Gonzago* is the poison in play of the deadly bout with foils. The King responds to the power of conscience by attempting to repeat the act of murder. Hamlet is committed to a deadly secret duel in which the odds are slightly in the King's favour.

Hamlet presents a familiar situation. The functions of society and the forms of law are used as a cover for the exercise of human passions which, if given full scope, would destroy for ever the law and society. The official forces of law and order are, whether they know it or not, committed to the support of a lawless and tyrannical oppression. Those who value the true harmony of society are themselves forced to act in secret and outside the law. It then becomes questionable whether it is possible to cure the poison of society without adopting the very methods of the tyranny that must be destroyed.

It is appropriate that the legal, moral, and political implications of this war should be raised over the grave of one of its more innocent victims. The argument between the Gravediggers about the propriety of the coroner's verdict on Ophelia is, like so many other arguments in the play, a dispute about the understanding and the will. In extended legal explanations and a display of aural Latin the First Clown considers in what circumstances a person who shows the will to seek her own salvation by suicide may properly be granted Christian burial. Shakespeare uses this argument about Ophelia's 'doubtful' (5 i 221: 3416) death to make an important contribution to the wider questions of the play.

W. L. Rushton pointed out the implications of the legal argument:

It seems that Shakespeare has made the first clown confound a *felo de se*, or one who is guilty of self murder, with a person who commits homicide *se defendendo*, in his own defence, or, as he miscalls it *se offendendo*; for, in answer to the second clown's assurance that 'The crowner hath sat on her, and finds it Christian burial', he says, 'How can that be, unless she drown'd herself in her own defence?' This is also apparent from his reasoning which, although it may appear absurd, is good law; for he evidently means, that if the water comes to a man and drowns him, not

wittingly, but against his inclination, he is as innocent of
suicide as that man is innocent of murder, who, *se defendendo*, in
his own defence, kills another who, *felleo animo*, presses upon him.[1]

The Gravediggers have raised a question rather than solved a problem.
Ophelia's death remains 'doubtful' (5 i 221:3416). Gertrude describes
it as an accident (4 vii 165:3156) but the Gravediggers and the Priest
have no doubts about the legal position. Only the intervention of the
King has mitigated the full rigour of the 'shards, flints and pebbles'
(5 i 225:3420) of the canonical law.

The question of Ophelia's responsibility merges, a few lines later,
into the question of Hamlet's responsibility for her death. Laertes holds
Hamlet accountable for the deaths of Polonius and Ophelia. There are
many critics who believe that Hamlet should be judged guilty on the
evidence provided by Shakespeare.[2] It is important, however, to
examine all the evidence that the dramatist has provided for his
audience. In the theatre they must judge by the evidence of their eyes
as well as their ears. In quick succession, Shakespeare provides two
violently contrasting stage pictures. In the inner-play they have seen
the act of poisoning twice committed. Both acts seem identical. In the
prayer scene Hamlet stands behind Claudius with drawn sword. In the
closet scene he thrusts at a man he believes to be Claudius concealed
behind the arras. Shakespeare asks his audience to 'look here upon this
picture and on this' (3 iv 53:2437).

Hamlet does not stab the King as he kneels in a position of submission and repentance because he hopes for a future opportunity in
which he can play the parts of Pyrrhus and Lucianus. Since the King,
despite his efforts to repent, is very far from a state of grace, the conditions for the 'perfect' revenge ironically exist at the moment that
Hamlet rejects this occasion. Yet the scene makes it clear that the
successful performance of such an act would be an acceptance of the
remedies favoured by Claudius (4 iii 9:2670):

King   Diseases desperate grown
        By desperate appliance are reliev'd,
        Or not at all.

The 'appliance' of Claudius, the remedy of murder, proves mortal to
the entire court. If he had administered it in the prayer scene Hamlet
would have been no less guilty of poisoning the state of Denmark.

---

[1] W. L. Rushton, *Shakespeare's Legal Maxims*, 1907, 47.
[2] Eleanor Prosser, *Hamlet and Revenge*, 1967, 192.

Like his mother and uncle, he would be something less than 'a beast that wants discourse of reason' (1 ii 150:334).

In the closet scene Hamlet is standing in front of his mother—whom he believes to be a murderess. She calls for help and is answered by a voice from the arras behind him. He believes it to be the King—whom he knows to be a murderer. He is, apparently, caught between his mother and Claudius—and in just these circumstances his father, he thinks, had been murdered. This is made clear in the exchange which follows the death of Polonius (3 iv 25:2406):

Queen	O me, what hast thou done?
Hamlet	Nay, I know not: Is it the King?
Queen	O, what a rash and bloody deed is this!
Hamlet	A bloody deed!—almost as bad, good mother, As kill a king and marry with his brother.
Queen	As kill a king!
Hamlet	Ay, lady, it was my word.

An audience may believe that, on this second occasion, they have seen performed the act of deliberate murder contemplated in the prayer scene. Yet they may also reflect that in the prayer scene Hamlet contemplates, but does not perform, an act of homicide that could be called murder. In the closet scene he performs, without consideration, an act of homicide which could be represented as the instinctive reaction of self-defence.

The play does not answer the question. The death of Polonius, like the death of Ophelia, remains 'doubtful' (5 i 221:3416). The actions of the prayer scene and closet scene remain comparable but not identical. The questions of moral and legal responsibility raised by the Clowns are not easy to answer. It is not remarkable, therefore, that critics should hold different opinions about the nature and degree of Hamlet's culpability. It is remarkable that Shakespeare should have provided, in a few short scenes, the evidence for both prosecution and defence.

As recently as 1961 the Privy Council overturned the decision taken *In re Polemis* of 1921[1] which had established the precedent that the author of a negligent act must be held liable for all the consequences

[1] A. L. Goodhart, 'Liability for Unforeseen Consequences', *The Listener*, 65 (6 April 1961), 603–4.

of that act. Shakespeare could hardly be familiar with such a decision but he, and the Tudor lawyers, were accustomed to the legal and moral problem. The decisions of 1921 and 1961 have a long history.

It seems a reasonable conclusion that a man who 'starts something' should be held responsible for what he has started. Such an idea is found in most early legal systems. Gradually, however, as the law develops, the idea that a man who starts something is therefore liable for all the consequences is abandoned. A man is only held liable if he has acted wrongfully:

> He acts wrongfully if, without lawful excuse, he intentionally
> injures another person; or if, as a reasonable man, he ought
> to have foreseen that his act might injure another person, and that
> he has not taken reasonable care to avoid causing that injury.[1]

It is evident that the murder of King Hamlet was a wrongful act. It seems probable that Claudius could be held liable for the consequences—but do these consequences include Hamlet's desire for revenge? Similarly it could be held either that the death of Polonius was a wrongful act or that it was a legitimate act of self-defence. In either case, is Hamlet responsible for the death of Ophelia? And if so, is one of the unavoidable consequences the vengeance of Laertes?

There is one further consideration. It is not always practicable to hold a man liable for all of the consequences of a wrongful act, since the consequences may be infinite:

> In June, 1914, Gavrilo Prinzep, in a remote town in Bosnia,
> pulled the trigger of the gun which killed the Austrian Archduke.
> He thus began a chain of events which has altered the lives of
> every one of us. It would, however, be absurd for any legal system
> to hold him responsible for everything that has happened since.[2]

The consequences of the original murder in *Hamlet* are infinite. They change the history of the state of Denmark. Is Claudius to be held responsible for the chain of events which kills Polonius, Ophelia, Rosencrantz, Guildenstern, Laertes, Claudius, and Hamlet? Does Hamlet share this guilt? Or can neither be held liable for the consequences of events which neither foresaw?

The question of a king's accountability was particularly acute for Tudor England. A king, and a man who kills a king, have each a very special responsibility. They are involved in acts of religious as well as political significance. Shakespeare avoids assigning total responsibility to any one individual. When Laertes, at the end of the play, cries 'The

[1] Ibid.   [2] Ibid.

King, the King's to blame' (5 ii 312:3801) he is still entirely ignorant of the murder of King Hamlet. His words can only refer to the terrible consequences of the wrongful act of the poisoned duel. Neither he nor Claudius can escape the blame. As reasonable men, they ought to have foreseen its possible deadly consequences. It is instructive that what overrode their judgment was the desire to retaliate or revenge themselves upon Hamlet. The audience are bound to extend Laertes's words and wonder whether Claudius ought not to have foreseen these consequences when he murdered his brother. What made disaster inescapable was his attempt, in full knowledge of the nature of the act, to murder his nephew.

If the consequences of a wrongful act are often unforeseen, the consequences of a cycle of revenge are often as infinite as they are wrongful. That the matter is of more than academic or theatrical interest may be suggested by the staged theatricality of the revenge cycle enacted in the forest of Réthondes on 21 June 1940:

> There stood the historic *wagon-lit* where, in November 1918, Marshal Foch and Weygand himself had received the defeated German emissaries. With characteristic efficiency, German Army engineers had hacked down the wall of the museum housing the railway coach and brought it out to where it had stood twenty-two years earlier. A large Swastika was draped over the monument to the 1918 Armistice. The cycle of revenge could not be more complete. France had chosen as the setting for the final humbling of Germany the Versailles Hall of Mirrors where, in the arrogant exaltation of 1871, King Wilhelm of Prussia had proclaimed himself Kaiser; so now Hitler's choice for his moment of supreme triumph was to be that of France's in 1918.[1]

The conventions of revenge may change, but its essential 'humanity' remains.

The war between Denmark and Norway which flickers restlessly off-stage in *Hamlet* threatened to become just such a cycle of revenge. Shakespeare slowly narrows the focus of his drama from the armies who march across his stage and through the language of his play to the situation within the castle of Elsinore. He further reduces it to the tensions of hatred and revenge within two family circles. Finally the audience are looking at these same tensions as they fight for the possession of the mind and emotions of a single individual. There is no need to update the play of *Hamlet*. It dramatizes the problems of the world

[1] Alistair Horne, *To Lose a Battle*, 1969, 507-8.

which we have created and in which it is doubtful if we can survive. In the centre of his war, beside the crash of the guns of Elsinore and the explosion of subterranean mines, Shakespeare has dramatized the power of conscience, understanding, and love which holds out the slender possibility that the killing may be stopped and the cycle of revenge broken.

The final stages of the play, after the burial of Ophelia, are of particular importance because they dramatize so clearly the forces whose victory in the mind of any individual threatens to prolong the more than Jacobean horror of the long war that mankind wages against itself. Claudius regards himself as a master gunner in such a war and his triumphs are regularly signalled by the crash of the great battery which Martin Holmes[1] has shown was one of the noted features of the Danish fortress in Elizabethan times. The metaphor of gunnery is one of the most important patterns of military imagery in the play.

Claudius uses the great cannon of the castle to emphasize his own power and position. At the beginning of the play the guns go off to accompany the King's 'rouse' (1 ii 127:310) celebrating 'this gentle and unforced accord of Hamlet' (1 ii 123:306). Claudius proposes to use the cannons during the duel (5 ii 260:3728):

King   If Hamlet give the first or second hit,
               Or quit in answer of the third exchange,
               Let all the battlements their ordnance fire;
               The King shall drink to Hamlet's better breath.

The effect is ironic because the King's position has radically changed. The guns now herald his own self-defeat. He makes the guns speak to heaven in celebration of the act of poisoning Hamlet. It is unwise of him to assume that the echo from heaven will be simply 'earthly thunder' (1 ii 128:311).

After the death of Polonius, Claudius, in speaking to the Queen, twice describes his position as being under imaginary cannon fire. On the first occasion he hopes that the poisoned tongue of slander, which normally spans the diameter of the world as easily as a well-aimed cannon hits the centre of a target, will miss his name 'and hit the woundless air' (4 i 44:2628 Q 4). The danger to his reputation fills his soul with 'discord and dismay' (4 i 45:2629).

Once Ophelia's madness is added to the death of Polonius, the King knows that there is no hope of slander missing his name. He feels himself wounded (4 v 91:2831):

[1] Martin Holmes, *The Guns of Elsinore*, 1964.

King   O my dear Gertrude, this,
              Like to a murd'ring piece, in many places
              Gives me superfluous death.

The 'murd'ring piece' is a cannon loaded with small shot, later known
as grape shot. When used at close quarters against infantry it does much
more damage than a single shell or cannon ball. The King's sorrows
which have arrived in 'battalions' rather than as 'single spies' have
brought their artillery with them.

The King's counterstroke, the poisoned duel itself, is also described
by Claudius in terms of artillery. He is afraid that his and Laertes's
attempt on Hamlet's life will expose their murderous intentions if it
is not immediately successful. He therefore proposes the second
stratagem of the poisoned cup (4 vii 150:3142):

King   If this should fail
              And that our drift look through our bad performance
              'Twere better not assay'd, therefore this project
              Should have a back or second that might hold
              If this did blast in proof.

The words contain what Edward B. Hungerford has called a *sub-
metaphor* or *buried metaphor*.[1] If Laertes puts up a bad performance
Hamlet will be able to see the aim (since 'drift' is the allowance for the
angle of deflection when aiming a cannon) behind the attempt. A gun
also has to be proved by firing on a test range. A gun which blasts in
proof explodes under the pressure of firing it and is more dangerous
to the gunners than to the enemy. If the cannon of the attempt on
Hamlet's life should explode in this fashion there must be 'a back or
second' gun ready to fire at once. Hamlet must not survive the barrage.

The cannon ball, or the thunder of artillery fire, was regularly used
by the Platonic emblem-makers of the Italian Renaissance as a conventional symbol for the prudent moral of *festina lente*—the slow haste of
prudence:

> The wise Federigo da Montefeltro who, as a successful *condottiere*,
> delighted in cultivating the arts of peace, expressed his faith in
> harmonious balance through the discordant symbol of a cannon
> ball, which he placed under the protection of the thundering
> Jupiter. On his medal the three stars in the sky form a constellation
> of Jupiter between Mars and Venus, and their symmetry is

[1] Edward B. Hungerford, '*Hamlet:* The Word at the Centre', *Tri-Quarterly*, No. 8
(Winter, 1968), 69–89.

repeated in the group of emblems below; the sword and cuirass belonging to Mars, the whisk broom and myrtle to Venus, while the ball in the centre is dedicated to *Jupiter tonans*, whose flying eagle carries the unusual still-life on its wings.[1]

The cannon ought to signify a princely attribute not confined to military strategy, a combination of force and prudence. The King's stratagem of the poisoned duel, however, is a misuse of force and extremely imprudent. He fails because he does not possess the kingly virtues symbolized by the fire of the guns. The success of the King's plot depends upon two factors. Hamlet must not notice that one of the rapiers is sharp, and Laertes must prove himself the better fencer. The King regards Hamlet in much the same way as he regards Laertes—a pattern of the honourable virtues of the Renaissance gentleman and, therefore, foolish and easy to manipulate. He has here made a series of miscalculations and mistakes which cause him to miscast his 'play' with foils. It is ironic that the King fails in his own part because he has not understood the character of Hamlet.

The King errs partly because he is blinded by his own preconceptions and does not understand the nature of the war in which he is engaged. He also does not possess enough information. Gertrude's account of the death of Polonius has been deliberately misleading. Claudius is never quite sure whether Hamlet's conduct is mere madness or whether the 'antic disposition' is merely a mask for a steady and unswerving determination. Once he has heard of the execution of Rosencrantz and Guildenstern, as Horatio warns Hamlet, he will no longer be in any doubt. This missing piece of information, which is vital to the King's calculations, only arrives with the English Ambassadors after he has lost his life.

The manner, and method, of their death is one of the questions of the play. The King determines to send Hamlet to England at a fairly early stage of the action. He expresses his intention to do so at the end of the nunnery scene and translates it into action after the play scene. The death of Polonius confirms the King's diagnosis of 'madness' and allows him to put his plan into instant effect. Only after the death of Polonius is the audience informed that Hamlet is on his way to execution in England. In an interesting example of dramatic foreshortening Shakespeare makes Hamlet aware, and suspicious, of the plan by the end of the closet scene.

Shakespeare uses Hamlet's discussion of the matter with his mother

---

[1] Edgar Wind, *Pagan Mysteries in the Renaissance*, 1967, 95–6, cf. 108–10.

to predict to the audience the future course of this action (3 iv 202: 2577 Q 1):

Hamlet   There's letters seal'd; and my two school-fellows—
            Whom I will trust as I will adders fang'd—
            They bear the mandate; they must sweep my way
            And marshal me to knavery. Let it work;
            For 'tis the sport to have the engineer
            Hoist with his own petar; and't shall go hard
            But I will delve one yard below their mines
            And blow them at the moon. O, 'tis most sweet
            When in one line two crafts directly meet.

Hamlet compares Rosencrantz and Guildenstern to a pioneer company engaged in a siege. They are driving a mine or subterranean gallery under the wall of a city or fortress in order to blow it up with a 'petar' or bomb. The correct defence is to dig a countermine below the original tunnel and 'blow them at the moon' with the force of their own explosive charge.

It is clear that such an operation requires careful and prudent management. Rosencrantz and Guildenstern are employed by the King on underground and secret operations. They are designed to secure another 'underground' operation—the burial of the King his brother in oblivion. Claudius, however, is ignorant of the appearance of that 'worthy pioneer' (1 v 163:860) the Ghost. He is unaware of the true extent to which his position has been eroded by Hamlet's countermines of memory. He proceeds with the arrangements for the 'shot' of the duel, confident in his own strategy and unconscious of the explosive charge that lurks beneath his schemes. Hamlet predicts that in this hidden, secret, and underground warfare his 'craft' will 'directly meet' that of his opponents and that he will prove more effective at such siege operations. In underestimating his enemy, Claudius has neglected the most elementary principle of military prudence.

The execution of Rosencrantz and Guildenstern is deliberately contrived by the dramatist. It would have been perfectly possible to make the point about Hamlet's readiness for combat by the episode of the pirate ship and remove him from the dangers of the voyage to England without ordering their judicial murder. The journey to England is more than a convenient way of removing Hamlet from the stage while the story of Ophelia and Laertes is developed. It provides the audience with essential information about Hamlet which is inaccessible to the King.

The King's first attempt to murder Hamlet relies on words—the words of the royal commission which the seasick and incompetent Rosencrantz and Guildenstern allow to be stolen from them. As Hamlet had inserted a speech in *The Murder of Gonzago* to catch the King's conscience, so he now forges the King's commission in order to bring this particular 'play' to a different and unexpected conclusion.

In planning his second attempt to murder Hamlet the King assures Laertes that (4 vii 134:3124):

> King   He, being remiss,
>   Most generous, and free from all contriving,
>   Will not peruse the foils; so that with ease
>   Or with a little shuffling, you may choose
>   A sword unbated, and, in a pass of practice,
>   Requite him for your father.

The King's description is both justified and disproved by the events of the duel. Hamlet does not peruse the foils, but he is not as free from contriving as the King imagines. He is a much more deadly and dangerous opponent than Claudius suspects.

The destruction of Rosencrantz and Guildenstern is a deliberate act of policy on Hamlet's part which is essential to the dramatic balance of the play. In the play and prayer scenes it is clear that Hamlet possesses the will to kill the King. The events on board the ship which carries him to England reveal a Prince who is the cunning master of exactly the devious and secret policies pursued by the King. It is not incompetence or lack of nerve which prevents him from turning these avenger's arts against the King.

If Hamlet did not possess the aggressive drive necessary to kill the King he would be a much less interesting character. The total psychology of the play would also be less alarmingly illuminating. The death of Polonius, the calculated arrangements for the execution of Rosencrantz and Guildenstern, and the leap on board the pirate ship reveal an extremely aggressive personality. Hamlet is capable of directing this aggression with a cold intelligence which is at least the political equal of the King's. Why, then, does he find himself inhibited from obeying the command of the Ghost and carrying out a satisfactory and bloody revenge?

Hamlet asks himself exactly this question throughout the play. He finds his conduct abnormal. Critics and clinical psychologists have not hesitated to agree with him. The counteraction of the King and Laertes has been prepared for them as well as for Hamlet. It asks them if they are sure they know what 'normal' or 'natural' behaviour should be in such circumstances. The price that has to be paid for exacting an aggressive, dominant, and successful revenge is the acceptance of the values of Claudius. The play asks its audience to consider whether it is not these values which are psychopathic and clinically abnormal.

Claudius believes that the normal response to such a situation is an overwhelming desire for aggressive revenge. He takes time and trouble to establish that this is, in fact, the attitude of Laertes before he unfolds his plan. He is interested in the quality of Laertes's remembrance for his father (4 vii 107:3105):

King	Laertes, was your father dear to you?
	Or are you like the painting of a sorrow,
	A face without a heart?
Laertes	Why ask you this?
King	Not that I think you did not love your father;
	But that I know love is begun by time,
	And that I see, in passages of proof,
	Time qualifies the fire and spark of it.

The King is anxious that Laertes will carry through the violent scheme of the play with foils and is not simply a man playing at a show of grief.

This is evidently the argument about 'playing' and 'show' that has been debated in the play since the first court scene. The King, naturally, believes that love is subject to time since he has observed its effect in the 'passages of proof' of his own marriage. The 'spark and fire' of Gertrude's love for her husband was clearly qualified by time. Like the Player King, Claudius here argues that Fortune is the greatest power in men's lives. It therefore follows that they must seize Occasion when she offers herself (4 vii 118:3112 Q 5):

King	That we would do,
	We should do when we would; for this 'would' changes,
	And hath abatements and delays as many
	As there are tongues, are hands, are accidents;
	And then this 'should' is like a spendthrift's sigh
	That hurts by easing.

Action must be the result of instant passion.

The King now reaches the crucial point in his argument. He returns to the imagery of disease as he refers to Hamlet. Since the King of

England has failed to cure him of the 'hectic' (4 iii 67:2731) of Hamlet, Claudius hopes to persuade Laertes to act as his surgeon (4 vii 123: 3112 Q 10):

King	But to the quick of th'ulcer:
	Hamlet comes back; what would you undertake
	To show yourself in deed your father's son
	More than in words?
Laertes	To cut his throat i'th'church.
King	No place, indeed, should murder sanctuarize;
	Revenge should have no bounds.

There could be no clearer statement of the ethics of revenge. It is Claudius who, for his own purposes, believes that revenge should have no limit. It is Laertes who is prepared to violate sanctuary in order to achieve it. The contrast between this desire to prove oneself in 'deed' and Hamlet, who has spent the play, prayer, and closet scenes anatomizing his role as his father's son in words, is deliberate and striking.

Claudius actually makes his appeal to the mind and conscience of Laertes. He has to rely upon words, first to persuade Laertes that it is Hamlet who is his enemy, and then to keep the Queen and court in ignorance of the fact that they will be watching a murder. The actual plan to dispose of Hamlet is described as an act of love. Killing Hamlet will be proof that Laertes really did love his father. It will also be a wager, or act of Fortune. The outcome of this wager, however, will not be left to chance. This appeal to conscience persuades Laertes to take part in an act which, if he had time to think and reflect, he would find against his conscience. The ungoverned, and perhaps excusable, passion of Laertes is now directed by a man whose memory, understanding, and will are coldly dedicated solely to his own preservation.

Hamlet also appeals to the conscience of Laertes. Before the play with foils the King makes a deliberately deceitful 'show' of reconciliation between Hamlet and Laertes. 'Come, Hamlet, come, and take this hand from me' (5 ii 217:3677). Hamlet responds in one of the most remarkable speeches in the play—asking for forgiveness from Laertes, but ascribing his fault to 'madness'. The audience are invited to make a comparison between Hamlet and Laertes. It is not one which will allow them the luxury of much moral indignation.

The offence for which Hamlet asks pardon is of so 'grave' a nature that it is difficult not to feel some sympathy for the embittered and unswerving purpose of Laertes. In the closet scene Hamlet had insisted upon his sanity and his ability to act as a responsible agent. It is surprising that he should here take refuge in the fiction of his madness. It would be possible to regard Hamlet's speech as an attempt by a Machiavellian intriguer to escape the just consequences of one crime while he meditates another.

Hamlet's final appeal to Laertes is expressed in a striking military metaphor (5 ii 232:3692):

> Hamlet   Sir, in this audience,
> Let my disclaiming from a purpos'd evil
> Free me so far in your most generous thoughts
> That I have shot my arrow o'er the house
> And hurt my brother.

The image of the arrow missing its mark is also used by the King while he is explaining to Laertes the necessity for the device of the poisoned duel. It is closely connected with 'the slings and arrows of outrageous fortune' (3 i 58:1712) and is part of a larger pattern of language which draws attention to the general ineffectiveness of all human action. The Player King gives the idea its most concise expression: 'Our thoughts are ours, their ends none of our own' (3 ii 208:2081).

Roger L. Cox has identified this tendency for all human action to 'miss the mark' with the Greek word *hamartia*.[1] Aristotle uses it in the *Poetics* in an attempt to define the nature of tragic error. Cox argues that it is more useful to examine the way in which it is used by St Paul in the Epistle to the Romans to identify the inescapable process of human error or sin. Hamlet's delay and his madness are now seen to be two similar aspects of the natural bias of sin in human affairs. Every man is condemned to commit 'the evil that he does not want'. On this interpretation any attempt to fulfil the command of the Ghost was bound to miss the mark and appear as madness and delay. In apologizing to Laertes for his 'madness' Hamlet is acknowledging his own share in this universal pattern of sin.

This interesting thesis overlooks one important aspect of the play. Hamlet's actions do not always miss their mark. On three occasions he appeals to the conscience and understanding of other characters. On each occasion his appeal finds its mark. In the play scene he catches the conscience of the King. In the closet scene he wrings the heart of the Queen. His request for forgiveness and pardon is an appeal to the

[1] Roger L. Cox, 'Hamlet's Hamartia: Aristotle or St Paul?', *The Yale Review*, lv (1966), 347–64.

conscience and understanding of Laertes. In the last analysis, even this appeal to an implacable avenger is not uttered in vain.

All of the characters, including Hamlet, find themselves gripped by passions which seem uncontrollable and which lead to murder or self-destruction. A man, however, who has committed the evil that he does not want need not abandon himself to despair. It is possible to mitigate the effects of the destructive actions of humanity. The appeal to understanding and conscience, and the hope of forgiveness, is the only possible hope of escape from the pitiless wheel of fortune to which humanity is bound by its passions. Hamlet, therefore, acknowledges his fault and asks for forgiveness—the exact act of contrition and repentance which the King was unable to perform in the prayer scene.

In the circumstances of Elsinore, Hamlet's appeal can only be effective if it is received in charity and answered with love. These are exactly the qualities of mercy which the King had declared could 'confront the visage of offence' (3 iii 47:2323). Claudius has rejected the possibility of pardon or forgiveness. He does not expect mercy, and neither he nor Laertes has any intention of showing any to Hamlet.

As Hamlet asks Laertes for pardon the King still stands between them in show of reconciliation. He is a man who has recognized within himself the claims of reason and the power of conscience. He has placed both at the service of his passion. This self-love is not governed by time and circumstance. It persists until consciousness itself has left his body. It is the demonic regard of the King for his own person and passion which devours the lives of all of the characters.

Laertes replies to Hamlet in words which are his own version of the damnation soliloquy (5 ii 243:3704):

> Laertes I do receive your offer'd love like love
> And will not wrong it.

He is determined to play his part in the poisoned duel and his answer is equivocal. He says that he will accept Hamlet's apology until he has had the advice of 'elder masters of known honour' (5 ii 240:3701). He has already taken such advice—from the King. Claudius and Laertes are determined to embark upon another act of 'madness', and it proves mortal.

The duel has its own harmony and laws which prescribe not only the manner of fencing but the conduct of the participants. In *Romeo and Juliet* Mercutio's description of Tybalt's style of fencing emphasizes the 'harmony' of the duel (*Romeo and Juliet*, 2 iv 19:1124):

> Mercutio O, he's the courageous captain of compliments. He

fights as you sing prick-song: keeps time, distance and
proportion; he rests his minim rests, one, two, and the
third in your bosom; the very butcher of a silk button, a
duellist, a duellist; a gentleman of the very first house,
of the first and second cause.

When Tybalt, according to the stage direction at 3 i 87, '*under Romeo's
arm thrusts Mercutio in, and flies with his friends*', he has committed two
crimes. He has broken the civil laws of Verona against duelling. He
has also broken the 'honourable' code of the duel itself in hitting an
unsighted and therefore disarmed opponent.

In their choice of an unbated envenomed sword and a poisoned cup
as weapons against Hamlet, Claudius and Laertes break every one of
the honourable codes and conventions which governed the practice of
fencing and single combat. The result, as Laertes admits to Hamlet, is
a 'foul practice' (5 ii 309:3798) whose very success is self-defeating. In
breaking even the recognized harmony of the duel Claudius has placed
in Hamlet's hands the perfect instrument for revenge and provided
the perfect occasion for its use. This court entertainment, which
Claudius has devised as the only acceptable solution to the problems of
the play scene, places the infinite questions raised by *Hamlet* in a context
where they must be resolved in a fashion so decisive that it brings the
endless debate to silence on the stage.

The attempt to kill Hamlet misfires because the Prince proves himself a better fencer than Laertes. Even the King's iron control over his
emotions might be a little shaken as he watches Hamlet win the first
two bouts. The 'back or second' of the poisoned cup proves even more
disastrous. The Queen drinks from it with the toast, 'The Queen
carouses to thy fortune, Hamlet' (5 ii 281:3758). As she raises it to
her lips the King is either unable, or unwilling, to prevent her. Divided
from his wife by the full length of the stage, Claudius is also separated
from her by his knowledge of his crime. Unable to explain his true
motives to his courtiers, he has been equally unable to share the true
basis of his marriage with the woman he loves. He cannot speak now
without betraying his plans. His only comment is, 'It is the poison'd
cup; it is too late' (5 ii 284:3763) and his only concern is to conceal the
Queen's death until both Hamlet and Laertes are also silenced. The
self-love of Claudius has destroyed even his passion for his Queen.

The King's despair, and the growing doubts of Laertes, are expressed
in an exchange that takes place while the Queen, already poisoned, is
wiping Hamlet's face (5 ii 287:3767):

Laertes	My lord, I'll hit him now.
King	I do not think't.
Laertes (aside)	And yet it is almost against my conscience.

The growing tension after the third inconclusive bout is resolved when Laertes overcomes his conscience and breaks another of the duel's conventions. He strikes at Hamlet before he is ready, with only minimal warning. It is possible that Hamlet's back is turned. The sudden thrust of Laertes completes the symbolism of the stage picture in the prayer and closet scenes. The sudden and secret attack is the only method open to a successful avenger of blood. Only when he has been hit by his own rapier and knows that he is dying by poison does the conscience of Laertes make him realize the full implications of his action. In the shadow of the grave Hamlet and Laertes finally exchange the love which had been offered and apparently accepted before the play with foils.

It is his own failure of love, his inability to stop Gertrude drinking from the poisoned cup, which seals the fate of Claudius. The Queen's dying cry to her son provokes the final confession and accusation of Laertes. What Claudius has tried to avoid throughout the play—a direct confrontation with Hamlet—is now inevitable. What finally kills the King is not only a sword-thrust but the dregs of his cup poisoned with his own 'union' which Hamlet forces down his throat. Laertes says that he is 'justly serv'd' (5 ii 319:3811) by 'a poison temper'd by himself' (5 ii 320:3812). What has killed Claudius is not simply the poison in the cup but his own pathological self-concern and total absence of feeling for any other person. This complete failure of compassion and humanity shows how much of his own personality Claudius had annihilated on his way to extinction.

Hamlet's admission of 'madness' and his apology to Laertes are part of an appeal to reason and conscience made by Shakespeare in a situation where the madness of intriguing passion threatens to destroy the essential humanity of the characters before it claims their lives. The King's self-love is a poison which threatens the state of Denmark because it would dissolve the bonds of all society. Shakespeare's dramatic method of the duel suggests that the claims of reason and compassion, the desire to ask for mercy and the power to grant it, are as deeply implanted in the human psyche, and as strong a force in human affairs, as the aggressive forces of lust and hatred. It is the conscience of Gertrude and Laertes which at last permits them to recognize and identify the terrible power that has destroyed them.

In the play this appeal to conscience is made through the consciousness of Hamlet. The command of the Ghost summons him from a student's life of contemplation to a world of action. The action, however, that he is called upon to perform requires both passion and understanding. He is correct when he hopes that he may sweep to his revenge with wings 'as swift as meditation or the thoughts of love' (I v 30:716). He is checked by the fact that, in the circumstances of Elsinore, the act of revenge will have to be an act of secret murder. Hamlet assures himself and the audience that he desires to commit this murder and intends to play the role of Pyrrhus and Lucianus. The playing of such a part, as the long war dramatized in the soliloquies and inner-play makes clear, requires exactly the single-willed mindless dedication to passion that Hamlet has condemned in Claudius and Gertrude.

In order to punish Claudius for his murderous and lustful passions, Hamlet must apparently abandon his own memory and understanding to the unrestrained power of his will. He seems to have done so in the damnation soliloquy. The desire to condemn one's enemies to eternal damnation, although a 'natural' and 'human' reaction, is also an expression of the total self-love that consumes Claudius. It can only be entertained by a man who has cast out love, charity and any form of fellow-feeling. Hamlet has never banished meditation or the thoughts of love. The troubled conscience of Claudius, shaken by the vision of the inner-play, saves Hamlet from himself. The reassertion of a murderous will then hurls the King on to his destruction.

The play's ultimate irony is that Hamlet does perform the task of vengeance by poisoning the King. In that moment, however, life is slipping away from him and from his victim. The poisoned cup of wine is, strictly speaking, superfluous. Hamlet fulfils his task, in a final paradox, by unpacking his heart with words—the same weapons which have prevented him from acting as a secret and murderous avenger.

The code of revenge, like the belief in fortune, depends upon a commitment to an unswerving sin-and-punishment morality. An eye is always exacted for an eye, and love and friendship always fly from bad fortune. Once this is accepted there is no reason why the killing should ever stop so long as any human participants in the deadly game remain alive. It is, however, clearly stated by Claudius, and his theology has never been impeached, that the grace of God and the power of love is sufficient to pardon even a brother's murder. There is some hope of breaking the chain of murder and sudden death if men can be brought to look at the reflection of their own crimes without being, as Claudius is, turned to stone.

Claudius articulates his repentance, but he acts according to his buried instincts of hate and self-preservation. Hamlet articulates his primitive feelings of hatred and his consuming passion for revenge. Instead, however, of acting upon these impulses he pauses for thought. In that pause Shakespeare develops, in the physical action, in the dialogue, in the meditations, and in the soliloquies Hamlet's consciousness of his own role. This examination of his own actions is a dramatization of the operation of conscience. Conscience requires the passion of human love, sexual, social, and compassionate. It is an examination of that hidden power which is the great 'unconscious' motivation and driving force of *Hamlet*.

Conscience or consciousness does not negate the drives of hatred and aggression. It has to struggle for existence in a world where its operation may sometimes seem cowardice, sometimes inexcusable dilatoriness, sometimes quixotic folly, and sometimes mere madness. It exists in Hamlet, in Ophelia, in Gertrude, and in Laertes. Only in Claudius does the appeal to conscience, the terrible self-knowledge granted by the inner-play, fail to produce any spark of human affection. This lack of conscience precludes any real understanding of his fellow human beings and thus prepares for the many miscalculations which lead him to death.

The consciousness of the possibility of human love gives the play its hope. It cannot save the characters, or the audience, from the destructive power of human hatred. It is one of the paradoxes of the play that the flame of love can only be kept alive by the rashness, anger, and passion which can also transform it to a poisonous venom that changes men into monsters. Claudius nearly succeeds in repeating his original crime. Hamlet can hardly escape from the envenomed sword or the poisoned chalice. Claudius, however, is not likely to escape the man who has sent Rosencrantz and Guildenstern to their deaths, who has seen the body of the girl he loves buried in the earth, and who is sufficient master of the soldier's art to defend himself in single combat against the admired fencing skill of Laertes.

In the graveyard Hamlet warns Laertes that he will respond in lethal fashion to any serious attack (5 i 252:3454):

Laertes   The devil take thy soul!

O   197

Hamlet   Thou pray'st not well.
I prithee take thy fingers from my throat;
For, though I am not splenitive and rash,
Yet have I in me something dangerous,
Which let thy wiseness fear.

Claudius's devices are overthrown because he is unaware of the existence of this skilful and determined opponent. The crime of Claudius against the King and state of Denmark is answered by an equal and opposite amount of violence. Such a response is natural and may be necessary. When Claudius moves to secure himself by removing Hamlet he finds himself engaged in a war or a duel whose conditions he has not fully understood. He is opposed by a man who has sufficient command of the necessary arts of actor, soldier, and politician to 'win at the odds' (5 ii 203:3660).

The final entry of Fortinbras emphasizes the necessity, in the delicate balance of human existence, of the military virtues. Without the presence of Fortinbras the audience would have less opportunity to appreciate the character of Hamlet. As the representative of the traditional heroic and military virtues, Fortinbras has never been in any doubt about his role. After his father's death he attempted to rectify his position by force of arms. Ordered to desist from a dishonourable course, he has obeyed and instead led his army on its 'honourable' campaign on the borders of Poland. He comes from there to claim his 'rights of memory' in the shape and form of the traditional heroic and kingly virtues.

Laertes, on the other hand, may be said to represent the traditional passions. Like Fortinbras, he has no doubts about the nature of his role. His words to the King (4 v 128:2878):

Laertes   To hell allegience! Vows, to the blackest devil!
Conscience and grace, to the profoundest pit!
I dare damnation. To this point I stand,
That both the worlds I give to negligence,
Let come what comes; only I'll be reveng'd
Most thoroughly for my father

are an expression of a desire to obey the revenge code whatever the cost and whatever the obstacles in the way. This determination makes him an inhabitant of the grim world where poison is secretly administered and passion is gratified by stealth.

The world of Laertes is the world of Claudius, just as the battlefield where Fortinbras is at home is the world of King Hamlet. All are secure in their roles and confident of their actions. The fact that Hamlet feels insecure in his role, and doubts the wisdom and necessity of his actions, is not necessarily an indication that he is a weaker character than these representatives of the older and the younger generation. It is an interesting commentary on our psychology that it should regard the roles of Fortinbras and Laertes as 'normal'. The problem of *Hamlet*, therefore, is not Hamlet's problem of delay. In that delay Shakespeare raises the questions of honour, love, and conscience which form so important a part of man's perpetual inquiry into the nature of his own existence.

The history briefly rehearsed by Horatio at the end of the play reminds the audience of the difficulty, and the importance, of that inquiry. The questions asked by the dramatic pattern of poison, play, and duel are directed at the guilty creatures sitting at a play. All are players in the losing game of chance that is human existence. The reason for the perpetual fascination of *Hamlet* is that Hamlet questions the definition of the roles that the audience are themselves called upon to play in the theatre of the world.

Hamlet is the thwarted successor to his father. He is called upon to prove himself his equal by avenging his murder. He is a son who must learn to accept the burden of his mother's guilt without allowing it to poison the springs of his own affection. He is a lover who so totally misjudges the nature of the girl he loves that he can only express his devotion over her grave. He is a man who longs to be able to give his hatred form in murderous action. He is also a man who attempts, as best he can, to oppose thought, truth, and integrity to a corrupt world of policy whose only enduring value is the love of self which overwhelms all understanding.

The play offers its audience some hope that it is possible to play these roles with a triumphant human dignity that can outface even the skull grinning in the graveyard. The play offers its audience the certainty that 'the rest is silence' (5 ii 350:3847). Critics naturally question, and disagree about, the way that Hamlet plays his role, because the role of Hamlet is designed to bring the performance of all human parts into debate and question. The pattern of poison, play, and duel reaches out beyond the stage and takes possession of the minds of its audience. It offers them a growth in consciousness and understanding.

The image seized upon by the Renaissance to symbolize the reconcilement of pleasure to virtue, which should have been the true outcome of the Judgment of Paris, was the unlawful union of Mars and

Venus. They had a daughter named Harmony. She inherits the contradictory characters of her parents, the god of strife and the goddess of love. The play of *Hamlet* ends upon this note of concordant discord which has been presented throughout the action by the warring elements of the soul and the symbolism of the three graces.

The play ends with a man in full armour who accords Hamlet a soldier's funeral, the rites of Mars which are also the values of fortitude and victory (5 ii 391:3900):

Fortinbras   The soldier's music and the rite of war
              Speak loudly for him.
              Take up the bodies. Such a sight as this
              Becomes the field, but here shows much amiss.
              Go, bid the soldiers shoot.

Horatio, the man who is not Fortune's fool nor passion's slave, has already promised to perform the last offices of friendship for the Prince. He accords Hamlet a celestial rite of passage which expresses also the values of Venus and human love (5 ii 351:3848):

Horatio   Now cracks a noble heart. Goodnight, sweet prince,
           And flights of angels sing thee to thy rest.

Both tributes are true, but since Horatio and Fortinbras both see Hamlet in their own terms, neither contains the whole truth.

In *De gli eroici furori* Bruno distinguishes between those who serve the myrtle, the plant of Venus, and those who gain the laurel, the crown of victory:

Those who can and do win praise for themselves by the myrtle are those who sing of love. If these bear themselves nobly, they win the crown of that plant consecrated to Venus who inspires them with her frenzy. Those who can praise themselves by the laurel are those who sing worthily of heroic things, who instruct heroic souls through speculative and moral philosophy, or who celebrate those heroic souls and present them as exemplary mirrors of political and civil action.[1]

Horatio praises Hamlet under the sign of the myrtle, Fortinbras praises him under the sign of the laurel. Their combination should mean that Hamlet has succeeded in keeping the flame of conscience and love still burning amid the heroic demands of the long war with

[1] P. E. Memmo Jr, *Giordano Bruno's The Heroic Frenzies: A Translation with Introduction and Notes*, 1964, 82.

Claudius. The play closes, as it opened, with the values of Mars. The question that remains is whether the human combination of the values of Mars and Venus is possible or attainable. Mars and Venus meet in the human mind. The play questions whether their union can ever produce harmony. The argument of the play is over. The argument about the play has begun.

BIBLIOGRAPHY

Only books and articles referred to in the text or notes, or books that relate to the issues in the text, are listed here. Fuller information is contained in Paul S. Conklin, *A History of Hamlet Criticism, 1601–1821*, Routledge & Kegan Paul, 1957 (Second edition); *A New Variorum Edition of Shakespeare: Hamlet*, ed. Horace Howard Furness, 2 volumes, New York: Dover reprint, 1963 (first published 1877); A. A. Raven, *A Hamlet Bibliography and Reference Guide, 1877–1935*, Chicago: University of Chicago Press, 1936; Clifford Leech, 'Studies in Hamlet, 1901–1955', *Shakespeare Survey 9*, Cambridge University Press, 1956; and the annual bibliography published in *Shakespeare Quarterly*.

ADLER, ALFRED, *Social Interest*, Faber & Faber, 1938.

ALEXANDER, NIGEL, 'Hamlet and the Art of Memory', *Notes and Queries*, New Series, xv (1968), 137–9.

ALEXANDER, PETER, *A Shakespeare Primer*, James Nisbet, 1951.
Hamlet: Father and Son, Clarendon Press, 1955.
Shakespeare, Oxford University Press, 1964.
Shakespeare's Life and Art, James Nisbet, 1938.

ALTICK, R. D., 'Hamlet and the Odour of Mortality', *Shakespeare Quarterly*, v (1954), 167–76.

AQUINAS, THOMAS, *Summa Theologiae*, ed. Thomas Gilby and P. K. Meagher, Eyre & Spottiswoode, 1964– .

ARISTOTLE, *see* Bywater.

AYER, A. J., *Philosophy and Language*, Clarendon Press, 1960.

BRADBROOK, M. C., *Shakespeare the Craftsman*, Chatto & Windus, 1969.

'Shakespeare's Primitive Art', *Proceedings of the British Academy*, li (1965), 216–34, Oxford University Press, 1966.

Themes and Conventions of Elizabethan Tragedy, Cambridge University Press, 1957.

BRADLEY, A. C., *Shakespearean Tragedy*, Macmillan, 1904.

BROOKE, NICHOLAS, *Shakespeare's Early Tragedies*, Methuen, 1968.

BROWN, JOHN RUSSELL, *Shakespeare's Plays in Performance*, Edward Arnold, 1966.

and HARRIS, BERNARD (eds), *Hamlet* (Stratford-upon-Avon Studies 5), Edward Arnold, 1963.

BRUNO, GIORDANO, *see* Memmo.

BULLOUGH, GEOFFREY (ed.), *Narrative and Dramatic Sources of Shakespeare*, 7 volumes, Routledge & Kegan Paul, 1957– .

BYWATER, INGRAM (tr.), *Aristotle on the Art of Poetry*, Clarendon Press, 1909.

CARLISLE, CAROL J., 'Hamlet's "Cruelty" in the Nunnery Scene: The Actors' Views', *Shakespeare Quarterly*, xviii (1967), 129–40.

CHURCHILL, G. B., 'Richard the Third up to Shakespeare', *Palaestra*, x (1900).

CLEMEN, W. H., 'Past and Future in Shakespeare's Drama', *Proceedings of the British Academy*, lii (1966), 231–52, Oxford University Press, 1967.

The Development of Shakespeare's Imagery, Methuen, 1951.

COX, ROGER L., 'Hamlet's Hamartia: Aristotle or St Paul?', *The Yale Review*, lv (1966), 347–64.

CUNNINGHAM, J. V., *Woe or Wonder: The Emotional Effect of Shakespearean Tragedy*, Denver: University of Denver Press, 1951.

ELIOT, T. S., 'Hamlet and his Problems' (1919) in *Selected Essays 1917–1932*, Faber & Faber, 1932.

EMPSON, WILLIAM, 'The Spanish Tragedy' (1956) in *Elizabethan Drama*, ed. Ralph J. Kaufmann, New York: Oxford University Press, 1961.

EVANS, BERTRAND, *Shakespeare's Comedies*, Clarendon Press, 1960.

FALK, DORIS V., 'Proverbs and the Polonius Destiny', *Shakespeare Quarterly*, xviii (1967), 23–36.

FERGUSSON, FRANCIS, *The Idea of a Theatre*, Princeton: Princeton University Press, 1949.

FORKER, CHARLES R., 'Shakespeare's Theatrical Symbolism and Its Function in *Hamlet*', *Shakespeare Quarterly*, xiv (1964), 215–29.

GARDNER, HELEN, 'Lawful Espials', *Modern Language Review*, xxxiii (1938), 345–55.

The Business of Criticism, Clarendon Press, 1959.

GELLERT, BRIDGET, 'A Note on *Hamlet*, 2 ii 356–357', *Notes and Queries*, New Series xv (1968), 139–40.

GIBSON, JAMES J., *The Senses Considered as Perceptual Systems* (1966), Allen & Unwin, 1968.

GILOT, FRANÇOISE, *Life With Picasso*, Nelson, 1965.

GODDARD, HAROLD, 'In Ophelia's Closet', *The Yale Review*, xxxv (1946), 462–74.

GOLLANCZ, ISRAEL, *The Sources of Hamlet: With an Essay on the Legend*, Oxford University Press, 1926.

GOODHART, A. L., 'Liability for Unforeseen Consequences', *The Listener*, 65 (6 April 1961), 603–4.

GRANVILLE-BARKER, HARLEY, *Prefaces to Shakespeare: Third Series*, Sidgwick & Jackson, 1937.

HARLOW, HARRY F., 'Love in Infant Monkeys', *Scientific American*, 200 (June 1959, No. 6), 68–74.

and HARLOW, MARGARET KUENNE, 'Social Deprivation in Monkeys', *Scientific American*, 207 (November 1962, No. 5), 136–46.

HAWKES, TERENCE, *Shakespeare and the Reason*, Routledge & Kegan Paul, 1964.

HEILMAN, ROBERT B., 'To Know Himself: An Aspect of Tragic Structure', *Review of English Literature*, v (1964), 36–57.

HOCKEY, DOROTHY C., 'Wormwood, Wormwood!', *English Language Notes*, iii (1965), 174–7.

HOLLOWAY, JOHN, *The Story of the Night*, Routledge & Kegan Paul, 1961.

HOLMES, MARTIN, *The Guns of Elsinore*, Chatto & Windus, 1964.

HONIGMANN, E. A. J. (ed.), *King John* (New Arden edition), Methuen, 1959.
'Shakespeare's Lost Source Plays', *Modern Language Review*, xlix (1954), 293–307.
'The Politics of *Hamlet* and the World of the Play', in *Hamlet*, ed. John Russell Brown and Bernard Harris, Edward Arnold, 1963.
The Stability of Shakespeare's Text, Edward Arnold, 1965.

HORNE, ALISTAIR, *The Price of Glory: Verdun 1916*, Macmillan, 1962.
To Lose a Battle, Macmillan, 1969.

HULME, HILDA M., *Explorations in Shakespeare's Language*, Longman, 1962.

HUNGERFORD, EDWARD B., '*Hamlet*: The Word at the Centre', *Tri-Quarterly*, No. 8 (Winter, 1968), 69–89.

JAMES, D. G., *The Dream of Learning: An Essay on The Advancement of Learning, Hamlet and King Lear*, Clarendon Press, 1951.

JAMES, HENRY, *The Art of the Novel: Critical Prefaces by Henry James*, ed. R. P. Blackmur, New York: Scribners, 1934.

JOHNSON, JERAH, 'The Concept of the "King's Two Bodies" in *Hamlet*', *Shakespeare Quarterly*, xviii (1967), 430–4.

JONES, ERNEST, *Hamlet and Oedipus*, New York: W. W. Norton, 1949.

JOSEPH, BERTRAM, *Conscience and the King: A Study of Hamlet*, Chatto & Windus, 1953.

KANTOROWICZ, ERNST H., *The King's Two Bodies: A Study in Medieval Political Theology*, Princeton: Princeton University Press, 1957.

KIRSHBAUM, LEO, 'A Census of Bad Quartos', *Review of English Studies*, xiv (1938), 20–43.

KNIGHT, G. WILSON, *Shakespeare and Religion*, Routledge & Kegan Paul, 1967.

The Wheel of Fire, Oxford University Press, 1930.

KNIGHTS, L. C., *An Approach to Hamlet*, Chatto & Windus, 1960.

KOTT, JAN, 'Hamlet and Orestes', *Publications of the Modern Language Association of America*, lxxxii (1967), 303–13.

Shakespeare Our Contemporary (Second edition), Methuen, 1967.

LAWLOR, JOHN, *The Tragic Sense in Shakespeare*, Chatto & Windus, 1960.

LEVIN, HARRY, *The Question of Hamlet*, New York: Oxford University Press, 1959.

LEWIS, C. S., 'Hamlet: The Prince or the Poem?', *Proceedings of the British Academy*, xxviii (1942), 139–54, Oxford University Press, 1943.

LORENZ, KONRAD, *On Aggression*, New York: Harcourt Brace, 1966.

MACK, MAYNARD, 'The World of *Hamlet*', *The Yale Review*, xli (1952), 502–23.

MAHOOD, M. M., *Shakespeare's Wordplay*, Methuen, 1957.

MAITLAND, F. W., *Selected Essays*, ed. H. D. Hazeltine, G. Lapsley, P. H. Winfield, Cambridge University Press, 1936.

MÂLE, E., *L'Art Religieux de la fin du Moyen Age en France*, Paris: Colin, 1908.

MEHL, DIETER, *The Elizabethan Dumb Show*, Methuen, 1965.

MEMMO, P. E. Jr, tr., *Giordano Bruno's The Heroic Frenzies: A Translation with Introduction and Notes* (Studies in the Romance Languages and Literature 50), Chapel Hill: University of North Carolina Press, 1964.

MORGANN, MAURICE, *An Essay on the Dramatic Character of Sir John Falstaff* (1777), ed. W. A. Gill, Clarendon Press, 1912.

MUIR, KENNETH, 'Imagery and Symbolism in *Hamlet*', *Études Anglaises*, xvii (1964), 352–63.

Shakespeare: Hamlet (Studies in English Literature 13), Edward Arnold, 1964.

NOSWORTHY, J. M., *Shakespeare's Occasional Plays: Their Origin and Transmission*, Edward Arnold, 1965.

PALMER, D. J., 'Stage Spectators in *Hamlet*', *English Studies*, xlvii (1966), 423–30.

PROSSER, ELEANOR, *Hamlet and Revenge*, Stanford: Stanford University Press, 1967.

RABKIN, NORMAN, *Shakespeare and the Common Understanding*, New York: The Free Press (Macmillan), 1967.

RANK, OTTO, *Art and Artist*, tr. Charles Francis Atkinson, New York: A. A. Knopf, 1932.

Beyond Psychology (1941), New York: Dover Books, 1958.

RIGHTER, ANNE, *Shakespeare and the Idea of the Play*, Chatto & Windus, 1962.

RUSHTON, W. L., *Shakespeare's Legal Maxims*, Henry Young & Son, 1907.

SALMI, MARIO, 'Gli affreschi del Palazzo Trinci a Foligno', *Bollettino d'Arte*, xiii (1919), 139–80.

SEZNEC, JEAN, *The Survival of the Pagan Gods*, New York: Pantheon, 1953.

SIMMONS, J. L., 'Shakespeare's *Julius Caesar*: The Roman Actor and The Man', *Tulane Studies in English*, xvi (1968), 1–28.

SPURGEON, CAROLINE F. E., *Shakespeare's Imagery and What it Tells Us*, Cambridge University Press, 1935.

STYAN, J. L., *Shakespeare's Stagecraft*, Cambridge University Press, 1967.

SYMONS, NORMAN J., 'The Graveyard Scene in *Hamlet*', *International Journal of Psychoanalysis*, ix (1928), 96–119.

TRACY, ROBERT, 'The Owl and the Baker's Daughter: A Note on *Hamlet* 4 iv 42–43', *Shakespeare Quarterly*, xvii (1966), 83–6.

TYNAN, KENNETH, 'Verdict on Cannes', *The Observer*, 22 May 1966, 24.

WALDOCK, A. J. A., *Hamlet: A Study in Critical Method*, Cambridge University Press, 1931.

Sophocles the Dramatist, Cambridge University Press, 1951.

WALKER, ROY, *The Time is Out of Joint: A Study of Hamlet*, Andrew Dakers, 1948.

WEITZ, MORRIS, *Hamlet and the Philosophy of Literary Criticism*, Chicago: Chicago University Press, 1964.

WEST, REBECCA, *The Court and the Castle*, Macmillan, 1958.

WILSON, JOHN DOVER, *What Happens in Hamlet*, Cambridge University Press, 1935.

WIND, EDGAR, *Pagan Mysteries in the Renaissance*, Faber & Faber, 1958 (Second edition, 1968).

YATES, FRANCES A., *Giordano Bruno and the Hermetic Tradition*, Routledge & Kegan Paul, 1964.

The Art of Memory, Routledge & Kegan Paul, 1966.

Theatre of the World, Routledge & Kegan Paul, 1969.

'The Stage in Robert Fludd's Memory System', *Shakespeare Studies*, iii, ed. J. Leeds Barroll, Cincinnati: University of Cincinnati, 1967. 138–66.

INDEX

Adler, Alfred, *Social Interest*, 86
Agrippa, Henricus Cornelius, 103
Alexander, Nigel, 47
Alexander, Peter, ix, xi; *Hamlet: Father and Son*, 139 n.
Altick, R. D., 161 n.
Aquinas, St Thomas, *Summa Theologiae*, 55, 103
Aristotle, 75; *Poetics*, 36, 37, 192
As You Like It, 14–15, 16, 146
Augustine of Hippo, St, 54, 95, 105, 130
Austria, Francis Ferdinand, Archduke of, 183
Ayer, A. J., *Philosophy and Language*, 108

Barroll, J. Leeds (ed.), *Shakespeare Studies*, iii, 102 n.
Beckett, Samuel, *Acte sans paroles*, 60
Berchorius, Petrus, 122
Blackmur, R. P., *see* James, Henry
Bradbrook, M. C., 92 n., 97 n., 113, 117
Bradley, A. C., *Shakespearean Tragedy*, 41
Brecht, Bertolt, 9

Bright, Timothy, *A Treatise of Melancholie*, 70
Brooke, Arthur, *The Tragical Historye of Romeus and Juliet*, 124
Brown, Professor John, x
Brown, John Russell, and Bernard Harris (eds), *Hamlet*, 178 n.
Bruno, Giordano, 64, 103–4, 126, 127–8
 De gli eroici furori (tr. P. E. Memmo Jr), 64–5, 66, 81, 104–5, 155, 169, 200; *see also* Yates, Dr Frances A.
Bullough, Geoffrey (ed.), *Narrative and Dramatic Sources of Shakespeare*, 115 n., 124 n.
Burbage, Richard, 96–7
Burghley, William Cecil, 1st Baron, 134
Burroughs, William, 9
Bywater, Ingram, *Aristotle on the Art of Poetry*, 36

Cannes Film Festival, 37
Carlisle, Carol J., 144 n.
Cartari, Vincenzo, *Le Imagini de i dei de gli antichi*, 138
Cecil, William, *see* Burghley, William Cecil, 1st Baron

Chapman, George, *The Revenge of Bussy D'Ambois*, 102

Chettle, Henry, *The Tragedy of Hoffman*, ix, 11–12, 34

Churchill, G. B., 115 n.

Cicero, Marcus Tullius, *De Inventione*, 103, 105

Clouzot, Henri-Georges, 37

Cox, Roger L., 192

Dover Wilson, John, *see* Wilson, John Dover

Elizabeth I, 97

Empson, William, 82–3

Epistle to the Romans, 192

Erasmus, 134

Falk, Doris V., 134, 161 n.

Fergusson, Francis, *The Idea of a Theatre*, 91 n.

Ficino, Marsilio, 97, 103

Foch, Marshal Ferdinand, 184

Foligno, Palazzo Trinci, 15–16

Forker, Charles R., 91 n.

Freudian criticism, 10–11, 12, 128, 166–7, 168

Gardner, Helen, 142 n.

Garland, John of, *Integumenta*, 122

Gellert, Bridget, 70

Genesis, 62

Gibson, James J., *The Senses Considered as Perceptual Systems*, 92–3, 94

Gilot, Françoise, *Life With Picasso*, 137–8

Giorgi, Francesco, *Harmonia mundi*, 79

Globe theatre, 15

Godard, Jean-Luc, 37

Goddard, Harold, 40–1

Goodhart, A. L., 182–3

Gorboduc, 107

Granville-Barker, Harley, *Prefaces to Shakespeare: Third Series*, 91 n.

Hamlet, Prince of Denmark
CHARACTERS
    Claudius, King, character, 56–7, 111, 158–9, 185–6, 193, 196–7; compared by Hamlet to King Hamlet, 54–5, 67, 155–6; conflict with Hamlet, 7, 19–20, 23–6 *passim*, 80–9 *passim*, 119–25 *passim*, 173–82, 187–91, 194–8; failure to repent, 21–2, 28, 85–6, 99; inner-play, Hamlet's weapon against, 13, 18–22 *passim*, 25–9 *passim*, 71–3, 91–5, 102–3, 105–18, 153–4; oblivion of King Hamlet's death, 51–4; position as king who is a murderer, 4–5, 7, 17, 84–5, 95, 176–8; responsibility for consequences of King Hamlet's murder, 183–4; treatment of Ophelia, 142–3; *see also* Gertrude; Ghost; Laertes; Polonius; Rosencrantz and Guildenstern

    First Player, 13, 62, 71–2, 76, 88, 90–4 *passim*, 95–9

    Fortinbras, King, 25, 42–3, 131

    Fortinbras, Prince, 25, 42–3, 63, 86–9 *passim*, 198, 200

    Gertrude, Queen, death, 194–5; Ghost invisible to, 157–8; Ghost's command to Hamlet on, 45–6, 50, 157–8; Hamlet's relations with, 153–60, 182; inner-play used by Hamlet against, 105–6, 108–9, 112, 149–50; marriage to Claudius, 35, 52–3, 54–5, 67, 80, 98, 125, 136, 137, 140–1, 144, 147, 154, 155–6, 157–60, 175, 194–5; marriage to King Hamlet, 54–5, 56, 155–6; oblivion of King Hamlet's death urged on Hamlet, 17, 163; *see also* Hamlet, Prince, Oedipus complex

    Ghost, 30–3, 44–5, 50, 74; commands to Hamlet, 43–6, 50, 157–8; dramatic function as 'historic' character, 33–7, 42–4, 57; Gertrude cannot see, 157–8; Hamlet's reaction to, 31–5 *passim*, 43–51, 57; King Hamlet's death related by, 43–5; *see also* Hamlet, King

    Gravediggers, 161–4, 180–1

    Hamlet, King, compared to Claudius by Hamlet, 54–5, 67, 155–6; duel with King Fortinbras, 25, 42–3, 131; Hamlet's remembrance of, 17,

Hamlet, Prince of Denmark (cont.)
CHARACTERS (cont.)

54–6, 67, 69, 106, 155–6; murder of, 19, 43–5, 51–4, 183–4; *see also* Gertrude; Ghost

Hamlet, Prince, 195–201; divided mind shown in soliloquies, 1–4 *passim*, 5–11, 12, 14, 23, 26–7, 28–9, 57–67; failure to understand passionate life, 119–31 *passim*, 153–4; harmony restored in mind, 168–72; ineffectiveness of action, 192–3; language, 112–13; Oedipus complex, 10–11, 80, 166–7, 168; *see also* Gertrude; meditations and soliloquies; Ophelia

meditations and soliloquies, 66–7, 68, 69–83 *passim*, 85–90 *passim* 1st meditation, 'The King doth wake tonight', 69; 2nd meditation, 'What a piece of work is a man', 69–71; 3rd meditation, 'Speak the speech', 13, 72–3, 99–101; 4th meditation, 'Give me that man/That is not passion's slave', 76–7, 79–80; 5th meditation, 'O the recorders!', 77–80; 6th meditation, 'Alas, poor Yorick', 89, 162, 163–4; 7th meditation, 'Not a whit, we defy augury', 89, 170

1st soliloquy, 'O, that this too too solid flesh would melt', 51, 54–5, 67, 69, 155; 2nd soliloquy, 'O, all you host of heaven', 46–9, 129; 3rd soliloquy, 'O, what a rogue and peasant slave am I!', 28, 31, 62–3, 71–2, 93; 4th soliloquy, 'To be, or not to be', 4, 62–3, 73–6, 87, 89, 140, 165; 5th soliloquy, ''Tis now the very witching time of night', 7–8, 22–3, 63, 76–7, 80–1, 115, 154; 6th soliloquy, 'Now might I do it pat', 7–8, 22–3, 63, 76–7, 80–3, 85–6, 99, 115; 7th soliloquy, 'How all occasions do inform against me', 2–3, 8, 55, 63, 86–8, 165

Horatio, 12–13, 30, 31, 42, 43, 49, 55–6, 69, 76–7, 79–80, 89, 200

Laertes, Freudian view of, 10–11,

166–7; Hamlet's admiration of, 120–1; Hamlet's contest with, 165–7, 197–8; Hamlet's duel with, 173–6, 183–4, 187, 189–95; instrument used by Claudius against Hamlet, 4, 23–4, 25–6, 121, 123–4, 160–1, 163, 174–6, 187, 189–91, 193–5; Ophelia's relations with, 132–4, 136; and Polonius, 3–4, 23, 49, 120–1, 123–4, 134, 198

Lucianus and Claudius, 22–3, 24, 27, 76, 94, 112, 114–18

Ophelia, 128–9, 131–2, 136–8; Claudius's treatment of, 142–3; and Hamlet, 105–6, 124–5, 129–31, 136–7, 140–52, 154, 159, 164–71, 197–8; Laertes's relations with, 132–4, 136; madness of, 40–1, 160–1; and Polonius, 4, 120–1, 129, 134–6, 143, 150, 151, 154; responsibility for death of, 165, 180–3 *passim*

Player King, 94, 110–12, 115, 116
Player Queen, 108–9, 115, 149–50
Players, dumb-show presented by, 22, 106–8, 114, 115, 147–8; Hamlet's advice to, 13, 72–3, 99–101; inner-play, 18–29 *passim*, 31, 72–3, 88–95, 102–18, 145–50, 153–4; *see also* First Player; Lucianus; Player King; Player Queen

Polonius, advice to Laertes, 49, 134; death, 3–4, 11, 23, 119, 120–1, 123–4, 150, 151, 154, 181–3; Hamlet's behaviour to Ophelia misinterpreted by, 129, 134–6, 143; instrument used by Claudius against Hamlet, 113–14, 125

Rosencrantz and Guildenstern, 23, 25, 69–71, 77–80, 83–5, 123, 173, 176–7, 187–9

IMAGERY AND CONCEPTIONS
banquet of sense, 156, 162
battle in the soul, 54–7, 62–6, 80–1, 95, 126, 166–72 *passim*, 178, 196
choice of life, book, flower, and sword, 129–31, 139, 140, 143, 151, 160, 168, 169; *see also* Raphael
colour, light and dark, 43, 51, 56, 74, 76
duel, military, 2, 6, 23–6, 73–5,

Hamlet, Prince of Denmark (cont.)
IMAGERY AND CONCEPTIONS (cont.)
88–9, 96, 132–4, 135, 173–5, 178–9,
185–8, 192, 193–4; *see also* Fortinbras, Prince; Hamlet, King; Laertes
  hawk, hand and saw, 70–1
  hunt of passion, 121–7
  Judgment of Paris, 96–9, 126–30
passim, 156, 166, 199
  memory systems, 47–9, 102–4,
105–12 *passim*
  mirrors, 13, 20–2, 100–1, 120
  music, harmony, 77–9
  Olympian gods, 54, 67, 69, 96,
155–6, 166–8
  play, theatre of the world, 2, 13–
19, 23–4, 26, 88–9, 92, 132–3, 135;
see also Players
  poison, disease and cure, 2, 6, 19–
24 *passim*, 26, 72, 109, 132–3, 161–2,
178, 190–1
  Prudence, 55, 57, 103–5, 126; *see
also* Titian
  sea, 73, 75
  sexual, the three graces, 132–7, 138,
140–59 *passim*, 165–70 *passim*, 199–
200; *see also* Raphael; Titian
  Time and Fortune, 15–16, 55, 75,
77, 84, 96, 104–6, 110–15 *passim*, 138,
160–1, 190
  traps, 113–14, 125, 135
  Yorick's skull, 118, 162–5 *passim*
Harlow, Harry F., 80 n.; *with* Mar-
garet Kuenne Harlow, 80 n.
Harris, Bernard, *see* Brown, J. R.
Heilman, Robert B., 25 n.
Henry IV, 40, 42
Heywood, Thomas, 15
Hinman, Charlton, *The First Folio of
Shakespeare*, ix
Hitler, Adolf, 184
Hockey, Dorothy C., 109 n.
Holmes, Martin, *The Guns of Elsinore*,
185
Honigmann, E. A. J., 115 n., 178 n.
Horne, Alistair, 162, 184
Hungerford, Edward B., 186

Isocrates, *Letter to Demonicus*, 134

James, Henry, *The Art of the Novel* (ed.
Blackmur), 6–7, 35, 60–2, 66, 125, 128,
164, 171
Johnson, Jerah, 176–7
Johnson, Dr Samuel, 82
Jones, Dr Ernest, *Hamlet and Oedipus*,
10–11, 166
Jonson, Ben, ix; *Bartholomew Fair*, 148
Julius Caesar, 38–40, 75

Kantorowicz, Ernst H., *The King's
Two Bodies: A Study in Medieval Political
Theology*, 177 n.
Kaufmann, Ralph J., *Elizabethan Drama*
(ed.), 83 n.
King Lear, Edmund in, 32; Lear in, 61
Kirshbaum, Leo, 115 n.
Knight, G. Wilson, *Shakespeare and
Religion*, 51
Kott, Jan, 150
Kyd, Thomas, *The Spanish Tragedy*,
101

Lawler, Professor John, x; *The Tragic
Sense in Shakespeare*, 59 n.
Locrine, The Tragedy of, ix, 107
Lorenz, Konrad, *On Aggression*, 144 n.
Love's Labour's Lost, 133
Lyly, John, *Euphues and his England*, 97;
Euphues: the Anatomy of Wit, 134

Macbeth, Weird Sisters in, 32, 50
Mack, Maynard, 18
Macrobious Theodosius, *Saturnalia*, 104
Maitland, F. W., *Selected Essays*, 177 n.
Mâle, É., *L'Art Religieux de la fin du
Moyen Age en France*, 16 n.
Marlowe, Christopher, *Doctor Faustus*,
60; *Hero and Leander*, 124; *Tamburlaine*,
5
Marx, Groucho, 64
Measure for Measure, 17
Medici, Lorenzo de', 97
Mehl, Dieter, *The Elizabethan Dumb
Show*, 107 n.
Memmo, P. E., Jr, *see* Bruno, Giordano
Merchant of Venice, The, 79
Middleton, Thomas, *Women Beware
Women*, 101

Midsummer Night's Dream, A, 150

Mirror for Magistrates, A, 124

Montaigne, Michel Eyquem, seigneur de, 139 n.

Montefeltro, Federigo da, Duke of Urbino, 186–7

Morgann, Maurice, *Essay on the Dramatic Character of Sir John Falstaff,* 40, 41

Muir, Kenneth, 25

Othello, 155; Iago in, 32, 144

Ovid, *Metamorphoses,* 122

Ovide Moralisé, 122

Palazzo Trinci, Foligno, 15–16

Palmer, D. J., 142 n.

Panofsky, Erwin, x

Pascal, Blaise, 139 n.

Peele, George, *The Arraignment of Paris,* 97

Picasso, Pablo Ruiz y, 137–8

Plato, 130, 139 n.; *Phaedrus,* 64, 65

Plowden, Edward, *Reports,* 176–7

Prinzep, Gavrilo, 183

Privy Council, decision *In re Polemis,* 182–3

Prosser, Eleanor, *Hamlet and Revenge,* 31 n., 181 n., 205

Proust, Marcel, 139 n.

Queen's Men, 114

Quintilian, 47

Rabkin, Norman, *Shakespeare and the Common Understanding,* 9

Rank, Otto, *Art and Artist,* 28; *Beyond Psychology,* 20–1

Rape of Lucrece, The, 98, 99

Raphael, ix, x, 129–30, 139–40, 143, 165, **Plates 1 and 2**

Richard III, 63–4, 114, 115 n., 144

Righter, Anne, *Shakespeare and the Idea of the Play,* 91 n.

Romeo and Juliet, 106, 124, 151–2, 169, 193–4

Royal Shakespeare Company, 60

Rushton, W. L., *Shakespeare's Legal Maxims,* 180–1

Sabie, Francis, *Pan's Pipe,* 97

Sainte-Beuve, Charles Augustin, 139 n.

Salmi, Mario, 16 n.

Sandys, George, *Ovid's Metamorphosis, Englished Mythologiz'd and Represented in Figures,* 122

Saxo Grammaticus, *Danish History,* 133

Scott, Sir Walter, *The Bride of Lammermoor,* 62

Serapis, statue of, 104–5, 115

Seznec, Jean, *The Survival of the Pagan Gods,* 16 n.

Shakespeare, William, ix, 35–42, 64, 126, 127–8; *see also* titles of plays; *Rape of Lucrece, The; Sonnets*

Shaw, George Bernard, 82

Sidney, Sir Philip, 64

Simmons, J. L., 38 n.

Sonnets (Shakespeare), 48, 64, 112, 133, 170–1

Sophocles, *Oedipus Tyrannus,* 27, 168

Spurgeon, Caroline F. E., *Shakespeare's Imagery and What It Tells Us,* 19

Stoppard, Tom, *Rosencrantz and Guildenstern Are Dead,* 129

Styan, J. L., *Shakespeare's Stagecraft,* 47

Symons, Norman J., 166, 167

Tempest, The, 35–8

Theobald, Lewis, 137

Thomas Aquinas, St, *see* Aquinas, St Thomas

Titian (Tiziano Vecelli), ix–x, 104–5, 137–9, 143, 165, **Plates 3 and 4**

Tourneur, Cyril, *The Revenger's Tragedy,* 101–2

Tracy, Robert, 'The Owl and the Baker's Daughter', 161 n.

Tragedy of Hoffman, The, see Chettle, Henry

Tragedy of Locrine, The, see *Locrine, The Tragedy of*

True Tragedie of Richard the Third, The, 114–15

Twelfth Night, 122, 135, 150–1

Tynan, Kenneth, 37

Ure, Professor Peter, x

Vecelli, Cesare, 104
Vecelli, Tiziano, *see* Titian
Verdun, 162
Versailles, Hall of Mirrors, 184

Waldock, A. J. A., *Sophocles the Dramatist*, 40–1
Weitz, Morris, *Hamlet and the Philosophy of Literary Criticism*, 32
West, Rebecca, *The Court and the Castle*, 137
Weygand, General Maxime, 184

Whitney, Geoffrey, *A Choice of Emblems*, 122
Wilhelm I, Kaiser, 184
Wilson, John Dover, *What Happens in Hamlet*, 32, 91 n.
Wind, Edgar, x; 75 n., 97, 104–5, 130, 138, 139–40, 186–7
Winter's Tale, The, 17–18
Wittenberg, University of, 8–9

Yates, Dr Frances A., x; 15, 47, 55, 79 n., 102 n., 103–4